# Understanding Indian Movies

Cognitive Approaches to Literature and Culture Series

Edited by Frederick Luis Aldama, Arturo J. Aldama, and Patrick Colm Hogan

Cognitive Approaches to Literature and Culture includes monographs and edited volumes that incorporate cutting edge research in cognitive science, neuroscience, psychology, linguistics, narrative theory, and related fields, insofar as this research bears on and illuminates cultural phenomena such as literature, film, drama, music, dance, visual art, digital media, and comics, among others.

The volumes published in this series represent both specialized scholarship and interdisciplinary investigation that are deeply sensitive to cultural particularities, but as grounded in an understanding of cross-culturally shared emotive and cognitive principles.

Understanding

# ndian Movies

## Culture, Cognition, and Cinematic Imagination

PATRICK COLM HOGAN

University of Texas Press
Austin

Printed in the United States of America
First edition, 2008
Requests for permission to reproduce material from this work should be sent to:
Permissions
University of Texas Press
P.O. Box 7819
Austin, TX 78713-7819
www.utexas.edu/utpress/about/bpermission.html
♾ The paper used in this book meets the minimum requirements of ANSI/NISO Z39.48-1992 (R1997) (Permanence of Paper).
Library of Congress Cataloging-in-Publication Data
Hogan, Patrick Colm.
Understanding Indian movies : culture, cognition, and cinematic imagination / Patrick Colm Hogan. — 1st ed.
p. cm. — (Cognitive approaches to literature and culture series)
Includes bibliographical references and index.
ISBN 978-0-292-71786-2 (cloth : alk. paper)
1. Motion pictures—India. I. Title. II. Series.
PN1993.5.I8H64 2008
791.430954—dc22

2007042909

*For Grinder (Hogie) and Tina*
*Vanu and Lovely*
*Api and Lily*

# Contents

# Acknowledgments

An earlier version of Chapter Four was presented as the keynote address at the 2004 conference of the Research Triangle South Asia Studies Consortium, North Carolina Central University, Durham. I am grateful to the participants, and especially to Mary Mathew, for their comments and questions. A fuller version was presented at the symposium on comparative literature, film, and cognitive neuroscience at the University of Copenhagen in 2004. I am grateful to Torben Grodal and the other participants in the seminar for the stimulating discussion that followed the talk. A version of one section from Chapter Five was presented at the colloquium in film studies at the University of Wisconsin at Madison in 2006. I am grateful to Ben Singer, David Bordwell, and other participants for their comments. Finally, I presented some of the ideas about mirth and childhood, treated in Chapter Three, at the seminar on cognition and literature at Yale University in 2006. I am grateful to Isabel Jaen-Portillo and the participants in the seminar for their observations. S. Shankar and an anonymous referee for the University of Texas Press gave careful, constructive suggestions which have certainly improved the manuscript.

Jim Burr of the University of Texas Press was an insightful and very helpful editor. I am indebted to him. I am grateful to Frederick Aldama for inviting me to submit the manuscript to Jim initially and for providing support throughout the process. Megan Giller expertly ushered the manuscript through production and Salena Krug did valuable copyediting on it.

Jonathan Frome provided invaluable assistance with technical matters regarding frame enlargements.

Lalita Pandit watched all the films with me (many times), constantly helped me with the language, and repeatedly pointed me toward illuminating connections and implications. Without her, this book could not have been written.

# Understanding Indian Movies

# Indian Movies and the People Who Love Them

## Universality and Cultural Particularity in the Cinema

For anyone interested in film, the importance of Indian cinema can hardly be overstated. It is the largest film industry in the world, and probably second only to Hollywood in global influence. Vijay Mishra points out that Indian films are seen "by an average of 11 million people each day" (1). Jigna Desai explains that "Indian cinema has a long past and has been an international cinema familiar to viewers from Russia and the Middle East to parts of Asia and Africa for many decades" (40). Kabir notes that "Indian films are unquestionably the most-seen movies in the world" (*Bollywood* 1).

Yet, as Desai also remarks, Indian cinema has been "unknown to many Westerners" (40). Fortunately, this is changing. The wide availability of DVDs with English subtitles has made Indian movies more accessible in the west. The presence of a growing Indian diaspora has also helped to introduce Indian films to English and American viewers. The expanding interest in Indian movies is evident in the recent publication of many works on Indian cinema, and perhaps even more importantly in the influence of Indian cinema on such popular western movies as *Moulin Rouge.* The growth of scholarly study on Indian films, along with the increased impact of these films on western directors, shows the degree to which Bollywood has made its way into the cinematic imagination of Europeans and Americans. As Hans Robert Jauss might put it, Indian movies have begun to affect our "horizons of expectation," the ways in which at least some westerners understand and respond to films.

But this impact has, in some ways, only rendered the apparent strangeness of Bollywood more salient. Indian films remain "distant" for most western viewers; they remain partially inaccessible, foreign, difficult to appreciate. Indeed, this is true not only for Europeans, but for many Indians. Recently, I was speaking with two Indian friends who asked how I could write about movies such as *Kabhi Khushi Kabhie Gham . . .* , how I could "get over" the treacly sentiment of these works. But I don't think that there is anything to get over in this case. In my view, K3G (as it is known) is not treacly nor fluffy, but a subtly crafted and highly ironic film.

Assuming I am right about this (as I hope readers will agree by the end of the book), why is it that so many viewers see K3G differently, mistakenly judging it to be both saccharine and moralistic? In part, this sort of misunderstanding has nothing to do with the "Indianness" of Indian movies. Rather, it is the result of a cross-cultural division between art and popular culture. My friends would not have been surprised had I expressed enthusiasm for work by an Indian art director, such as Satyajit Ray. Indeed, much of the academic work on Indian cinema has been organized around the division between popular and art films. As Mishra notes, "Indian critics such as Chidananda Das Gupta . . . have divided Indian cinema into two almost irreconcilable parts: an art cinema meant for the self-conscious transnational aesthete (and therefore eminently suitable for critical analysis) and a popular variety (a lower form and therefore not an art object) meant for the general population and the diaspora" (xviii). This is not to say that all writers necessarily valorize "art." Some critics reverse the standard hierarchy, celebrating popular work at the expense of the "difficult" filmmakers. As Prasad puts it, "popular Indian cinema has attracted a considerable amount of attention as the site of an authentically folk culture" (15).

My own view on this issue is closer to that of Leslie Fiedler, who rejected the "unfortunate distinction" between "High Literature and low" (13) from early on. There are popular works that are complex and worth close examination, and popular works that are simplistic. There are art films that are complex and worth close examination, and art films that are simplistic. For this reason, I will not pay a great deal of attention to the division between popular and art cinema, mainstream and alternative films.

The division will enter only in the second chapter, when I pair a paradigmatic alternative film, *Nishānt,* with a paradigmatic popular film, *Sholay.* I will point to differences between the two. However, I hope to show that the similarities between the two are profound and consequential as well.

In any case, the art/entertainment opposition is not the only factor inhibiting viewers' comprehension and appreciation of Indian films. Indian movies are as complex as literary and cinematic works anywhere else. They require the same plenary attention, the same reflection and detailed analysis. We should not expect viewers to understand intuitively all the subtleties of Indian films any more than we would expect them to understand intuitively all the subtleties of European or American films. This too is true for both Indian and non-Indian viewers.

My primary aim in writing this book is, therefore, to provide an account of Indian films that helps viewers comprehend and (critically) appreciate those films. Indeed, I hope to provide a way for viewers to understand and respond fully to a range of Indian movies, not only the specific films I analyze. In other words, I hope to provide the reader with knowledge and skills that are generalizable, knowledge and skills that will help him or her to view, and to enjoy, a wide range of Indian movies.

In connection with this, I have tried to choose films that allow me to explicate generalizable cultural particulars (not particulars that are peculiar to a given film). Moreover, I have sought to relate these particulars to more accessible cross-cultural patterns. For example, just as biblical stories have had a great influence on western literature, stories from religious epics frequently structure plots in Indian films (the general point is widely acknowledged, though not often considered in detail; see, for example, Dissanayake and Sahai, *Sholay,* 9–12, and Mishra 4). Just as Aristotelian ideas of unity and Romantic theories of expression have influenced European drama, the theory of rasadhvani has had effects across Indian arts (a point also noted by some authors, though rarely developed; Joshi provides an interesting exception). I have set out to explicate these and related topics in such a way that the reader can follow their development in the individual films I am analyzing, understand their generalizability to other works of Indian cinema, and recognize their relation to cross-cultural patterns.

Consider rasa theory, the theory of aesthetic emotion initially developed in ancient Sanskrit texts. First, I discuss the cross-cultural, indeed universal, principles manifest in rasa theory—universal principles that have led some cognitive scientists (such as Keith Oatley) to take up rasa theory in a neurocognitive context. Second, I treat the cultural particularity of the theory, countering the objection of some critics that it is "ill-defined" (Dwyer and Patel 28). It is important to consider such culturally particular accounts of emotion because emotions involve processes. These processes are initiated by particular sorts of cues and are often sustained by particular decisions and actions on the part of the people experiencing the emotions. In my view, the emotions are the same across cultures. However, the cues and related responses may differ. The differences are superficial, but they may be consequential in particular cases. Take a very simple example. Suppose Sunil and Bob meet an attractive and engaging young woman who has colored the part in her hair. Sunil realizes that this means she is married, thus he does not open himself to the possibility of romantic involvement with her (e.g., he does not approach or address her in certain ways, imagine his future relationship with her in certain ways, and so forth). Bob, in contrast, does not understand this. Over the course of several weeks, he develops romantic feelings for the young woman. In part, this development is out of his control. But in part it results from his initial openness to seeing this woman in a particular (romantic) way, with all the actions, interpretations, and imaginations that such openness entails. The same point holds for literary experience, and bears directly on the importance of rasa theory. The culturally specific aesthetic practices articulated in rasa theory bear on the way viewers open themselves to particular emotions in particular contexts. In connection with this, then, I analyze three films in terms of rasa theory. The purpose of the analyses is not only to show something about these three movies, though all three films are important and influential. It is also, and even more significantly, to provide the reader with knowledge and skills that he or she may extend to other Indian films.

An examination of cultural particularity is, then, central to the following analyses. However, my treatment of cultural particularity is somewhat different from that of most writers in cultural studies over the last few decades. Specifically, I hope to advance readers' understanding and appreciation of Indian film, not by insisting on cultural differences, but by locating cultural particularity within cross-cultural patterns. I pursue the second task primarily by drawing broader theoretical principles from cognitive neuroscience. But why should cognitive neuroscience provide understanding and appreciation in a way that, for example, post-structural approaches have not? Why should we consider empirical studies of emotion and the human brain any more illuminating to ordinary viewers than, say, Homi

Bhabha's reflections on "temporality as the desire of the daily plebiscite" (310)?

Here, I need to set out some basic ideas of the book. First, understanding and appreciation are based on shared principles. This is true both within and across cultures. Suppose I am talking with Jones. I understand what Jones means because I share a range of principles with him. My understanding of Jones is not based on my differences from him. It is based on my similarities with him. At least until recently, it was commonplace in the humanities to argue that we understand the Other only by affirming his or her difference. This idea responds to a real problem, but it offers a solution that is itself no less problematic. The problem is projection. I may assume that Jones and I share certain ideas or attitudes that, in fact, we do not share. Thus I may falsely attribute particular sorts of commonality. However, the solution to this problem is not to affirm difference. Indeed, affirming difference is ultimately a matter of giving up on agreement, discussion, mutual influence, even mutual comprehension. The solution to projection is, rather, to figure out just what our commonalities really are. The solution is to get our shared principles right—a point made, in somewhat different terms, by Kwame Appiah, among others (see Appiah 58).

If the problem of misunderstanding arises between two people in the same culture—and we all know from experience that it does—the danger of misunderstanding seems all the more acute for people in different cultures. Here, too, humanists have often maintained that it is particularly crucial to affirm cross-cultural difference. But, in fact, if the problem of projection increases across cultures, so too does the problem of affirming difference. Indeed, it becomes politically acute—and in precisely the opposite of the way commonly assumed by writers in the humanities. It has overwhelmingly been the assertion of difference, not the assertion of sameness, that has been politically deleterious. Affirmations of difference have underwritten all forms of cultural supremacism. No one claims that his or her culture is better than another culture because the two are the same; one claims superiority only over cultures that one believes are different.

In cross-cultural study, then, it is crucial neither to project false commonalities nor to affirm difference, but to determine just what it is that we actually do have in common. The shared principles that define our commonality are what linguists call "universals."[1] Universals are the only basis on which we can build cross-cultural understanding. The point applies not only to conversation, but to all types of communication, including those embodied in literature and film. Indeed, the point applies not only across but within cultures. In conversation, in literature, and in film, the most fundamental principles that my neighbor and I have in common are not cultural. The fact that we both have access to the same kitchen appliances would be meaningless if it were not for the fact that our memories are structured in the same ways, our cognitive processes are virtually identical, our emotional propensities differ only marginally. What connects us most deeply to one another are just those universal principles that we share with contemporary Indian (or European or Chinese or African) filmmakers, ancient Indian (or European or Chinese or African) poets, and, indeed, everyone else.

In sum, our understanding of Indian cinema—or, for that matter, any cinema—must first of all be based on universal principles, on ideas, sensitivities, impulses that we share, whatever our national origin or cultural milieu.

The most fundamental universal here concerns art itself. Every culture produces verbal art (see Kiparsky 195–196). Why is that? The answer to this question is suggested by the literary theories that have been produced by every major literary tradition.[2] Though the emphases differ, these traditions (European, Indian, Middle Eastern, Chinese, and Japanese) all indicate two main purposes for verbal art—roughly, "to teach and entertain" (in Sidney's famous phrase [138]). Recent work by evolutionary psychologists, such as Steven Pinker, draws similar conclusions (*How* 539). I would say more technically that the main purpose of literary art is to communicate emotion. (This is sometimes viewed as a Romantic idea. But, in fact, it is stressed by early Greek, Sanskrit, Japanese, Arabic, and Chinese theorists, well before the development of Romanticism.) Its second purpose, usually considered more elevated, is to communicate themes. In other words, verbal art is cross-culturally understood to involve feeling in every case. In addition, theorists tend to see the articulation of consequential ethical, political, or religious ideas as important for verbal art, if sometimes absent from purely entertaining works. While emotions and themes may be communicated in different ways, the most common way of communicating them in verbal art has been through narrative—narrative itself being a universal property of verbal art. With the development of the cinema, these universals come to be manifest in fiction film as well.

But these universals clearly leave a great deal up in the air. Indeed, to some extent, they rephrase our dilemma. If the main purposes of art—including film—are to communicate emotions and themes, usually by way of narrative, then we are still left with the problem of how we experience these emotions or understand these themes and narratives in particular cases. In other words, we need more detailed, more fully specified universals. We need precisely articulated principles of emotion, theme, and narrative that we share cross-culturally. It is not sufficient to state the general principle that everyone has verbal art and that this art vaguely includes some sort of emotion, theme, and narrative.

This is what leads me to cognitive science. The research programs gathered together under the rubric of cognitive science provide us with the best current understanding of precisely what it is that cultures share, because they provide us with the best current understanding of what people share. From narrative structure to visual construction, cognitive neuroscience—though far from infallible—comprises the best complex of theories available.

This is not to say that I intend simply to draw on already established cognitive results. In a very real sense, there are no results that are established in this way. To study Indian film through cognitive science is a worthwhile undertaking only if it is simultaneously a testing and development of cognitive ideas. It should not simply be an application of those ideas, an attempt to fit works into a theory that is accepted as if it were a religious dogma. Rather, a cognitive study of Indian movies, or of anything else, should be part of an ongoing research program that works through the received ideas of neuroscience and related fields, sometimes modifying or even rejecting those received ideas. My hope, then, is that the various cognitive analyses in this book will not only enhance our understanding of Indian cinema and clarify the basic principles of cognitive neuroscience as they bear on the study of film. My hope is that they will also advance the study of cognitive universals, along with our understanding of the relation between universals and cultural particularity.

In connection with this, the main body of the book is organized by reference to the fundamental universals of narrative, theme, and emotion. In separate chapters on each topic, I consider both the cross-cultural patterns (e.g., universal story prototypes) and their cultural specifications. Of course, film does not communicate its emotions and themes solely by way of narrative. It includes sound and visuals. Indeed, even narrative information may be suggested by such formal features as camera work or song. In the fourth and fifth chapters, then, I turn to music and visual style. Here, too, there are universal and culturally particular elements.

In the course of the book, I discuss eleven films in some detail. I have tried to include instances of the major categories in Indian cinema. However, my selection is not in any way proportionate to the actual production percentages of various types of film. Rather, I have chosen films that I feel merit consideration, films that, in my view, have achieved some sort of artistic excellence. Four of these films come from the 1950's, the "golden age" of Bollywood—"the most creative and innovative decade in Hindi cinema" (Kabir, *Bollywood,* 16). Another four have been produced since 1990, reflecting my view that Indian cinema has experienced a sort of renaissance in that period. While most of the films are in Hindi or Urdu, one is in Tamil and one is in English. I have included films by some of the directors who are often considered the best in mainstream Hindi cinema— Guru Dutt, Mehboob Khan, and Raj Kapoor (see ibid., 123, and the quotation from Johar on 124; see also Thoraval 71)—and an award-winning film by one of the best-known directors of the alternative cinema (Shyam Benegal). One chapter treats the highest-grossing Hindi film; another treats what is probably the most widely known work in Tamil (the only one readers are likely to find in the local Blockbuster). There are films by Muslims (Mehboob Khan and Muzaffar Ali) as well as Hindus, and so forth. In short, though not quite representative, the selection of films is diverse along several important axes and should therefore allow the reader access to a wide range of movies beyond those discussed directly in the book. The one obvious gap is the absence of any film by Satyajit Ray. I have chosen not to include Ray as he is the most widely discussed Indian filmmaker in the English-speaking world. As such, his work is less in need of examination. Given limited space, it is, I believe, better to include a less frequently analyzed director in his place.

More exactly, the first chapter treats plot, considering the three universal narrative prototypes—romantic, heroic, and sacrificial tragi-comedy—and their cultural particularization in three Indian films. The chapter begins by explaining the three prototypes, their structure and origin. It goes on to examine an instance of each type. First, it takes up the romantic structure in relation to Ajit Chakrabarty's *Ardhangini*. Cross-culturally, the romantic plot treats the desire of two lovers to be united and the social opposition that temporarily prevents their union. This social opposition is commonly based on some status discrepancy between the lovers (e.g., class difference). *Ardhangini* specifies this plot by, in effect, making the obstacle one of caste. I say "in effect" because the treatment of caste in the film is unmistakable, though it is only implicit. Indeed, this is one reason for the effectiveness of the film. Chakrabarty also draws on Hindu myths of Śiva and Pārvatī to develop the narrative and characterization.

The heroic plot has two components. In one, the national hierarchy is threatened by a rebellion; in the other, the nation as a whole is threatened by an out-group, commonly through invasion. To treat this genre, I take up Guru Dutt's widely misunderstood film, *Baaz* (*Falcon*). In recent years, Guru Dutt has come to be admired as one of the greatest directors of Indian cinema. However, *Baaz* is almost uniformly viewed as a failure, even an embarrassment. At best, it is simply passed over by critics. This is, I believe, a serious error. Indeed, I would argue that *Baaz* is one of Dutt's finest works. Part of the difficulty is that the political aims and historical references of Dutt's film have not been recognized. In particularizing the heroic plot, Dutt collapses the history of European colonialism into a single narrative. He alludes to a range of historical persons and events in order to present a story that is not about a particular usurpation of social authority. Rather, it treats a sort of repeated usurpation that extended over centuries. Moreover, Dutt directs this entire condensed narrative toward what was, at the time of the film's production, a current political concern—the continuation of Portuguese colonialism in Goa.

Finally, sacrificial tragi-comedy treats communal devastation (e.g., famine) and the offering of a sacrifice to end that devastation. In order to discuss this structure, I turn to a celebrated Tamil film, Santosh Sivan's *The Terrorist*. Sivan's film is also historical, presenting a fictionalized version of the assassination of Rajiv Gandhi by the Liberation Tigers of Tamil Eelam (LTTE), a group seeking a Tamil homeland in Sri Lanka. Sivan clearly uses a sacrificial plot to characterize the main character's suicide bombing. To develop this plot, he also draws extensively, though implicitly, on a sacrificial Tamil epic, *The Ankle Bracelet,* that appears to have influenced the leader of the LTTE.

The second chapter turns to theme. To a great extent, universal themes of narrative may be derived from the narrative prototypes and from the general structure of stories. In fact, Chapter One necessarily treats some of these themes. Rather than repeating topics treated in the preceding chapter, I focus on a single theme associated with heroic tragi-comedy, a theme of particular importance in an Indian context—violence. This theme is bound up with a surprising recurrent feature of heroic narratives. Specifically, heroic tragi-comedies often end, not with the victory of the heroes, but with some sense of remorse over the misery produced in the course of securing that victory. They end, in other words, with an "epilogue of suffering."[3] I consider two films in this context. The first, *Nishānt,* involves a clear epilogue of suffering, particularized in such a way as to support nonviolence. It reinforces its thematic point by using a central Hindu epic, the *Rāmāyaṇa,* as a narrative model. The second film, *Sholay,* also draws on the *Rāmāyaṇa.* But, in contrast with *Nishānt,* it alters standard motifs of the epilogue of suffering in order to oppose the political valorization of nonviolence, a valorization most famously supported by Mahatma Gandhi. These two films appeared in the same year (1975). The former is a paradigm of the Indian art cinema, and the recipient of numerous awards (Best Film and Best Screenplay from *Film World* magazine and the National Award for Best Film). The latter is one of the biggest popular blockbusters in the history of Hindi cinema.

Chapter Three considers emotion. It begins with an outline of a cognitive account of emotion. It then turns to the theory of aesthetic emotion or "rasa" that arose with classical Sanskrit traditions in the arts and that has continued to be important in Indian classical dance, music, and elsewhere. Rasa theory is fundamentally a theory about empathy and the particular forms empathy may take in relation to a literary work. Romantic love was the emotion most emphasized in rasa theory. However, since most of the films discussed in the preceding chapters are romantic, I set that rasa aside to consider three other emotive genres—those focusing on anger, sorrow, and mirth. In connection with this, I briefly consider evolutionary psychology, arguing that, in the case of these three emotions, empathic responses have a special, adaptive relation to children.

To treat empathic anger, I take up Shekhar Kapur's *Bandit Queen*—according to Shyam Benegal, "possibly the greatest film ever made in India" (Gokulsing and Dissanayake 109). This film treats the life of Phoolan Devi, India's notorious "bandit queen." It has a particular political purpose—to make viewers angry enough about caste and gender oppression to do something about them when they leave the theater. It systematically develops our empathic anger in the course of the film. Moreover, it does so to a considerable degree by stressing physical cruelty to a child, the young Phoolan.

For empathic sorrow, I turn to the most famous melodrama of Indian cinema, Mehboob Khan's *Mother India.* I begin this section by considering cognitive accounts of melodrama. I go on to discuss how the self-sacrifice that characterizes melodrama is often a parental self-sacrifice for the benefit of a child and that, in keeping with this, empathic sorrow is particularly intensified by separation in attachment relationships (e.g., mother/child relationships). *Mother India* has been one of the most successful and one of the most lauded films of Indian cinema (see Sumita Chakravarty 149 and Chatterjee 79–80). It makes particularly subtle use of mother/child attachment and separation. First, it repeatedly reverses the parenting roles, making the tiny Birju mother his own parents. Second, it reverses the final sacrifice, for in the end the mother feels that she must kill her own son. Khan draws extensively on Kṛṣṇa legends to develop his characters and the audience's relation to those characters. He also draws on Marxist ideas to present an implicit criticism of independent India—a criticism inseparable from the emotional response fostered by the film.

Finally, I consider mirth. I argue that mirth has an evolutionary function in giving us pleasure in the oddities of actions, speech, and appearance that are characteristic of children, though by no means confined to children. To explore this, I look at a work by a comic genius of Indian cinema, Raj Kapoor. Specifically, I examine *Shree 420,* often considered Kapoor's best film (see, for example, Thoraval 88). In this work, Kapoor presents us with an allegory of Indian self-government (*swa-raj*) as the character Raj has to choose between the westernized elite, represented by Maya (whose name means *illusion*), and the people who embody both learned and popular Indian traditions, represented by Vidya (whose name means *knowledge*) and Ganga Ma (Mother Ganges). As in *Mother India,* the argument of the film is fundamentally in keeping with Marxist ideas, specifically those advocated by the All-India Progressive Writers' Association. However, in this case, the themes of the film are developed through mirth. Moreover, that mirth is clearly bound up with Raj's childlike character. Indeed, our affinity with Raj is in part dependent on the affection we have for him as a sort of child.

The fourth chapter turns to sound, specifically music. Most Indian films are musicals. Many western viewers find the use of song and dance in Indian films to be disorienting. Even Indians often dismiss the song interludes as fluff. However, they are quite serious productions, often the most complex and significant sections of a film. In this chapter, I address the functional relation of the musical interlude to the three main components of narrative film—plot, theme, and emotion. For example, I argue that the freedom of the interlude allows filmmakers to communicate narrative and thematic ideas that would otherwise be difficult to present, especially in the Indian cinema with its strict codes of censorship. I illustrate the often remarkably subtle use of interludes in these three areas by treating one of the greatest box-office successes in the history of Indian film, *Kabhi Kushie, Kabhie Gham . . .*

The fifth chapter considers the other sensory mode of cinema, vision. It begins by dividing the discussion into editing and lighting/color. I discuss some of the universal principles of vision as these bear on cinema, and particularly as they bear on our emotional response to films. From here, I examine the ways in which the standard system of editing, called "continuity editing," both accords with our perceptual tendencies and may be violated in such a way as to produce particular perceptual, emotional, and thematic effects. To develop this point, I consider Muzaffar Ali's *Umrao Jaan* (which received the Filmfare Award for Best Director). This film concerns the life of a girl who is kidnapped and sold into prostitution at a young age, then grows up to be an accomplished poet, singer, and dancer. Ali uses the story to present themes drawn from Ṣūfī mysticism—themes of the illusory character of material life and the ultimate identity of one's soul with God. In the course of the film, Ali repeatedly violates standard principles of continuity editing. He has two purposes in doing this. First, he wishes to intensify our emotional response by violating our expectations in particular ways. Second, he wishes to make thematic points by frustrating—and thus redirecting—our interpretations, at times by creating impossibilities in the story world.

Finally, I consider the operation of color and lighting. In the course of her controversial, award-winning film, *Fire,* Deepa Mehta makes systematic use of colors to communicate her main themes and manipulates lighting for both thematic suggestions and emotional effects. Indeed, *Fire* is a film that is almost impossible to understand if one does not pay attention to visual style. For example, Mehta repeatedly associates the women in the film with the colors of the Indian flag (orange, white, and green), suggesting that the hope for India's future lies in new forms of connection undertaken by women. The first sexual union of the two main characters—Radha and Sita—presents the viewer with a particularly striking image. One of the women is in orange. The other is in green. They are separated by the white bedsheets. But this is not only a union of women. It is also a union of communities (orange representing Hinduism; green representing Islam). When they are finally and fully joined at the end of the film, Radha and Sita meet in a Ṣūfī shrine, Ṣūfism itself being a union of Hinduism and Islam. Mehta stresses and emotionally enhances her thematic points by the systematic use of two lighting techniques. First, she associates diffuse, boundaryless, bright light with repressive religious orthodoxy. In contrast with this, she gives us sharply outlined silhouettes to communicate an almost tactile sense of union between the women.

• • •

Again, Indian cinema is one of the most vibrant in the world. It is not only entertaining, but beautiful, moving, and thematically subtle. My hope is that readers of the following chapters will not only learn something about these particular films, but will be inspired to go and watch more Indian movies, appreciating them more fully. Such appreciation derives simultaneously from an understanding of cultural variations and from a sensitivity to cross-cultural constancies. The patterns in these films are not idiosyncratic. They are cultural specifications of emotional, narrative, perceptual, and other universals. In relation to this, I hope the following analyses help to advance our understanding of film generally—its narrative organization, thematic structures, and emotional impact, as well as its use of music, editing, light, and color. Moreover, insofar as it advances our understanding of film, I hope it advances, in some degree, our understanding of the human mind as well. The creation and experience of art are universal processes of the human mind. They are central to human life, both individual and collective. For example, it is virtually impossible to imagine even a single human life, not to mention an entire culture, without the telling of stories. If our cognitive science does not encompass such processes, it is fatally incomplete.

CHAPTER ONE

# From Mythical Romances to Historical Sacrifices

## Universal Stories in South Asia

### *Ardhangini, Baaz,* and *The Terrorist*

Humans think about and respond to categories by way of prototypes.[1] This includes the category of *stories.* Prototypes are, roughly, standard cases of a certain group (e.g., birds). They do not provide necessary and sufficient conditions for membership in the group. However, they most often guide our thought about the group. Thus for most of us the prototype of a bird is more or less a robin. In judging whether something is or is not a bird—or whether it is a "normal" bird or a "strange" bird—we commonly compare it to that prototype. If asked to draw a bird, imagine a bird, or describe a bird, we are likely to come up with something along the lines of a robin. However, a robin does not provide a definition of the word *bird.* We can perfectly well accept that an ostrich is a bird, though it is not very much like a robin, and thus we might say that, though an ostrich is a bird, it is not very "bird-like." The same point holds for stories. We consider some stories more story-like than others. The story-like stories are prototypical.

It is well established that our prototypes vary with context. Our prototype for a dog is different in the context "Manhattan apartment" than in the context "farm in Iowa" (see Kahneman and Miller 140). The same point holds for plots and for the emotion concepts that are crucial for the production and reception of plots.

Recent research indicates that prototypical narrative structures show remarkable cross-cultural consistency. Specifically, research on canonical narratives from Europe, the Middle East, Africa, South Asia, East Asia, and the Americas indicates that there are three cross-culturally recurring narrative prototypes—romantic, heroic, and sacrificial. These prototypes all involve a protagonist pursuing some goal, specifically some form of happiness. They are distinguished, first of all, by the type of happiness the protagonist desires. We may isolate different types of happiness by reference to context. In a personal context, happiness is defined by romantic union. In a social context, it is a function of social authority and power. In a physical context, it is a matter of health and sustenance—specifically, plenty or abundance. These prototypes generate the three cross-cultural genres. For instance, romantic plots are driven by a protagonist—or, in this case, often two protagonists—pursuing romantic union. All three genres may be referred to as "tragi-comedies" as, in their full form, they involve an apparent loss of the animating goal before it is achieved. Thus, in the romantic plot, the lovers often seem to be separated permanently (e.g., by death) before they are finally brought together.[2]

It is important to stress that narrative prototypes do not provide necessary and sufficient conditions for being a story. Thus they do not cover all stories in all traditions. However, they do appear to characterize the majority of those stories. They regularly guide our production and reception of stories. But they do not determine that production and reception. Moreover, there may be considerable variation even in stories derived from a particular prototype.

As the last point indicates, prototypes are somewhat abstract. They are not fully particularized stories. To get a story, we need to "fill in" the prototype. We do not do this in a random manner, but by following principles. We may call them "development principles." For example, one very simple development principle is to add physical and psychological features and personal and social relations to the characters. A second development principle is to draw such features and relations from real persons or from other fictional characters.

Though most (perhaps all) development principles are universal, it should be clear that rules such as those just mentioned will produce different results in different circumstances. First, an individual author's experience and understanding of persons and characters will be to some extent unique. More important for our purposes, there will be patterns across individuals that are not universal, but a matter of culture, literary tradition, or historical period. These patterns develop in two ways. First, in many cases, the facts about the world will be different. The general types of personal and social relations are, at some level, universal. However, people do not enter into precisely the same personal and social relations in different cultures or historical periods. Moreover, in one sense, even physical and psychological properties change historically and culturally. For example, everyone has the same basic emotions. However, in particular cultural conditions sexual jealousy or hatred of out-groups may be fostered, while in other conditions they may be inhibited. In keeping with this, the "actional and expressive outcomes" of emotion (i.e., what one does when one feels an emotion)—including the ways in which one envisions and selects action—vary to some extent culturally and historically.

Beyond differences in facts themselves, there are further differences across authors' and readers' understandings of those facts. Cultures do not have precisely the same ideas about emotion, even for those aspects of emotion that are in fact universal. An author may, then, develop characters in keeping with culturally specific ideas about emotion (e.g., the Renaissance psychology of humors) such that the characters reflect those ideas more than actual patterns in real life. On the other hand, authors do not invariably adhere to cultural clichés. Indeed, they not infrequently contradict standard ideas. Thus one also has to be aware that common views about a topic (e.g., emotion) do not determine any given author's representation of that topic.

In introducing development principles, I referred to two sources for the specification of character prototypes—real life and earlier fictional works. In fact, we seem to process information about persons in much the same way whether we are reading about a fictional character, reading about a public figure, or hearing about what a friend did yesterday. This suggests that real versus fictional may not be an operative division in these cases. Rather, we might more usefully distinguish between experiential or personal sources of specification, on the one hand, and literary or historical sources, on the other. This division is useful because individual, biographical sources tend to be idiosyncratic, while literary and historical sources tend to be more generalizable across authors in a particular culture or historical period. Indeed, that generalizability is largely what defines a tradition.

But here we might ask—just what developments justify generalization in these cases? How do traditions—particularly literary traditions—develop so as to be shared by many individuals? After all, there are countless literary works, and countless aspects of those works. Similarly, there are countless historical events. How do patterns form across this diversity?

Here we come to another universal, indeed another universal that has culturally particularistic consequences. Literary traditions are selective and hierarchical. They do not simply accept all stories as equal. The most obvious way traditions select and hierarchize is through the creation of canons. However, I would like to emphasize another aspect of selection and ranking within tradition. The crucial division, I believe, is not between canonical and non-canonical works. Rather, it is between paradigmatic works and all others, for paradigmatic works are the works that define literary excellence, whether narrative, emotional, or moral/thematic. All major literary traditions appear to make this division. There are even universal patterns in the general nature of these works. Perhaps most important, paradigmatic works are often religious or political—in a broad sense, one may say "national"—stories, stories that present fundamental principles about spiritual and social authority. On the other hand, there are, of course, differences in the precise stories that achieve this status in different traditions. The sacrificial story of the Fall of Adam and Eve and the redemption of humanity is a paradigmatic religious story in Christian traditions. This is in many ways strikingly different from the heroic and romantic story of Rāma, Sītā, and Rāvaṇa that is a paradigmatic religious story in Hindu tradition.

Paradigms are crucial for the specification of prototypes in any given tradition. In applying development principles, authors do not draw on all works (or historical events) equally. They draw on works based, in part, on their salience. To put it differently, some characters, events, and scenes are prominent and easily accessible in our memory. In isolating useful features for filling out a prototype (e.g., when defining individual character traits), we are most likely to draw on those prominent and accessible structures. Authors will differ individually in which works are most salient for them. However, across a wide range of authors, paradigmatic works are the ones that will recur most frequently. Indeed, that cognitive prominence is part of what defines such works as paradigmatic. When paradigmatic works serve as models for subsequent works, that further secures their place as paradigms by enhancing their saliency for still later writers. Thus the Bible is not only important as a text in itself; it is important as the source for a range of canonical works from explicit retellings, such as *Paradise Lost,* to the countless novels, plays, and poems that implicitly rely on parallels between their own events and the Passion of Jesus or the Fall of Humankind. More relevantly for our purposes, the *Rāmāyaṇa* bears both directly and indirectly on the development of countless romantic and heroic plots in India from Sanskrit drama through the most recent Bollywood films. Each new use of that poem reaffirms its paradigmatic place.

Of course, our cognitive tendency to rely on salience does not lead only to paradigmatic literary works. It leads also to common figures—indeed, paradigmatic figures—in cultural discourse, prominently including important persons or events from history. For example, in American culture, George Washington has a certain salience as a paradigmatic political leader, a salience that operates without reference to any particular canonical text. A similar point may be made about Gandhi in India, or about the 1857 uprising. These too enter into the specification of narrative prototypes.

Finally, salience leads us to pressing social and political concerns in an author's environment. These include concerns that, however important at the time, have not been incorporated prominently into subsequent cultural traditions. It is particularly easy to overlook these concerns and, as a result, to misunderstand (and underestimate) a work. For example, Guru Dutt's *Baaz* responds in part to the then-current political situation in Goa. However, most viewers of the film today are likely to be both ignorant about and indifferent to that situation.

In sum, stories result from the application of development principles to prototypes. Both the prototypes and the development principles are largely universal. However, the development principles necessarily refer to particulars that are not universal. These particulars are, rather, a matter of individual experience, cultural tradition (literary and historical)—prominently including paradigms—and pressing current affairs. In this way, our understanding of a given story needs to combine two things: first, sensitivity to the universal structures that organize and orient cultural and socio-political particulars; second, comprehension of the cultural and socio-political particulars that specify, extend, and revise those universal structures.[3]

In this chapter, then, I will consider three exemplary Indian films, one for each of the three universal narrative prototypes. I will begin each discussion with a sketch of the universal structure. I will then consider the way in which the film both manifests and specifies that structure, prominently by drawing on one or more literary paradigms of Indian tradition. In the course of the three analyses, I will outline some of the paradigms that are most crucial for understanding Indian cinema. In the Hindu tradition, these paradigms include the two great Sanskrit epics, the *Rāmāyaṇa* and the *Mahābhārata* (cf. Mishra 4), along with some childhood and adolescent stories of Kṛṣṇa, some stories of Śiva and the Goddess, and other materials. For South Indian works, we need to add the great Tamil epics to this list. Paradigms in the Muslim tradition include such allegories as *Laylā and Majnūn,* as well as a range of Qur'ānic stories, many of which are familiar to Europeans and Americans from the Torah and the Bible. In the following sections, I will take up the *Rāmāyaṇa,* some stories of Śiva and the Goddess, and one of the Tamil epics. I will also treat some of the historical and contemporary socio-political events and conditions that bear on these films. Historical concerns are prominent only in *Baaz.* However, their presence in this film is exemplary of the larger tradition. Specifically, *Baaz* refers centrally to the 1857 uprising or "Mutiny." This is perhaps the most frequently invoked historical event in Indian cinema. Finally, all three films make direct reference to pressing socio-political concerns. Thus they illustrate nicely the ways in which current events combine with literary paradigms—and, in the case of *Baaz,* historical paradigms—to concretize universal prototypes. They also illustrate the ways in which our experience of Indian cinema is impoverished when we do not recognize the socio-political issues engaged by particular films, just as it is impoverished when we fail to recognize the literary and historical resonances of those films, or the universal patterns those films instantiate.

## The Shadow of an Untouchable: Romantic Tragi-Comedy and Ajit Chakrabarty's *Ardhangini*

Cross-culturally, romantic tragi-comedy is the most common narrative genre. It derives from the personal prototype for happiness, romantic union, which is to say, enduring union with a person for whom one feels a fusion of sexual desire and affection. Since that is the defining happiness prototype of the genre, it is the defining goal of the main characters; its achievement is what makes the plot resolution comic. The positive emotional impact of any comic resolution, romantic or otherwise, is enhanced by difficulty of achievement (see Ortony, Clore, and Collins 71–73 on the general relation between difficulty of goal achievement and the intensity of the resulting emotion). If the lovers fall in love and are joined, we are pleased. But we are more pleased by the union if the lovers fall in love, struggle against great odds to be united, then finally succeed. As a result, the middle of the prototypical romantic tragi-comedy involves the separation of the lovers. Our anxiety about the separation and our joy at the eventual union are often further intensified by making each condition apparently eternal. When the lovers are separated, it seems that they will never be rejoined. When they are united, they will "live happily ever after." Indeed, their final union is often spiritualized, implicitly or explicitly extended to an afterlife. In keeping with this, the separation of the lovers is often associated with death, literally or metaphorically. It is unsurprising in this context that romantic plots frequently make reference to religious ideas and practices, and often borrow from paradigmatic religious narratives.

Since the narrative middle requires the lovers to be separated, there must be some reason for their separation. In keeping with the division of happiness prototypes, the reasons are commonly physical, personal, or social. Physical problems are the least common. However, they can figure importantly, particularly in certain forms of melodrama. In these cases, the blocking agent for the lovers' union may be a fatal illness (such as cancer), a debilitating accident, or a natural catastrophe (such as famine).

Personal conflict is a more usual way of blocking the union of the lovers. This commonly takes one of two forms. The more common form is a love triangle in which one of the lovers cannot make up his or her mind about his or her true love. In a common Hollywood variant of this, suggested also in such Hindi films as Tripathi's *Kavi Kalidas,* this lover seems oblivious to the fact that he or she is really in love with one of the rivals, and treats that person merely as a friend. The other recurrent form of personal conflict involves some ethical dilemma, some sort of moral duty that prevents the lover from committing himself or herself to the beloved. One common version of this involves a devoted child who feels he or she cannot abandon his or her parents (as in one segment of Bimal Roy's *Sujata*). This is particularly common in melodrama, especially if the parent is alone and physically ill. Other variants include devotion to the nation (as in Roy's *Bandini*) and commitment to a child or younger sibling (as in Dutt's *Kaagaz ke Phool*).

The most common means of blocking the lovers' union is social. In the usual form of this structure, some representative of society forbids the lovers' marriage on the grounds that it violates traditional social principles. This representative may be a political or religious figure. More commonly, it is one of the lovers' parents. In some cases, the problem is simply that the lovers' choice of one another usurps the authority of the parent, who claims the right to make this decision. Most often, however, there is a combination of paternal authoritarianism and group hierarchy, so that the father objects to the marriage because the lovers are from different classes, castes, or races. This gives rise to a love triangle plot as well. But this love triangle is very different from the one in which the lover is uncertain about his or her own preferences. In this case, the rival is placed between the lovers by the social representative, not by the beloved. For example, in what is probably the most common version of this plot, the rival is the man chosen by a father for his daughter.

Social authority or group hierarchy is commonly the ultimate reason for the separation of lovers, even in cases where personal or physical factors enter. Indeed, it may even be the reason for a physical calamity. In the case of personal conflict, the feeling of duty toward a sickly parent may be created by that parent as a strategy for preventing the union of the lovers. Moreover, in cases where the beloved cannot decide who it is that he or she loves, the root of the conflict may be in the parents' plotting on behalf of the rival—or in the beloved's own ambivalence about the crucial social hierarchy (e.g., his or her uncertainty about the wisdom of marrying outside his or her class, caste, or race).

Thus we have an ending for the romantic plot (union, if the plot is a comedy) and a middle (separation, usually due to social interference based on group hierarchy). The beginning of a romantic plot simply requires that the lovers fall in love. This is a surprisingly simple matter. One might expect that authors would have to take pains to convince us that two people are right for one another—and sometimes authors do that. But, more often than not, authors just have the lovers meet and their fate is sealed. Whether we are discussing the great Sanskrit classic *Abhijñānaśākuntalam* or *Romeo and Juliet,* it seems that most readers or viewers find it sufficient for the lovers to see one another and express their love (first to us, then to one another). After that, almost everyone seems to want the lovers to be united. Almost everyone is vehemently opposed to the authorities who try to separate the lovers. Indeed, it takes a great deal of effort to make the audience unsympathetic to the lovers' preferences. (A good way of doing this is to make the beloved unfaithful or physically abusive.) In this way, the beginning of the romantic plot is not difficult to establish.

Before going on to *Ardhangini,* I should say something about character. Romantic plots commonly have two main characters, the lovers, though we are often more closely aligned with one of the two (i.e., the narrative usually focuses more fully on one). Obviously, there are blocking characters, which is to say, characters who impede the lovers' progress toward union. Parallel to the blocking characters, there are "helpers," characters who aid the hero and heroine. These helping characters are often involved in elaborate schemes to unite the lovers. In this way, the helping characters may also instantiate another universal type—the "internal author." By "internal author," I mean a character who manipulates the actions and experiences of other characters with (often implausible) precision and ease. Such a character, who recurs across literary traditions,[4] is a sort of parallel to the author, for this character controls other characters in much the way the author does. (Of course, in the case of the internal author, that control is indirect, the result of clever strategies, not mere dictation.) The humor of romantic plots is often taken up by the ancillary characters. In treatments of romance that aim to be more amusing than romantic, blocking and helping characters may be the focus of attention (cf. Frye 166–167).

*Ardhangini* fits the romantic structure perfectly. But it also varies it in interesting ways, and specifies it by reference to cultural paradigms and contemporary political concerns. Specifically, *Ardhangini* is the story of a girl, Chhaya (meaning "shadow"), born at a moment of disaster for her family. Just as she enters the world, her mother dies, her father loses his job, and the family home is burned. For this reason, she is stigmatized. She is characterized as cursed and inauspicious. The opening scenes of the film elaborate on the social consequences of this stigma. Eventually, Chhaya's status as inauspicious will inhibit her marriage to Prakash (meaning "light"). Thus the opening serves to establish the social hierarchy that blocks the union of the lovers.

But there is more to the opening than this indicates. Chakrabarty has already begun to specify the romantic plot in politically consequential ways, in ways directly related to social conditions at the time. After Chhaya is born, there is a brief scene when she is a young girl. We then have a series of shots of her feet as she walks along the road. Her shadow is clear. At one point, we cut to a man who has evidently just left his home in the morning and glimpsed Chhaya. He turns away, lamenting and invoking the god, Rāma, "Ram, Ram! Why did I have to see the face of that cursed girl?" In the course of the walk, Chhaya changes from a child into an adult. She arrives home and discusses the marriage of her friend, Leela. She cannot attend the marriage because she is inauspicious.

Chhaya seems to be the victim of bizarrely irrational prejudice. Because her family suffered a series of disasters when she was born, she is blamed for anything that goes wrong around her. But Chakrabarty is using this scenario to criticize other tendencies within Hindu society. For example, widows were considered inauspicious and excluded from festive occasions in some parts of India. This is an unkind practice in any case. However, it was particularly unkind in a society that practiced child marriage, and thus a society that sometimes had child widows. Moreover, in some areas, widows were not allowed to remarry. In this way, if a girl was widowed in childhood, she may have had to spend the rest of her life in social isolation. The film suggests a criticism of such practices surrounding supposedly inauspicious persons.

But widowhood and related taboos are not Chakrabarty's main target. Chakrabarty's central concern is to expose the irrationality of untouchability. The man's reaction on seeing Chhaya in the morning is designed to suggest a caste Hindu finding it inauspicious that he has seen an untouchable. (Wolpert points out that, in some cases, untouchables were "obliged to wear warning bells . . . so that at first sound of their remote approach," high-caste Hindus "might shield their eyes" [*India* 130; see also Mukherjee 41].) The focus on her shadow, and the fact that she is named "Shadow," are designed to recall the idea that untouchables are so polluting that one should not even have contact with their shadows. As Zinkin explains, "a high-caste Hindu is polluted . . . if his shadow is crossed by that of an Untouchable." Indeed, the two points are related. Zinkin goes on to point out that the "taboo" on the untouchable's shadow "produced unseeability" (13). Chhaya's exclusion from the wedding ceremony is designed to recall caste-based exclusions as well. This was a topic of direct political concern at the time. For example, the 1955 "Untouchability (Offences) Act" forbade, among other things, the exclusion of untouchables from "religious ceremonies" (Galanter 242). When she approaches the wedding, she is rejected due to her "cursed shadow," which is almost an unequivocal reference to untouchability. Later, when Prakash's family considers arranging his marriage with Chhaya, they are warned, "Even her shadow is unfortunate"—again, a statement that makes sense within the context of untouchability taboos, but otherwise may be difficult to comprehend.

Without recognizing the many allusions to untouchability, a viewer is likely to miss, not only the main themes of the film, but its emotional force as well. Superficially, it seems to be a film that makes easy criticisms of a fairly blatantly crazy idea—that Chhaya is inauspicious because several disasters befell her family when she was born. In fact, the political brilliance of the film, and its emotional power, derive from the fact that Chakrabarty is not criticizing some silly aberration in a local community. Rather, he is criticizing an enduring social practice. The film's criticism of this practice is more powerful precisely because Chakrabarty pretends that he is not treating caste at all. The absurdity and cruelty of the prejudice against Chhaya are obvious. The point is that caste prejudice is no less absurd and cruel. Any viewer who thinks of Chhaya's suffering as undeserved should think the same thing about the suffering of untouchables. Emotionally, this also makes Chhaya's fictional suffering into something other than a fanciful story; it is a version, actually a very mild version, of the suffering experienced by millions of real people.[5]

Untouchability was a theme of particular importance at the end of the 1950's, when Chakrabarty made his film (and when Bimal Roy made *Sujata*, which also treats untouchability). Though the Indian constitution outlawed caste discrimination, discriminatory practices persisted after Indian independence in 1947. In 1956, the government instituted new measures to secure the rights of untouchables or, as they prefer to be called, Dalits. But that same year, the major political leader of the Dalit community, B. R. Ambedkar, abandoned hope of ever reforming Hindu caste practices. As a result, he publicly renounced Hinduism and, with a group of a half-million other Dalits, converted to Buddhism (see Chandrasekhar xvii–xviii). Over the next five years, the number of Dalit conversions to Buddhism was staggering (see Mahar, "Preface," xxxi). In some ways, this manifested a sort of crisis about untouchability. Indian independence was widely seen as the beginning of a new period of liberation from old disabilities, not only for the nation, but for the various groups that constituted the nation. Dalits were one of the most important groups of this sort. But after more than a decade of independence, it seemed that little had changed. For example, Galanter quotes the Chief Secretary of Uttar Pradesh in 1959 that there was "no appreciable improvement in the treatment given by members of the so-called higher castes to persons belonging to the [low castes]. The practice of untouchability continues unabated. . . . The provisions of the Untouchability (Offences) Act are being disregarded on a large scale" (262).

Given the structure of romantic tragi-comedy, untouchability was a likely candidate for inclusion in romantic plots of the period. Perhaps what is most interesting here, however, is that intercaste marriage—thus marriage across a hierarchical divide of just the sort emphasized in romantic tragi-comedy—was a crucial issue in the politics of the time as well. In a sense, activism around untouchability had already incorporated the concerns of the romantic plot before Chakrabarty, Bimal Roy, and other writers and directors of the late 1950s incorporated the issue of untouchability into their romantic plots. One of the main pieces of legislation affecting Dalits was the 1954 Special Marriage Act. This was seen as crucial because, as Sripati Chandrasekhar explains, "a major reactionary prop of the traditional caste system was its inherent ban on intercaste marriages" (xxvi). Chandrasekhar goes on to explain that the legislation did not change practices, largely due to the interference of parents, especially in the arranged marriage system. "The young bride and groom," Chandrasekhar writes, "have, by and large, no say in choice of partners. The elders, normally conservative, choose to unite persons who . . . belong to the same caste" (xxvi). Chandrasekhar's analysis and criticism of caste discrimination are, in this respect, indistinguishable from the implicit analysis and criticism one would expect from a romantic tragi-comedy. It does not seem to be mere coincidence that he is addressing the period in which Chakrabarty made *Ardhangini* and the context in which the initial audience would have seen this film.

One common response to caste discrimination was rationalism, a thorough attack on superstition and an opposition to religious thought, often including advocacy of atheism (see, for example, Chandrasekhar xix–xx). Chakrabarty certainly opposes irrationalism and superstition in the course of the film. But he does not opt for atheism, at least not overtly. Rather, he draws directly on Hindu tradition to develop his criticism of untouchability. Chakrabarty does not refrain from criticizing Hindu religious beliefs. However, Chakrabarty—along with the script writers Adil and Bhushan—implicitly distinguishes among different tendencies in Hindu thought and practice, using the tolerant strains to criticize the intolerant ones. For this purpose, he draws on—and revises—religious and literary paradigms in his specification of the romantic plot.

Chakrabarty's social criticisms, and his use of Hindu tradition in support of these criticisms, are already suggested in the opening scenes of the film. When he is informed that his child is a girl, Chhaya's father does not respond with a lament, as would often have been the case at the time. Rather, he replies that she is a form of the goddess Lakṣmī. While not a literal claim that Chhaya is an incarnation of a divine being, the comment nonetheless serves to suggest a connection between Chhaya and the two main incarnations of Lakṣmī, Sītā and Rādhā. Sītā was the beloved of Rāma in the *Rāmāyaṇa* while Rādhā was the beloved of Kṛṣṇa. Rāma and

Kṛṣṇa were incarnations of Viṣṇu, the consort of Lakṣmī and one of the three all-encompassing deities in the Hindu pantheon (along with Śiva and Brahmā). The story of Rāma and Sītā and the story of Kṛṣṇa and Rādhā are paradigmatic romantic tragi-comedies. It is worth reviewing both.

The *Rāmāyaṇa* has two components. One treats the kingship of Ayodhyā. Rāma should succeed his father, Daśaratha. However, one of Daśaratha's three wives extracted a promise from Daśaratha. As a result, her son, Bharata, is to be crowned king while Rāma is to be exiled. Bharata refuses this arrangement, but Rāma agrees, leaving for exile. While in exile, Rāma encounters the terrible demon, Rāvaṇa, who is a threat to the stability of the entire universe. Rāma defeats Rāvaṇa and returns home to Ayodhyā in triumph. Bharata, who never assumed the kingship, turns over the throne to Rāma. As will be clear when we treat heroic plots in the following section, this part of the story is a highly prototypical heroic tragi-comedy. It is perhaps worth mentioning that Hindus commonly view Rāma's rule or "Rāmarājya" as defining the perfect social state. The *Rāmāyaṇa* explains that one aspect of this rule was keeping the caste hierarchy in place. For example, when a low-caste boy violated the law by studying sacred scripture, Rāma beheaded him.

The other part of the *Rāmāyaṇa* is romantic. In some versions, this part begins with Rāma and Sītā falling in love before their marriage is arranged (see the Tamil version of Kamban, retold by Narayan [24–30], and the very influential Hindi version of Tulasidasa [131–133]). It then moves to the fixing of their marriages—in which, by a delightful coincidence, they are betrothed to one another. When Rāma is exiled, Sītā joins him. Unfortunately, she is kidnapped by Rāvaṇa and held in his palace. Eventually, Rāma defeats Rāvaṇa and rescues Sītā. However, when Sītā approaches him, he rejects her on the grounds that she has lived with another man. Sītā protests that she always remained faithful to Rāma. To prove her innocence, she must pass through a fire unburned. She does this and Rāma accepts her, explaining that he knew all along that she was innocent. When they return to Ayodhyā, the people begin to gossip that Sītā—who is now pregnant—was unfaithful with Rāvaṇa. Rāma decides that it will cause problems for the kingdom if Sītā remains there as queen. He calls his brother Lakṣmaṇa and instructs him to take Sītā to the woods and abandon her. Lakṣmaṇa tells Sītā that they are going for an outing. However, when they arrive at their destination, he abandons her. She is given shelter by a hermit, who helps her raise her twin sons. Many years later, she meets

Rāma again. Rāma explains that he will take her back if she goes through another fire ordeal. She refuses and calls to her mother, the earth, to take her back. The earth opens; a throne appears; and Sītā descends into the earth on the throne.

Sītā is widely considered the ideally chaste and ideally obedient Hindu wife who worships her husband as her god (see, for example, Kinsley 70–80). In fact, her character is much more complex, as a number of writers have noted. Nonetheless, her popular image is one of entirely selfless devotion to her husband.

This contrasts strikingly with Rādhā, who is unabashedly sexual in her pursuit of Kṛṣṇa. She is married to another man, but she goes out in the night to meet her lover (Kṛṣṇa), whom she chides for his fickleness. Allegorically, the idea is that her devotion to God supersedes her devotion to anything in this world, including her husband. But at the literal level of the story, Rādhā's behavior is, to say the least, unconventional. (On Rādhā's adulterous love and its allegorical interpretation, see Chapter Six of Kinsley.) Whenever Kṛṣṇa plays his flute, Rādhā runs to join him, her heart filled with love and desire. Kṛṣṇa has a parallel relation with all Rādhā's fellow milkmaids (for God must love all his devotees). But that does not diminish his relation with Rādhā. Indeed, in his divine dance, Kṛṣṇa multiplies himself into many Kṛṣṇas, each one paired with a different maid (see Hawley 14).

Broadly speaking, *Ardhangini* sets up an opposition between the romantic plot of the Rāma/Sītā story and that of the Kṛṣṇa/Rādhā story, combining the latter with elements from stories of Śiva and his consort Pārvatī. To put the matter a bit crudely, Chakrabarty links the oppressive, hierarchical aspects of Hinduism with Rāma while connecting the disruptive elements with Kṛṣṇa and, somewhat less consistently, with Śiva. This is suggested already at the beginning of the film, when the man walks into the street and sees Chhaya. He invokes God, asking "Why did I have to see the face of that cursed girl." When addressing God, he does not use a generic term, but calls out specifically "Rāma, Rāma!" (also transliterated as "Rām, Rām!").

In contrast, Chhaya's one friend is named Lila (alternatively, "Leela"), after the play of Kṛṣṇa with Rādhā and the milkmaids. Lila is marrying a man named Murari, which is one of the names of Kṛṣṇa. As the story develops, these two become the helper figures who make it possible for Chhaya and Prakash to be united. The film relies in part on their relation to Rādhā and Kṛṣṇa in order to give religious authority to the union of

Chhaya and Prakash. There is also a subplot involving these two newlyweds in which they continually try to meet, not unlike Rādhā and Kṛṣṇa. In this case, the interfering figure is Murari's mother. This is a comic twist on the prototypical romantic structure, for here the parent prevents the union of the lovers after they are married, not before. Moreover, rather than the usual exile and danger of death surrounding the lover, here the mother believes that she herself will die if the lovers are united. (She comes to this conclusion on the basis of astrology, one of the superstitions criticized in the film.) Finally, it is only by cleverly exiling the mother that the lovers manage to be united—though, in keeping with the usual comic structure, the entire family is reunited at the end.

Returning to the main plot (we stopped with Chhaya unable to attend her friend's wedding), it is not long before the central romance is kindled. In this case, Prakash's mother comes to visit Chhaya's father, accompanied by her brother and young nephew, Bablu. The purpose of their visit is to arrange a marriage between Prakash and Chhaya. From the outset, viewers are likely to find the three- or four-year-old Bablu reminiscent of the baby Kṛṣṇa. In addition to his appearance, which recalls popular icons of the tiny God, he assumes great authority in the family's activities. For example, in a charming and funny, but nonetheless serious way, he evaluates the potential bride on Prakash's behalf.

Given Bablu's approval, everything seems settled for the marriage of Chhaya and Prakash. But then the mother learns that Chhaya is "inauspicious." She writes a letter breaking off the engagement. Before Chhaya opens the letter, she infers that it is from her future in-laws. Happily imagining her marriage, she plays on a swing in the courtyard of her father's house. The swing is traditionally associated with the union of Rādhā and Kṛṣṇa. Thus the image serves to link Chhaya's happiness with Kṛṣṇa stories. Needless to say, her feelings change when she reads the letter. Hearing the letter's contents, Chhaya's father is both angry and despondent. Though deathly ill, he drags himself into the courtyard and faces the statue of Viṣṇu and Lakṣmī. He chastises Viṣṇu for making a world in which some people (whom He has created) so terribly mistreat other people (whom He has also created). The speech is in keeping with one tradition of Hindu devotion, in which the devotee complains about the supreme God's indifference and even unkindness (see, for example, 52–65 of McDermott).

When her father dies, Chhaya leaves to visit her only friend, Lila. Murari and Lila determine to bring Chhaya together with Prakash. They devise an elaborate scheme that ultimately succeeds in uniting the two. In this way, they take up the standard helper role. They combine this with the internal author, for they in effect write the scenario for the lovers in the way an author does. However, Chakrabarty, Adil, and Bhushan also vary these character types. The standard romantic plot begins with the lovers meeting and falling in love, then being separated, then recruiting the help of friends. Here, the lovers have been separated before even meeting and the helpers, operating entirely on their own, come up with the plan to unite them.

The scheme works. Chhaya and Prakash meet and fall in love, entirely unaware that they were earlier betrothed to one another. This may allude to a common theme in Hindu romantic literature. It is a cross-cultural commonplace that lovers feel they are destined to be together. In the Hindu tradition, this takes a particular metaphysical form. The lovers have been together in previous lives. They are fated to be rejoined because their love continues from birth to birth. The relevance of this idea is made clear in the subplot when Murari tells Lila that, even if his mother keeps them apart in this life, they will be joined in all subsequent births.

The romance of Prakash and Chhaya generally proceeds well, though they do encounter some difficulties. Most important, Chhaya herself worries that she may be inauspicious—and thus dangerous for Prakash, whose job as an airline pilot is perhaps particularly susceptible to ill fortune. She explains her social disability to Prakash, who brushes off the idea of being inauspicious as merely a matter of people's imagination.

It is only at this point that Chhaya learns that Prakash is the same person she was supposed to marry earlier. This causes a more serious crisis. Chhaya tells Prakash that he should forget her, because she does not want to come between a son and his mother. In a Hindu context, this is a very orthodox and noble sentiment. However, here it is virtually impossible for a human spectator to wish that Prakash will forget Chhaya. Moreover, it is clear that Chhaya does not really want this either. After she says this, Prakash walks away and picks up his coat. Everyone must assume that he agrees and is leaving. Reaction shots of Chhaya show that this is how she understands Prakash's actions, and, as Meena Kumari's facial expression makes clear, the thought is devastating. Prakash explains that he took her home believing that his mother would accept her and adorn her with bangles as a new bride. As he reaches into his coat pocket for the bangles, he explains that now he will have to put the bangles on her himself. He then slips a bangle onto her wrist. This is a gesture that recurs in romantic Indian films. It is always resonant. Here it is very moving.

The immediately following scene is the wedding. In many romantic plots, this would be the end. The couple is married and lives happily ever after. However, the subplot has already suggested that this is not the case. The union of the lovers is not assured by marriage, for the interfering parent—in this case, the mother—may only become more effective after the ceremony. Indeed, here, the mother does not even see the bride until after the ceremony. She is so shocked that she nearly manages to get herself burned in a fire. She rejects Chhaya unequivocally. Prakash comments, "So the mother's heart has lost against illusion." The theme is in part Hindu. Several important strands of Hinduism assert the illusory nature of the changing and differentiated material world, contrasting it with the unchanging, unified world of spirit. However, the word used by Prakash is not *māyā,* and it may suggest errors that result from superstition more than errors that result from a belief in material reality, with its social distinctions and harmful desires.

In any case, by threatening to leave, Prakash convinces his mother to accept Chhaya in her home. However, she is systematically duplicitous about this acceptance. She welcomes Chhaya fully when Prakash is present. But she mistreats her when he is away.

Chhaya has two well-wishers or allies in the house. They operate in part to link the story with mythic prototypes. Before going on with the plot, it is worth considering these characters and the mythic prototypes.

Chhaya's first ally is Bhola, the servant. "Bholā" is "a name for Śiva" (McDermott 173). At one point, Bhola laments, "It feels like the entire house has been set on fire." He goes on to tell Chhaya, "You will turn into ashes if this goes on." Given his name and the name of the film, it is almost impossible not to read these lines as an allusion to the famous myth of Satī, who entered the sacrificial fire and "was reduced to ashes" (*Śiva Purāṇa* 415) when her father, Dakṣa, insulted her beloved husband, Śiva. Crucially for our purposes, Dakṣa's complaint against Śiva was a matter of caste. Śiva, he maintained, was "a resident of cremation grounds," thus associated with the untouchables who handle corpses; he was "lacking in nobility of birth and pedigree" and "an outcaste," which is to say, someone who is below the lowest orders of the caste system (*Śiva Purāṇa* 396–397). Eventually, Satī was reborn as Pārvatī and reunited with Śiva (in a divine instance of lovers being reunited across births). Their union is so complete that they become a single body (see, for example, *Śiva Purāṇa* 474), iconically represented as the divine androgyne, half male, half female. Together, they form the ardhanārīśvara and she becomes his female half, his *ardhānginī.* (Kinsley points out that the same claim is sometimes made regarding Rādhā and Kṛṣṇa as well [92].) It is important to note that this is not some mere accident. Metaphysically, it was necessary for Śiva and Pārvatī to become one because, ultimately, the two can never be separated to begin with. It is not possible to have male without female, day without night, subject without object (see Kinsley 50)—or light (prakash) without shadow (chāyā/chhaya; cf. the *Devī-Māhātmya* on the goddess in the form of shadow [Coburn 53] and the *Śiva Purāṇa* on "the Chāyāpuruṣa . . . who is called Śiva," puruṣa meaning person, spirit, or even universal spirit, and chāyā meaning, of course, shadow [1568]). Along with the references to the *Rāmāyaṇa,* this allusion to the burning of Satī prepares us for the end of the film.

Eventually, Bhola feels that he cannot live in the house any longer. Chhaya tries to stop him from leaving. He explains that his dharma or ethical duty requires it. The implication is clear. Throughout the history of Hinduism, there has been a conflict between two sorts of dharma—"universal" dharma, which applies to everyone and which stresses nonviolence and truth (see O'Flaherty, "Clash," 96), and caste dharma, which is specific to one's caste and, in certain cases, is bound up with violence and falsity. "Violence" here refers to the infliction of harm—in action, word, or even intent. Moreover, this applies not only to harm for which one is directly responsible, but even to harm that one simply allows (see Patañjali 53). Bhola cannot stay in the house because to stay there as a servant, following his duty to obey Prakash's mother, would be to cooperate tacitly with violence. The issues of falsity and violence are brought out more fully in the following sequence. Bhola tells Prakash's mother that Chhaya is not inauspicious, but her thoughts about Chhaya are. (Note that the point applies directly to untouchability and pollution: it is not Dalits who are polluted, but the thoughts of bigots.) Prakash's mother strikes Bhola when he says this. Bhola responds, "This is not a slap of an employer to an employee," thus an action that might possibly be judged in terms of caste dharma (where corporal punishment of social inferiors is permissible). Rather, "This is a lie's slap to truth," thus a violation of universal dharma. As is usually the case in romantic plots, the film is opposed to an ethics of subordination, represented by the interfering parent, and supportive of an ethics based on individual resistance to social hierarchies. But, here again, the universal principle has been expressed in a culturally particular way, in this case by tacit reference to two competing types of dharma in Hindu tradition.

Chhaya's other ally in the home is Bablu, whose relation to Kṛṣṇa is developed, beyond his iconic appearance, in the course of several scenes. In one scene, Chhaya prays before an icon of Kṛṣṇa playing the flute. Bablu brings flowers. She looks right; the camera cuts to Bablu's face, then back to Chhaya; she looks forward; the camera cuts to Kṛṣṇa's face (see Figures 1.1–1.4). It is not absolutely necessary to see the shots of Bablu and Kṛṣṇa as parallel. In context, however, we are certainly encouraged to do so. There is a similar, but even more forceful use of editing later in the film. Prakash's mother is praying to Kṛṣṇa, just after she has evicted Chhaya from her home. Chakrabarty cuts to a shot of Bablu weeping (see Figures 1.5 and 1.6). The editing serves to connect Bablu with the deity to whom Prakash's

*1.1. Chhaya looks right . . .*

*1.2. . . . cut to Bablu.*

mother is directing her prayers. It also serves to suggest Kṛṣṇa's response to that eviction.

There are more narratively based connections as well. Like the child Kṛṣṇa, Bablu is very mischievous. In one particularly striking scene, he tries to steal milk. The child Kṛṣṇa was so notorious for stealing butter that he is often referred to as "the butter thief"; Hawley stresses that this involves imagery of milk, for butter is "the concentrated form of milk" (112–113). Of course, the child Kṛṣṇa is not only misbehaved. He is a great protector of his devotees and the people in his village, battling demons on their behalf. In keeping with this, Bablu destroys a dangerous ritual designed to kill Chhaya.

A broader set of Kṛṣṇa parallels—and their opposition to Rāma stories—are also developed through the subplot. For example, Murari and Lila de-

*1.3. Chhaya looks ahead . . .*

*1.4. . . . cut to Kṛṣṇa.*

*1.5. Prakash's mother looks up toward Kṛṣṇa (off camera) . . .*

*1.6. . . . cut to Bablu.*

vise a plan to get Murari's mother to leave them alone. Murari dresses as a priest, concealing his true identity. When his mother invokes Rāma, he corrects her, insisting that she invoke Murari (thus Kṛṣṇa) instead. At one level, this is simply a pun on the name of the character Murari. However, at another level, the implication is that the romantic joy and affirmation of life desired by the young couple are to be found in the model of Kṛṣṇa and his Lila/līlā (play—in this case, amorous play), not in the life of Rāma and Sītā.

Again, Chakrabarty incorporates important links with stories of Śiva as well. Shortly after their marriage, Prakash refers to Chhaya, saying "my Goddess is at my side," suggesting the image of the ardhanārīśvara. Subsequently, Chhaya complains to her mother-in-law that a mother should give her daughter nectar (*amrit*), but that she has offered only poison. This alludes to a famous myth in which the gods churn the primeval sea to produce nectar. Instead, they produce poison, which they offer to Śiva. Śiva agrees to hold the poison in his throat forever to protect the universe. The main point of the allusion is clear. Prakash's mother is behaving in the same selfish and broadly destructive manner as the lower deities of the myth. Two further points are important. First, Chhaya implicitly identifies herself here, not with the goddess, but with Śiva—which, of course, fits the idea of ardhanārīśvara perfectly for, as ardhanārīśvara, the god and goddess are one and the same. Second, there is a direct parallel with Śiva's holding of the poison in his throat. Specifically, Chhaya refuses to speak about her mother-in-law's cruelty. She insists that it is her duty to swallow back the words that would express her mother-in-law's poisonous actions. She must do this in order to protect the family, just as Śiva must swallow back the poison in order to protect the universe.

Of course, the film is not confined to myth. Indeed, the mythic resonances operate in the service of the film's political concerns. As the story proceeds, the connections between Chhaya's "inauspiciousness" and untouchability become increasingly clear. At one point, Chhaya confronts her mother-in-law, who shouts, "Don't you touch me!" Later, Prakash's uncle berates her with the words, "Don't disgrace me by touching my feet." (Touching someone's feet is a sign of respect in Hindu culture. Obviously, however, untouchables are not supposed to touch the feet of their caste superiors.) At another point, Chhaya picks up Prakash's picture and her mother-in-law tells her, "Even your shadow shouldn't fall on him." The identification, though still implicit, is unmistakable.

Returning to the plot, we find Chakrabarty, Adil, and Bhushan rearranging the usual romantic structure in a noteworthy way. Again, despite the (tacit) caste conflict, the lovers are not separated after their first meeting and before their public marriage. They were, in a sense, "separated" after they initially expected to meet. But, having met, they seem to have proceeded smoothly to romantic union. In this way, the usual tragic separation—what makes the romantic plot into a *tragi*-comedy—has been delayed to a remarkable degree, considered relative to the standard structure. However, at this point, after the public marriage, both exile and imagery of death, even the threat of actual death, enter. First, Prakash's plane is lost. Thus he is away from his beloved, and feared dead. During this time, Prakash's mother evicts Chhaya from her home. Just at the moment

Prakash returns, Chhaya is run over by a car. Though the exile of Chhaya is due to parental interference, the separation of the lovers is ultimately a physical matter, a matter of a lost airplane and an automobile accident. The point fits with the tendency of melodrama to rely on physical causes for separation of the lovers. (Perhaps these give rise to melodrama because physical causes seem beyond human control in a way that other forms of blocking are not.)

Following a standard motif in Indian tragi-comedy (extending back to Sanskrit drama), the hero goes temporarily insane when separated from his beloved. Eventually both Prakash and Chhaya recover. Well again, and aware of all that has happened, Prakash decides to take Chhaya and leave his family for good. In the prototypical romantic tragi-comedy, the final union of the lovers includes a reconciliation with the family. It appears that *Ardhangini* will vary this standard pattern as well, granting the lovers final union only in separation from the family.

It is at this point that the various mythological strands of the plot come together to make a remarkably powerful conclusion. Prakash is packing to leave. His mother comes into the room to beg him to stay. She explains that it is Dīpāvalī, the festival of lights, when Rāma came to meet his mother, "a day of union for the mother and son." (The use of Dīpāvalī in relation to family union or separation is a recurring theme in Indian cinema.) Here we are asked to see Chhaya and Prakash in relation to Sītā and Rāma.[6] But precisely how? The way in which we are to understand this relation, here and elsewhere, is finally made clear in Prakash's reply: "Mother, neither are you Kausalya, nor am I Rama." The effect is very powerful. Here, Prakash replies to the common Hindu idea that every son should be like Rāma and every parent should be revered as Rāma revered his parents. He implies that there are other obligations, and that it is wrong to impose the ethics of the *Rāmāyaṇa* on real life. Through Prakash, Chakrabarty implies a criticism of the ideology that identifies Rāma as the incarnation of dharma, the personification of everything that is moral. Chakrabarty has set up his hero, not to parallel Rāma, but to contrast with him. (Recall how Rāma abandoned his wife rather than supporting her in the face of social opposition.)

On the other hand, things are not entirely simple here. When Prakash's mother tries to restrain him physically, he pushes her away and she falls to the ground. No matter how bad she has been, it is difficult for an Indian audience to feel unmoved when an old mother is pushed to the ground by her son. Moreover, she has been humanized by an earlier scene in which she confesses her self-doubts to Kṛṣṇa. Now, rejected by her son, she appeals tearfully to Chhaya.

When Prakash's mother leaves, Chhaya asks Prakash to stay just for Dīpāvalī. She then explains that he has no choice but to listen to her because she is his ardhānginī. Here, at last, we receive an explanation for the title of the film. Conversely, the fact that the title is *Ardhangini* tells us that this is a thematically crucial point in the film. In contrast with the immediately preceding references to Dīpāvalī, it suggests that we should understand the ideal of the film, not in relation to Rāma and Sītā, but in relation to the ardhanārīśvara, the unified, androgynous form of Śiva and Pārvatī.

The events that follow serve to extend these points. As Prakash's mother is distributing the lamps for Dīpāvalī, one accidentally falls and begins a fire. She notices this when the fire has already spread. At first, she calls out to Chhaya. But then she thinks that the only way she can retain her son is if Chhaya dies. She runs outside, believing that she has left Chhaya to perish in the fire. Unknown to her, however, Chhaya is outside and the person trapped inside the building is Prakash, as the outside latch on his door has fallen, locking him in.

When Chhaya learns of the fire, she runs inside to rescue her husband. Most western viewers will recognize that, for its time, this was quite a novel plot development in the sense that it is typically the brave man who rescues the endangered damsel. The affirmation of female agency and strength is certainly one important aspect of this scene. However, the greatest emotional force of the scene, and its primary thematic significance, derives from its mythological resonances. The episode simultaneously recalls the fire ordeal of Sītā and the self-sacrifice of Satī. In effect, it rejects both models. As to the Sītā/Rāma parallel, the episode is a sort of fire ordeal for Chhaya. She is called on to prove her devotion to her husband by passing through the fire. But it is not a pointless ritual, based on a crazy belief that chastity will protect a woman's body from injury by fire. It is practical and necessary. It is brought about by real need. At the same time, it is not insignificant that Chhaya is able to pass through the collapsing house unharmed. It is difficult not to see her safety as bound up with her moral qualities.

A parallel point holds for the allusion to Satī. The relation of Satī and Śiva is similar to that of Chhaya and Prakash in the sense that Satī enters the fire willingly and as a direct expression of her love. It is not a test set up for her by Śiva. But it is nonetheless a pointless exercise that only causes Śiva greater misery. Instead of sacrificing herself, Chhaya saves her husband. In context, her act is not only moving, but socially significant. Chakrabarty indicates that the ideas of female duty represented by Sītā and even by Satī are mistaken. A valid ideal is seen, perhaps, only in Pārvatī—born after the death of Satī to be joined with Śiva in one body as his ardhānginī.

After this, the reconciliation of standard romantic tragi-comedy can proceed in the usual way. Prakash's mother renounces her former behavior, embraces Chhaya, and calls her "daughter." Murari and Lila arrive on the scene and express their concern over the fire. Prakash explains to them that it "is not the home burning, but the illusions and inauspiciousness."[7] The flames, he tells them, are Agni, the sacrificial fire that carries offerings to heaven. It is, in other words, the very fire through which Sītā walked, unharmed; the very fire that consumed Satī in her self-sacrifice (and that thereby allowed her to be reborn as Pārvatī and to become half of the ardhanārīśvara).

In these sections, the film turns somewhat from the themes of caste discrimination to themes of the oppression of women. Like many directors of the 1950's, Chakrabarty was concerned with a range of social issues. He saw different forms of oppression and discrimination as interrelated and he used this film to oppose more than one entrenched, discriminatory practice in Indian society. On the other hand, by this point we cannot forget that Chhaya has been consistently linked with untouchability. The conclusion thus elevates this untouchable girl to the level of the most revered goddesses of Hindu devotion—a point with both emotional and thematic consequences.

Though romantic plots are notorious for leaving some aspects of the plot unresolved, Chakrabarty is not so lackadaisical. In a delightful coincidence, he has Murari's mother arrive back on the scene just at this moment. Murari embraces her and presents her with two grandsons, proving to her that her life was not endangered. The twin sons of Lila complete not only the romantic plot (which often leads to the birth of children), but the borrowings from and response to mythology. The difficulty with Rādhā and Kṛṣṇa is that they cannot be a normal couple, since Rādhā is someone else's wife. Thus they can never have children. The difficulty with Sītā and Rāma is that Rāma abandons his wife just when she is pregnant. Chakrabarty wishes to preserve the romantic love and sexuality of Rādhā and Kṛṣṇa, but to incorporate the possibility of having children. He does this by transferring Sītā's twins to Lila. In the final shot of the film, the entire family is reunited—and, to connect Chhaya with motherhood as well, Chakrabarty has Bablu leave his father and embrace Chhaya.

In sum, the film manifests the romantic structure very clearly. Chakrabarty specifies this structure in a way that extends its anti-hierarchical themes in a culturally specific way. He does this, first of all, by pointing to a real, debilitating social hierarchy that affects literally millions of people. Moreover, in treating this hierarchy, he draws on paradigmatic romantic stories of Hindu tradition—not only to develop the resonances of his own film, but equally to comment on those paradigmatic stories and to criticize the values they underwrite in contemporary Indian society.

## Violent Love, National Duty: The Heroic Tragi-Comedy of Guru Dutt's *Baaz*

Heroic tragi-comedy derives from the social prototype for happiness, which is group domination. "Domination" here refers to a combination of power and esteem. Group domination has two aspects. The first is individual. It concerns one's position in a given in-group. The second is collective. It concerns the position of the in-group relative to out-groups—for example, one's nation relative to other nations. These two components in the happiness prototype yield two components in the heroic plot. Specifically, the heroic plot prototypically involves a hero seeking a position of authority within an in-group that itself is seeking to establish authority over out-groups.

Before going on to the (tragic) middle, it is worth dwelling for a moment on the function of respect in the resolution of heroic tragi-comedy. The esteem of the in-group for the individual hero is invariably important for the ideal of social happiness. A heroic plot is not genuinely comic if the protagonist achieves power, but is despised by his or her people. In contrast, the esteem of the out-group may or may not be significant. The heroic plot is comic when the in-group (e.g., the home nation) defeats its enemies. It does not necessarily matter whether or not it wins the respect of those enemies. Indeed, one could distinguish antagonistic from conciliatory (or dehumanizing from humanizing) versions of the heroic plot, depending on whether out-group esteem is presented as valuable or not.

The heroic plot develops in the usual manner whereby the middle involves, not merely the absence of the resolving ideal (i.e., group domination), but its opposite. Thus, the hero not only lacks a position of power and respect. He or she is rendered utterly powerless. In the most prototypical version, the rightful leader (e.g., the hereditary monarch) is denied his or her position and disgraced. This routinely occurs through imprisonment or through exile. Moreover, the in-group (e.g., the home nation) not only does not dominate out-groups (e.g., other nations). It is subordinated to them, or threatened with such subordination. This subordination commonly takes the form of military invasion. The enemy may be represented as disdaining the home society or merely having power over it. There seems to be an inverse correlation between the attitude of the enemy and the value of out-group respect in the comic resolution. Specifically, if the out-group disdains the in-group (e.g., characterizes its members as racially inferior), then the comic resolution may involve humiliating members of the out-group rather than winning their esteem. The respect of the out-group members seems much more likely to have a positive value if members of that out-group did not disdain the in-group initially.

The beginning of the heroic plot usually intensifies the subsequent events by giving positions of authority and esteem to the hero and his or her society, positions of authority that are subsequently lost. Often, the hero is about to achieve the highest position of power and respect when some usurpation occurs. For example, he or she may be on the verge of coronation when he or she is suddenly displaced (examples range from *Hamlet* to the *Rāmāyaṇa*). Moreover, the society is commonly stable and prosperous when the threat of invasion arises. On the other hand, the society is usually not as stable and prosperous as it is following the defeat of the enemy and the restoration of the hero to his or her rightful place of leadership. That final resolution is often associated with the establishment of a utopia, as in the case of the "Rule of Rāma," the paradigm of a perfect society in the Hindu tradition.

As the preceding outline shows, there is something peculiar about the heroic plot. It is, in effect, two plots. These plots are often interwoven by connecting the invasion with the usurpation. Specifically, the usurper is often in league with the invader. Alternatively, the weakening of the society caused by the usurpation is what allows for the invasion. As a result, the most prototypical way of defeating the threat from the out-group is for the hero to return from exile and lead the defense himself or herself. In keeping with this, the most common way for the hero to regain his or her position of power and authority is through defeating that enemy. In all these ways, the *Rāmāyaṇa* provides an exemplary instance.

Since the heroic plot is rather complicated, it is worth recapitulating the structure briefly by reference to what is probably its most common form. The hero is about to be put in a position of national leadership (e.g., crowned king), a position he or she deserves. However, some usurper prevents this. The ruler is then exiled, and is commonly feared dead. Meanwhile, the nation is threatened with conquest by one of its enemies, and may even be defeated temporarily. If the enemy triumphs over the home society, this is often due to an alliance between the enemy and the usurper (though it may also be due to the usurper's incompetence). The hero returns and defeats this enemy, commonly overcoming the usurper as well. If the enemy not only dominated the home society, but denigrated it, this defeat may involve the enemy's humiliation. In any case, by defeating the enemy, the hero re-establishes himself or herself as the rightful ruler. He or she at last achieves his or her rightful position and is able to lead the nation to unimagined prosperity. Thus the hero achieves the highest position of power and esteem in a nation that is itself at the apex of power and, in relevant cases, esteem.

The main protagonists in a heroic tragi-comedy are, of course, the usurped leader and the defender of the in-group against the enemy. Again, these two roles are frequently filled by one character. On the other hand, in some cases the two roles are distinct. Thus there is often a primary leader (e.g., a king) and some associate (e.g., a great warrior) who is not merely a helper, but a main hero, thus a primary focus of audience interest. (There are obvious reasons why readers may be more able to identify with someone who ably defends his or her nation than with the unique individual who inherits the throne.)

As usual, there are helping characters and blocking characters. Helping characters are of the standard varieties—loyal servants, devoted friends, and so forth. Blocking characters figure more crucially and are of two sorts, defined by the two plot sequences—out-group enemies or invaders and in-group usurpers. The invading enemy often mirrors the in-group in its social structure. Thus the primary blocking figures in the invasion/defense part of the heroic plot are commonly a leader (e.g., a foreign king) and a loyal soldier. The usurper commonly mirrors one or the other hero as well. Indeed, he or she is often a close relative of the rightful leader, a relation that serves to intensify the emotional impact of the betrayal.

Since the romantic plot is the most common of the three structures, the heroic plot is often interwoven with a romantic plot. In one common variant, the beloved is from the enemy side and the conflict between the societies provides the social inhibition that separates the lovers.

*Baaz* fits the prototype very closely, while also varying it in some intriguing ways. The plot concerns an Indian prince, Ravi, whose father has died and who should soon be crowned. However, his kingdom is occupied by the Portuguese. The Portuguese present themselves as partners, but it is clear that they in fact rule the country. The sinister General Barbosa is in charge of the colony. He is assisted by his loyal captain. Thus we have a variation on the standard invasion plot. The invasion has already occurred. The in-group hierarchy retains its leader. But his power is minimal. Despite all this, we still have the standard hero, a leader who is about to achieve his position of authority through coronation. We also have the standard enemy, a foreign leader and his loyal soldier.

Barbosa insists that Prince Ravi must go to Portugal for the coronation. This is a peculiar twist on the exile sequence. First, it is demanded by the foreign leader, not the in-group usurper. Second, it is an exile that will, supposedly, allow him to attain his rightful position. On the other hand, this is not unrelated to the usual exile motif. As it turns out, Ravi's cousin, Yashwant, is plotting to take the throne. Ravi's trip will facilitate this. Thus we have the standard intensification of the usurpation by making it a familial conflict. It also turns out that Yashwant is closely connected with the Portuguese, whose domination Ravi has resisted, however weakly. Thus we have the common alliance between the usurper and the invader.

A second sequence of events concerns Nisha. Nisha is a brave young Indian woman who leads a rebellion on a slave ship, takes over the ship, and uses it to harass the Portuguese. By chance, she is brought together with Ravi, when she attacks the ship that is transporting him to Portugal. They work together, eventually defeating the Portuguese and restoring Ravi to the throne. Thus Ravi and Nisha form the common leader/warrior duo. However, there is an obvious difference here. Ravi is male and Nisha is female, which is quite rare. This innovation allows an easy incorporation of the romantic plot. Ravi and Nisha fall in love. But Nisha does not know that he is the prince. When she discovers this, she briefly assumes that he cannot marry her because she is a commoner (a version of the usual social separation of the lovers). As it turns out, however, their romantic union is blocked only by the political situation, which has made both of them outlaws. Interestingly, there is a Portuguese woman, Rosita, who tries to seduce the prince, but fails. Thus we have the elements of the more common romance plot in which the lovers are from different sides in a national conflict. Indeed, Dutt stresses Rosita's advances in order to make it clear that the prince feels nothing for her.

The preceding point goes along with the film's general attitude toward the Portuguese. The ideal of in-group authority here is clearly one of power alone. It does not in any way involve respect from the enemy. The Portuguese have been disdainful of Indians. Dutt portrays them as cruel and racist. Thus the ideal resolution does not include securing their esteem. (Indeed, one of the thematically crucial songs in the film involves a repeated call for "revenge," not reconciliation.)

Of course, these heroic (and romantic) patterns do not appear in their abstract, cross-cultural form. Dutt necessarily specifies them. He does this, in part, by reference to myth and religion. Ravi's mother worships the Goddess in one of her many forms and Nisha's men hide in a cave that is also an ancient temple to the Goddess. Though her precise identity is not entirely clear in the film, there are hints that Dutt means to point us toward a specific form of the Goddess—Durgā, who protects the world against demons.[8] More important, Dutt draws on Indian history and current political conditions to particularize his story. Or, rather, Dutt began his work on the film with a concern over contemporary political events and their history. In this way, the political particulars inspired the film. The narrative prototype was not specified by the political issues; the political issues were there first and Dutt organized them by using the narrative prototype. More exactly, Dutt's film has a direct political purpose—to oppose the continuing Portuguese control of Goa and to support the incorporation of Goa into India. To treat this issue, he draws on the entire history of colonialism in India. His aim is, evidently, to remind the viewer of that history in order to inspire patriotic feeling for India and a sense of outrage at colonialism, especially Portuguese rule over Goa.

The film takes place at the start of the European colonial period in an area of Portuguese domination—historically, domination often marked by "sheer destruction" (Marques I: 232). After the credits, Dutt shows us a foreign flag, marked by a prominent cross signaling the foreign religion as well. The first scene takes place in a market. A woman complains that trade has been ruined by the Portuguese. This reprises a common anti-colonial theme that the political economy of colonialism systematically degrades the economy of the colonized country (through the extraction of resources, harmful regulation of local trade and manufacture, etc.). Here, colonial exploitation is a matter of blatant thievery. Soldiers simply take goods from the vendors without paying. One young woman refuses to salute the soldiers, proudly asserting that she is "Hindustani." This is anachronistic in that it is unlikely rebels would have envisioned themselves as Indian at the time (rather than, say, loyal subjects of a particular kingdom). Indeed, anachronisms are spread throughout the film. But these are not accidental. They are there by design. Dutt's purpose is not to dwell on the past. It is to comment on the present as a result of that past. Again, the film implicitly advocates the end of Portuguese rule in Goa and the incorporation of Goa into independent India. Indeed, the film's depiction of Portuguese domination is not solely, or perhaps even primarily designed to reflect the historical practices of the Portuguese in the early colonial period. Rather, it is designed to condemn the fascism of Portugal's government in the 1950's, its recalcitrance in negotiations over Goa, and the reported mistreatment of anti-colonial activists in Goa (see Chapter Fourteen of Marques vol. 2; see also Kay 306).

As the film continues, a group of young women stage a sort of market uprising against the Portuguese. The predominant figure in this battle is Nisha, who pelts the soldiers with vegetables until she is whisked away by a young man that we later learn is Prince Ravi. Ravi helps her escape from the soldiers and their romance begins. However, he does not inform her of his identity.

Meanwhile, Ramzan Ali has violated the Portuguese monopoly on trade. He is therefore being sought for punishment. Moreover, the General declares that anyone aiding Ali will be subject to the same punishment. We subsequently learn that Nisha's family is harboring Ali. It is important that Nisha's family is Hindu, while Ali is Muslim. Dutt is not advocating a vacuous form of nationalism. He is advocating nationalism of a particular kind. Crucially, this nationalism is one of thorough Hindu/Muslim unity, a willingness of Hindus and Muslims to risk their lives for one another, on behalf of the nation and against the colonizers. Indeed, he is implicitly drawing on the standard metaphor of the nation as a family when he has Nisha refer to Ali as "Ramzan Uncle." This thematic concern relates to an entire history of colonial Hindu/Muslim relations from the early Portuguese anti-Muslim practices (see Wolpert 137–138) to the (then very recent) violence of the India/Pakistan partition in which roughly a million people were killed (see Wolpert, *A New History*, 348).

The following scene shows the Portuguese whipping Indians, then cuts to a scene of the General receiving a massage and making racist comments. The point of this sequence is too obvious to require comment. We are subsequently introduced to Rosita and Yashwant.

The Queen Mother appears at this point, offering worship before a shrine of the Goddess. Ravi has just returned from his meeting with Nisha. The conjunction suggests a possible link between Nisha and the Goddess, especially in light of Nisha's militancy and the Goddess's militant forms. The connection will be developed in the following scenes. The Queen Mother also explains at this point that Yashwant "dreams of being a king," thus introducing the usurpation plot. This is followed by the scene in which the General explains that Ravi must go to England if he is to be crowned.

After this, we return to Nisha's family. Her father and Ramzan Ali are arrested. They are taken before the General, but refuse to bow before him. Several prisoners list atrocities committed by the Portuguese soldiers. It is clear that the colonizers are inhumanly cruel and that there is no possibility for constructive engagement with them. The only option is expelling them entirely.

Nisha petitions the Queen Mother as the latter is worshipping the Goddess. Here again there is a suggestion of a connection between Nisha and the Goddess, though at this point in the film, the precise nature of the connection is not clear. (Indeed, it is not even clear that the connection is with Nisha rather than with the Queen Mother.) The Queen Mother explains that she is powerless to aid Nisha's father. Nisha and her sister therefore take up arms in an attempt to free him. This begins to suggest that the film may be using the heroic plot to oppose Gandhian nonviolence and to advocate militarization of the new state along with support of armed rebellion against colonialism elsewhere (e.g., in Goa). In fact, this does seem to be one main purpose of the film. However, in this particular instance, the militant scheme is foiled and the sisters are captured. Thus the film's attitude toward violence is not entirely clear at this point.

Meanwhile, the prince has been put on a ship for Portugal, thus developing the exile part of the standard narrative. Rosita is also on board and tries to seduce him. His resistance inverts the more common development of the romantic plot "across enemy lines."

At this point, a new Portuguese arrival approaches the General with a Buddha statue. He talks about how people can be brought down with cannons or with opium. The reference to opium anachronistically alludes to the British imposition of opium importation on the Chinese, a notorious part of British colonial domination in East Asia (for a summary of the relevant history, see Garraty and Gay 938–940). The purpose of the allusion is to extend the film's incorporation of European colonial history. The film refers not only to events across the entire period of European colonialism in India. It also points toward European colonialism elsewhere, suggesting the continuity of all forms of colonialism. In this way, Dutt takes up the heroic plot to criticize, not only Portuguese colonialism in Goa, and not only European colonialism in India, but European colonialism generally. Correlatively, he uses the film, not only to foster Indian nationalism, but to foster a spirit of solidarity among colonized and formerly colonized people. This also indicates why the film is so apparently anti-European. It condemns Europeans far more harshly than was most often the case in Indian writings. The general racism and cultural disdain of European colonialists becomes more obvious when one recognizes that it covered the entire non-European world. The point is extended from India and China to Africa by the fact that the man with the Buddha statue is a slave trader. In connection with this, the General sells him his prisoners, including Nisha and her family.

On the ship, the slave trader behaves brutally. He throws a number of men overboard as he calculates that he will not be able to sell them. This act furthers the implicit connection of the film with colonialism in Africa and the African slave trade. On seeing Nisha, the slave trader takes an immediate interest in her. Among other things, he puns on her name, reminding the audience that "Nisha" means "night." Since "Ravi" is a name of the sun (see Daniélou 97), this hints at a kind of cosmic complementarity. It may suggest the sort of divine connection that we found in *Ardhangini*. In other words, this romantic plot too may draw on the male and female aspects of divinity in modeling its lovers. The point has obvious relevance for their role as national leaders against colonialism (e.g., in suggesting an association between divine preference and anti-colonial struggle and in affirming equality of the sexes in the new nation). In keeping with one common version of the love triangle, the slave trader in effect abducts Nisha, taking her to his own quarters. In an Indian context, any abduction of this sort is likely to recall the abduction of Sītā. However, this Sītā does not wait to be rescued by Rāma. Rather, she takes matters into her own hands. When tied to the mast and denied food and water, she calls on the other Indians to revolt. Ultimately, she leads an uprising on the ship—what is usually called a *mutiny.*

I emphasize the term *mutiny* here because the film at several points alludes to the revolutionary upheavals that shook British India in 1857. Commonly referred to as the "Sepoy Mutiny," these constituted a widespread uprising against British domination and served as an inspiration for later nationalists. The "mutiny" or uprising of 1857 is particularly relevant to Nisha, for her militancy, and particularly her ability to fight, almost certainly alludes to two figures in Indian culture—one mythological, the other historical. The first is the goddess Durgā, whom I have already mentioned. The second is the Rāṇī of Jhansi. The rāṇī was a ruler who took part in the 1857 mutiny and is renowned as one of its most courageous fighters. In Indian popular imagination, she is the female paradigm of militant nationalism. In connection with this, she is sometimes referred to as the "Joan of India," on the model of Joan of Arc (see Wolpert, *A New History,* 227).

The song that Nisha sings to inspire the revolution stresses self-esteem, thus the struggle against cultural imperialism that was so important to Dutt and his contemporaries. It ends with a remarkable call for everyone to "pick up the torch of revenge and walk tall." In response to this, a chorus of mutineers cries, "Revenge! Revenge! Revenge!" In addition to taking a stand on the issue of Goa, then, the film is indeed taking a stand on Gandhian nonviolence. The film is, in effect, asserting that violence is both justified and necessary when one faces a violent enemy. Gandhi's advocacy of nonviolence entailed a complete opposition to "return[ing] blow for blow." Indeed, Gandhi insisted that his followers should avoid "wishing that some harm should be done to the enemy," or even categorizing anyone as an enemy (138). In obvious and sharp contrast with Gandhian ideas, Dutt is explicitly calling for the isolation of enemies and the enacting of vengeance against them. In terms of the heroic plot, this is clearly the version in which the enemy is dehumanized. The crucial point here is that the call for revenge is paired with the call for pride in oneself. Here, as elsewhere, the enemy is dehumanized precisely because the enemy previously dehumanized the national in-group.

In another anachronism that serves the contemporary political purposes of the film, there is a celebration after the victory in which one of the victors says, "Hail Hindustan!" Here, too, the point is not that Indians had national consciousness about India centuries before the film was made. Rather, the point is that all events of rebellion against colonialism—from early resistance against the Portuguese through the 1857 uprising and beyond—are part of the heritage of contemporary nationalists. Indeed, these events constitute precisely the heritage that contemporary nationalists must take up and follow through—prominently, in evicting the Portuguese from Goa.

To clarify the position of the film on violence, Dutt includes a fascinating and disturbing sequence right after this. The first ship they encounter is the one carrying Prince Ravi. The rebels, led by Nisha, defeat the Portuguese. They gather the prisoners. Tillu, Nisha's second in command, asks if they should throw the prisoners in the sea. At first, Nisha hesitates. Then she agrees. The execution of prisoners is simply a war crime. But Dutt seems to find it perfectly acceptable. He certainly gives us no reason to be critical of Nisha or her decision, and the action is the only one consistent with the call for revenge (as opposed to a call for, say, freedom and justice). I suspect that there are two reasons for this, one contemporary, one historical. As to then-current events, this is a sort of extreme response to the Gandhism that was dominant in India at the time and a way of asserting support for the militant movement in Goa, the Azad Gomantak Dal. As to earlier history, this seems to be a sort of retrospective justification of a war crime often attributed to the Rāṇī of Jhansi. During the mutiny, a number of Europeans had taken refuge in a fort. They agreed to come out from the fort when they were promised safe conduct. However, they were killed (see Taylor 170–171). It is not clear that the Rāṇī actually knew that the English were to be killed. Nonetheless, she was widely blamed for the atrocity. The film seems to suggest that such an execution of prisoners is not an atrocity, but a justifiable act of vengeance in a time of war.

Nisha does spare the Indians on the ship, including the prince. However, she still does not know his identity and puts him to work swabbing the decks. She also spares Rosita, who claims to be Indian. One of the Indians taken prisoner is a farcical Brahmin character played by the great comic actor, Johnny Walker. This character's primary concerns are avoiding danger, getting out of work, and most important of all, eating. Viewers familiar with the conventions of Sanskrit drama will recognize this immediately as the *vidūṣaka* character, one of the most common character types in ancient Indian drama. I suspect that Dutt put this character here not only for comic relief, but to extend the film's treatment of cultural heritage by including the Sanskrit literary tradition. (Prince Ravi's romantic/heroic character is also standard in Sanskrit drama, and the theme of the king concealing his identity from his beloved turns up there as well. Both may be seen in, for example, the great paradigm of Sanskrit drama, *Abhijñāśakuntalam*. However, these features are less distinctive of the Sanskrit tradition.)

For some time, the heroic plot is, so to speak, put on hold as the romantic plot advances on board the ship. For our purposes, the crucial aspect of this ancillary narrative is its integration with the heroic plot. This integration comes when Nisha indicates that her commitment to the nation, her complete devotion to her "duty," prevents their romantic union—an inversion of a cross-culturally common theme in which the political duties of the man prevent his union with his beloved. (We have seen a version of this in Rāma's exiling of Sītā.) Taking up the imagery of the goddess Durgā, Nisha says, "Time has armed me with a sword. And I won't let go of the sword for love." Ravi replies, "I don't just love you. I love your sense of duty too." The sequence suggests that the love plot operates not only literally, but allegorically. The union of Ravi and Nisha is a union of different classes in the population. Most obviously, they are the social elite and the ordinary people who will eventually rule the free nation together.

Lest this all seem too Hindu-centric, Dutt turns to the Muslim tradition as well. Specifically, the crew affirms that, in struggling against the Portuguese, they wish to be shahīds. The concept of the shahīd is somewhat complex. First of all, it refers to someone who bears witness to Allāh even when faced with an obstacle or trial. Bearing witness in the face of a trial is called "jihād." In other words, contrary to common belief, "jihād" does not mean "holy war." It means, again, struggle against obstacles or trials to witness for Allāh (see, for example, Maulana Ali 402n.1073, 761n.1902, and Waines 92). Thus one may engage in a jihād against one's own greed, insofar as greed is inhibiting one from witnessing for Allāh. The most severe form of trial is, of course, one that threatens one's life. This may come in the context of battle, and in this case a jihād is a holy war. In any case, the greatest form of witnessing occurs when one gives up one's life in jihād. Thus shahīd simultaneously means "witness" and "martyr," for the martyr is the paradigm case of the witness (cf. Maulana Ali 209n.598 and Giffen 101). This assertion by the crew—that they wish to be shahīds—is obviously related to the preceding assertions by Nisha that her duty requires her to fight with a sword and that "I can sacrifice even my life to my duty." All of them are shahīds in bearing witness for the nation in this (holy) anti-colonial war. As we will see again in *Sholay,* an appeal to the Islamic idea of jihād and the Islamic ideal of the shahīd is common as a way of opposing Gandhian nonviolence.

Meanwhile, in keeping with the tragic middle of the heroic plot, the people in the kingdom come to believe that their prince has been killed. Moreover, in keeping with the standard usurpation sequence, Yashwant is to be crowned. Nisha and her men land and hide in a cave temple, with a huge icon of the goddess carved into one of the walls. Ravi rides off in the night to tell his mother that he is alive, but he is captured by Yashwant. This has consequences for the love plot as Nisha briefly feels that she has been betrayed. More interestingly, it fuses the separation of lovers in the love plot with the confinement of the rightful ruler in the usurpation plot. Specifically, in the love plot, the male lover is often exiled while the female lover is confined at home. Here, we find the male lover imprisoned (thus confined at home) while the female lover is effectively exiled. In the heroic plot, we often find the rightful ruler either imprisoned or exiled. He or she (usually he) must be aided by the faithful soldier in escaping from prison or ending the exile. Nisha takes the place of the faithful soldier here, again contradicting our gender expectations.

At this point, there is a brief dialogue between Prince Ravi and General Barbosa that explores some of the themes that are important to the film. First, Barbosa explains that the Portuguese gained control of Ravi's kingdom by helping him fight against his enemy, the Zamorin. Understanding this requires some historical background. The Zamorin was the ruler of Calicut. Ravi takes up the historical role of the prince of Cochin. According to Danvers, Cochin was more than once threatened by the Zamorin of Calicut and called on the Portuguese for aid, first in 1504 (see Danvers I: 93–116, 488–490). In connection with this, there are two incidents that seem to have provided sources for Dutt's story. The first involved an alliance of the King's cousin, not with the Portuguese, but with the Zamorin (see I: 204–205). The second, which occurred eighty years later, includes a more thematically significant parallel with the narrative situation of *Baaz.* As Danvers explains, "The King of Cochin, having assigned over all the Customs of his territories to the Portuguese, caused thereby great discontent to his people, who, feeling themselves robbed of their just rights, banded themselves together to the number of 20,000, swearing to die in defence of their liberties." The result was that the Portuguese commander,

"Not feeling himself in a position to resist their demands . . . suspended . . . that agreement" (II: 54).

The main importance of the reference to the Zamorin is in emphasizing the ways in which colonialists generally gained control over India by taking advantage of internal divisions within India. It was not the intrinsic strength of the Portuguese (or British) that allowed them to conquer and exploit Indians. Rather, the film suggests, it was the disunity of India, whether that disunity was a matter of region, religion, caste, or something else. However, it is also interesting that Dutt changes the history of the mass rebellion. First, he makes it a conflict in which the Portuguese are on one side and the Indians, both prince and people, are together on the other side. Second, he implies that the conclusion is permanent. There are obvious political reasons for both changes. The permanence of the solution connects the historical events with the condition of the new, independent India. The aligning of the people and the ruler allows Dutt to provide a positive model for the nation, a model in which different, hierarchized social groups join together for the good of all. However, it is no less noteworthy that Dutt does this by making the history fit more closely the prototypical plot of heroic tragi-comedy. He took two incidents from history. Like everything in real life, these incidents were more complex and ambiguous than a simple usurpation or invasion. He combined these events and simplified them into the form of heroic tragi-comedy. This is not surprising. Romantic, heroic, and sacrificial tragi-comedy not only organize fictions. They also orient the ways in which we emplot life. We think about the world in the form of stories. As a result, we are likely to understand the world—its events, its political struggles and personalities, its important social issues—through narrative prototypes. Chakrabarty, along with screenwriters Adil and Bhushan, did this with respect to untouchability, using romantic tragi-comedy. Dutt appears to have done this with respect to Indian colonial history—in particular, the then-current situation in Goa—using heroic tragi-comedy. In other words, I suspect that Dutt was not only making a good fictional story when he combined and reshaped historical events. He was, to some extent, trying to make sense of the history, and he was tacitly drawing on narrative prototypes to do so.

In any case, in direct, if implicit, contrast with the internal divisions condemned by the film, Ravi goes on to praise Nisha as a "worshiper of the nation." Barbosa presses Ravi to reveal Nisha's location. Now Ravi affirms the true unity of the nation, a unity that lies below its superficial divisions. Specifically, he replies that Nisha is "in the hearts of the children of Malabar." The answer is suggestive in several ways. It indicates that the "worship of the nation" that characterizes Nisha is in fact latent in the hearts of all the "children" of the nation. More important, it implies that at the time of the film's making Nisha continued to live in the hearts of the people of India, and perhaps especially in the hearts of the people of Goa. In this context, Nisha may be understood once again as the Rāṇī of Jhansi, or more generally as the rebels of 1857, or more broadly still as all those who fought against colonialism. Their spirit now lives in the hearts of the people of India. It is their anti-colonial heritage that animates current nationalism. Indeed, it is no accident that Nisha has the nom de guerre "Baaz," for "heritage" is one of the meanings suggested by the term. In music, "baaz" refers to the style which musicians have derived from their particular lineage of instruction (see Vijay et al. 154). Here, we may see it as the attitude of uncompromising patriotic duty—indeed, patriotic witnessing in jihād—derived from a particular national lineage.

In keeping with the tragic middle of the heroic plot, Ravi is now condemned to death. There is a lengthy sequence during which he rides to his execution, singing. The lyrics of the song all take up metaphors of what he might have been, but was not—"The one who nearly made it, that kind of destiny I am. Look at me, O God. . . . I am a colourless picture. . . . I'm the arrow that missed its target, the one who made it but didn't," and so on. The emotional and thematic force of the song will be lost on any viewer who does not recognize that the entire sequence alludes to the exile of the last Mughal emperor, Bahadur Shah, after the 1857 uprising.[9] Just as Ravi is to be buried alive, the Shah was sent off to a sort of living death in exile. Bahadur Shah was a renowned poet and his verses are often seen (sometimes anachronistically) as expressing the misery of that exile and of the stifling of Indian independence. More important, the lines sung by Ravi echo Bahadur Shah's most frequently quoted poem (see, for example, Ahmed 85). This poem too draws on metaphors of what this king might have been, but was not. He explains, for example, that he is "the spring of the garden, laid waste by fall" (Kanda 101). When Majrooh Sultanpuri wrote the lyrics for Ravi's song, he appears to have modeled it on this famous poem by Bahadur Shah.[10] This gives the scene historical resonance. It supports, and is in turn supported by, the link between Nisha and the Rāṇī of Jhansi. It also serves to stress the Muslim heritage of the nation—which is, of course, crucial in a film that calls for national unity.

Nisha manages to rescue Ravi, in keeping with one common version of the heroic plot in which the loyal soldier rescues the ruler. When they return to the caves, she worries that their difference in class means that they cannot be married. Ravi insists that she is superior to him and makes it clear that there is no obstacle to their union. This is obviously part of the romantic plot. However, it has consequences for the heroic plot as well. It suggests (somewhat naïvely) that the new India has not roused the masses simply in order to install a new ruling elite. Rather, the ordinary people are superior to the political leaders. The latter will govern the country only in full union with the former.

Here we begin the sequence of events that will lead to the final resolutions of both the usurpation and invasion parts of the heroic plot. Ravi goes off to gather soldiers from across the nation. Yashwant's coronation day has arrived. In a somewhat confusing sequence, Nisha stages a classical dance recital before Barbosa and Yashwant. Thematically, the point is to affirm indigenous tradition against the cultural hegemony imposed by the colonizer. However, it is not clear just how this relates to the literal plot of evicting the Portuguese and restoring Ravi. The song accompanying the dance is clearly a call to action. Nisha sings, "Your memory invokes challenge" and "Your time has come." The message, apparently bearing on the people of Ravi's kingdom, is addressed more significantly to Dutt's contemporaries sitting in the movie theater. He urges the latter to remember their heritage of anti-colonial struggle, the "memory" of which "challenges" them to further resistance. Specifically, they should take up the challenge of anti-colonialism and free Goa. Moreover, they should continue the work of cultural decolonization represented by the use of classical Indian dance in this scene. The connection with the new independent India is suggested by such lines as "Wake up, the morning has broken. The night is over." This chorus indicates that it is no longer necessary to remain subservient to the colonizers. It is no longer the night of colonial domination. Indians must recognize that it is a new day and act accordingly—ridding themselves of the last vestiges of colonialism.

Ultimately, Nisha flees with the Portuguese in pursuit. The Portuguese enter the temple and engage in a battle beneath the statue of the Goddess, a shocking sacrilege for a Hindu audience. Eventually, Nisha returns to

*1.7. Nisha is burned at the mast.*

her ship only to be ambushed. Barbosa reports the results of the battle, explaining that the rebels have lost. Both prophesying the future and implicitly appealing to the audience in the theater, Nisha responds, "If not today, some other day this dream will be fulfilled. For it's not just my aim but the whole of Malabar's." It is impossible not to hear this declaration as a direct statement about the then-current condition of Goa and an appeal to Goans and Indians to fulfill this dream, a dream that had not died, but also had not been fulfilled for centuries.

After this, Barbosa has Nisha tied to the mast of the ship and tells his soldiers to set the ship on fire. The subsequent shots of Nisha amid the flames (see Figure 1.7) allude in part to the burning of Saint Joan, as depicted in films such as Dreyer's *Passion of Joan of Arc*. The connection is relevant in many ways. It is relevant because, as a military leader for her nation, Nisha herself is directly parallel to Joan. It is relevant because Joan was a martyr, a *shahīd*. It is relevant because the Rāṇī of Jhansi is often referred to as the Joan of India. Of course, the burning does not allude only to Saint Joan. There are also Hindu associations here. As with Chhaya, Nisha's fire ordeal recalls both the trial of Sītā and the sacrifice of Satī. Nisha too is passing through fire for the sake of the kingdom and for the sake of her partner. Here, as elsewhere in Indian cinema, undergoing the fire ordeal is the most sublime act of the heroine. In this case, it is taken up for nationalist purposes.

As Nisha's ship burns, Ravi arrives on the shore leading a popular revolution against Portuguese rule. He himself kills Barbosa. The people chase Yashwant along the shore. His fate is clear. The two strands of the heroic plot have been resolved. The invasion has been repulsed. The rightful ruler has been restored.

But there is still something left outstanding. Obviously, the love plot is not resolved—or it has been resolved tragically with Nisha's death. Moreover, there is something left out of the heroic plot as well. The second hero, the loyal soldier, seems to have died. This note of sorrow is not unheard of in heroic tragi-comedies. It is one of the reasons that the endings of heroic plots are often less fully comic than the endings of romantic plots.

Ravi is able to pull Nisha from the water. At first, it seems that she is dead and the scene calls to mind Śiva carrying the charred remains of Satī. But Nisha revives. As a literal plot development, this may not make much sense. However, as allegory, it is perfectly reasonable. The spirit of popular defiance seemed to have died, but it remains alive. Ravi's final speech is not a comment on his own kingdom, but on the new nation of India, and on its mission to liberate and incorporate—or "welcome"—the people of Goa: "Our nation is free now. Did you hear? We're free. Look. See how eager the flag of independence is to welcome you."

In sum, with only slight variations on the universal plot structure of heroic tragi-comedy, Dutt has fashioned a story that is profoundly resonant both culturally and historically. He has used that socially particularized universal story to organize and interpret a contemporary political situation and to give emotional force to a concrete political program.

## Make Love, Not War: The Anti-Sacrificial Tragi-Comedy of Santosh Sivan's *The Terrorist*

Sacrificial tragi-comedy is formed from the third universal happiness prototype, plenty—first, plenty of food; more generally, abundance of everything that sustains life. The first crucial point to make about the happiness goal in a sacrificial narrative is that the bounty toward which the story aims is not only bounty for the hero or heroine individually, but for the entire society. This generalization to society is important. It results from the fact that happiness goals should not be provisional but, as far as possible, eternal. After all, it is not true happiness if it is riddled with insecurity. That is why there is a social component to the personal and physical prototypes, as well as the social one. Eternity in romantic love is a matter of joining with one's beloved. But it will not be untroubled unless there has been social reconciliation, so that the couple will not be subjected to repeated interference. Obviously, plenty cannot be sustained individually. The work that produces plenty is social work. The conditions that produce plenty (e.g., rainfall) are socially shared conditions. Indeed, this social extension is more crucial in the sacrificial plot than in the romantic plot. Fundamentally, the romantic plot requires only that the blocking characters be neutralized. It requires only that society not bother the lovers. In the case of sacrificial plots, however, the narrative requires a much more thorough integration of the individual hero or heroine with the society. The society as a whole must produce the wealth that sustains the individual. In this way, the sacrificial narrative is, in its actual development, almost as thoroughly social in character as the heroic narrative. Indeed, this is one reason why the conclusion of the heroic narrative is commonly a utopia marked prominently by agricultural plenty and the absence of disease. The ideal rule of society is bound up with the ideal physical condition of its members.

In my experience, Americans today find the sacrificial plot the most alien, the most difficult to accept as universal—even though most of them are Christian and the story of Jesus is a paradigmatic sacrificial tragicomedy. The problem, I take it, is that, living in a society where plenty is as close as the nearest Super Stop & Shop, it is difficult to imagine the acquisition of food as constituting much of a story. But, in fact, for most of human history, food was easily the most important of the three prototypes for happiness, the one that consumed most of the energy of most people most of the time. Indeed, it is difficult to understand how people bothered about romantic and heroic plots, given that so much of their life was taken up with concern over their next meal.

In keeping with the usual principles of narrative construction, the middle of the sacrificial narrative is the opposite of the goal. Specifically, it is not merely the absence of plenty. Rather, it is complete devastation. Since the end is most crucially bounteous food, the middle is most commonly famine. However, since plenty is inseparable from other aspects of physical health, the middle may also be developed in terms of other overpowering threats to health, such as epidemic disease. Another way of thinking about the three narrative structures is in terms of reproduction. The romantic plot takes up personal reproduction, thus sexuality. The heroic plot takes up the reproduction of social structure and culture. The sacrificial plot considers the physical substrate for social and sexual reproduction—thus food and general health. The middle of the sacrificial plot treats whatever devastates the physical basis of reproduction. Famine is the most prototypical case of this.

The devastation of plenty raises a problem for the beginning of the sacrificial plot. The suffering that marks the narrative middle is usually the result of malevolence. Controlling parents keep the lovers apart. A sinister enemy invades the kingdom. Of course, the hero or heroine may contribute to this in some way. A lover may be ambivalent about a tabooed marriage. The ruler may be too trusting of a rebellious relative. A hero's faults and errors may be stressed, particularly in tragic versions of romantic or heroic plots, as Aristotle famously noted. But these faults and errors tend to be less significant than the malevolence of blocking characters. The situation is very different in sacrificial plots. The only agent who could possibly cause famine is divine. Thus the only fault that could bear on famine is some offense to a controlling deity. Moreover, this offense must somehow implicate the entire community, for it leads to punishment of the whole group. In keeping with this, the beginning of the sacrificial plot is some communal fault, some crime committed by the entire society or by a representative of the society—often the current political or religious leader or a founding ancestor (such as Adam). This crime is typically related to reproduction. It is most often a sin involving food itself or sexuality.

Thus we have the beginning (sin), the middle (devastation), and the end (plenty). However, it is not yet clear just how one gets from the middle to the end. The heroic plot commonly solves the problem of this transition by combining its two constituent plots so that the exiled leader defeats the invasion and thereby regains his or her rightful position. Even without this, the general outlines of the transition are suggested by the nature of the resolution—the rightful leader must defeat the usurper and the home society must repel the invading enemy. The romantic plot has no standard transition. But in this case any sort of plotting will do. Again, the goal itself suggests different possible means. After all, the hero and heroine usually need to do nothing more than outwit their parents. The difficulty with the sacrificial plot is that there is no question of defeating or outwitting God. Moreover, in this case, the devastated society is more deeply blameworthy than the heroic or romantic protagonists, even when the latter are unusually bad. The obvious and universal response to this collective guilt is reparation. The society must atone for the initial sin. Atonement is always a matter of sacrifice. One gives up something that one values as a form of self-punishment. That sacrifice is most obviously a matter of social power (as when one resigns a position), sexual enjoyment, or physical well-being. All three occur in sacrificial plots. However, the last is the most common. In keeping with the general principles of emotional intensification in narrative, that sacrifice is standardly developed into its most extreme form. The greatest sacrifice of physical well-being is, obviously, the sacrifice of life. In consequence, the most prototypical form of the sacrificial plot moves from devastation to plenty by way of sacrifice, most often the sacrifice of human life. Clearly, this cannot be the sacrifice of the entire community. It is most prototypically the sacrifice of some uniquely innocent member of the community.

The characters follow directly from the plot. Commonly, there is some individual who is particularly responsible for the initial sin. In addition, there is often some tempter figure who seduced that individual into sin. Eve, Adam, and the Devil, in the Judeo-Christian and Muslim stories of the Fall, provide obvious instances. In explicitly political versions of the sacrificial plot, the seducer is often from some enemy out-group (e.g., a foreign nation) while the "sinner" is a (representative) member of the in-group. Particularly in versions of this sort, these guilty parties may be singled out for sacrificial punishment.[11] However, even in these cases, there is most often an innocent sacrificial victim as well. Ancillary characters in this narrative may include a figure who organizes and presides over the sacrifice, commonly a priest. Moreover, the sacrifice is frequently tied to ritual. There may also be a punishing deity or other characters. Again, the central narrative of Christianity comes to mind, with the punishing God, the uniquely innocent sacrificial victim (Jesus), and the ritualization of the victim's death in Christian services.

In discussing *Ardhangini* and *Baaz,* we saw how universal narrative prototypes served to organize political and social concerns, while at the same time being particularized by those concerns. The relation between prototypical emplotment and current events and conditions is even more striking in the case of *The Terrorist.* This is because the contemporary history depicted by the film was already emplotted in a prototypical narrative form by the people who made that history.

Specifically, *The Terrorist* presents a fictionalized account of the assassination of Indian Prime Minister Rajiv Gandhi by a suicide bomber working for the Liberation Tigers of Tamil Eelam (LTTE). The LTTE is a militant group whose aim is to establish a Tamil homeland in Sri Lanka. The majority of Sri Lankans are Sinhala-speaking Buddhists. A minority are Tamil-speaking Hindus. Following independence, the latter group experienced discrimination in education and employment, prominently including discriminatory legislation based on language (see, for example, Swamy 15 and 25), as well as anti-Tamil violence (see Swamy 13, 25, 40, 60, 77, 79–84). An escalating series of conflicts gave rise to a Tamil separatist movement, the most forceful component of which has been the LTTE. (For an illuminating treatment of this history as it bears on the film, see Pandit, "Inside.") The LTTE leader, Velupillai Prabhakaran, cites an incident from his childhood as crucial in leading him to militancy. He "was four years old when a Hindu temple priest was savagely caught by a Sinhalese mob and burnt to death during the anti-Tamil carnage of 1958" (Swamy 23). Prabhakaran explains that "the widespread feeling was: when a priest like him was burnt alive, why did we not have the capability to hit back?" (quoted in Swamy 23). Initially, the Tamils looked to India as a source of support, for most Tamil-speaking Hindus live in India, forming the majority population in the Indian state of Tamil Nadu. However, in 1987, the government of Rajiv Gandhi sent "peacekeeping forces" to Sri Lanka. The Tamil militants felt that the Indian forces were not there to keep peace, but to suppress the rebellion—and ultimately to assert Indian hegemony in Sri Lanka. At certain points, the Sri Lankan government appears to have agreed about India's hegemonic aims (even going so far as to give covert support to the LTTE against the Indian Peace Keeping Forces [see Pandit, "Inside," 96]).[12]

Many Tamils clearly viewed their situation as one of devastation, devastation requiring sacrifice. That sacrifice took the political form of suicide bombing. Indeed, the tactic was pioneered by the LTTE. (As Kennedy and Power point out, "Military analysts believe that terrorist groups like al-Qaeda have studied the tactics of the LTTE, especially their ruthless use of suicide bombers, or Black Tigers" [23].) In many ways, the LTTE bases its political policies and military strategies—as well as its ability to recruit new militants—on a tacit sacrificial emplotment of its own history and its own condition.[13] This is particularly clear in the case of Rajiv Gandhi. Gandhi in effect collapsed the roles of tempter and sinner. On the one hand, he was one of "us"—not Tamil, but Hindu and Indian, thus a political figure who should have continued his mother's policies of giving covert support to the rebels. (Rajiv's mother, Indira Gandhi, had been prime minister of India before Rajiv.) On the other hand, he was, in their view, the foreigner who infiltrated Sri Lanka to dominate it. Killing him was a way of purging these two figures who had violated the moral order. Moreover, the death of the suicide bomber was not merely an unfortunate side effect. It was, rather, a necessary sacrifice. Put differently, suicide bombing is not simply an efficient way of killing a political opponent, at least not in all cases. Rather, it is a way of making the sort of sacrifice that is necessary to end social devastation. It is guided not only by practical considerations of efficiency in killing, but also by a narrative understanding of politics, an understanding structured by the universal prototype of sacrificial tragi-comedy.

Though I cannot imagine Sivan was self-consciously aware of this emplotment, he was nonetheless sensitive to it. His treatment of the story highlights and even enhances its relation to sacrificial emplotment. For example, in Sivan's fictionalization, Malli is recruited to kill herself and an Indian VIP who is harming the movement. She is trained by Perumal, who takes up the priestly role. The rehearsals he sets up for Malli have a markedly ritualistic character; they are more like ceremonies than practice sessions. More important, one striking difference between the universal sacrificial prototype and the LTTE emplotment of the Rajiv Gandhi assassination concerns food. Famine and drought, or related problems, have figured importantly in the case of other political movements that drew particularly on the sacrificial plot. For example, much Irish nationalist struggle has had a sacrificial orientation. This is inseparable from the fact that the "potato famine" or "Great Hunger" of the 1840s stands as the most salient instance of the devastation caused by British colonialism in Ireland. But there is no obvious way in which such concerns enter in the Sri Lankan case. In *The Terrorist,* however, Sivan introduces them in a remarkable, creative way. When Malli goes to India, she obviously needs a cover story. (She can hardly say that she is there to assassinate someone.) The cover story is that she is doing research on agriculture. In other words, Malli is supposedly there to do things that will eventually aid the production of food back in Sri Lanka—precisely what the sacrificial narrative says she is doing in killing herself and the VIP.

Of course, it is crucial that this is a cover story, not the truth. Indeed, Sivan makes it clear that, in his view, sacrifice of this sort does not bring life. It brings only further death. This is particularly emphasized through the sub-plot, and through a crucial change in the main plot, a change that makes Sivan's film deviate decisively from historical events.

As I noted in discussing *Baaz,* romantic tragi-comedy is the most frequently recurring prototype. For this reason, it is often combined with other narrative structures. In the case of *Baaz,* we saw it reinforcing the heroic plot. Such reinforcement seems to be the usual case. However, two prototypes may be joined in contradictory ways as well. In other words, the romantic plot may undermine or inhibit the achievement of heroic or sacrificial goals. Indeed, this is rendered particularly easy by some salient differences between the romantic plot, on the one hand, and the heroic and sacrificial plots, on the other. First, both the heroic and sacrificial plots tend to support social hierarchies very strongly. Both value obedience and structures of authority—primarily political, in the case of the heroic plot; primarily religious, in the case of the sacrificial plot. In contrast, the romantic plot is very forceful in its opposition to authority. Secular and religious authorities tend to block the union of the lovers. The entire thrust of the romantic plot is to overcome the power of those authorities and free the lovers, so that they are able to unite with one another. Second, the sacrificial plot tends to condemn sexuality as sinful, as a source of devastation. Heroic plots do not necessarily involve sexuality. However, if it is part of the heroic plot per se, then it is often treated as a sort of distraction from the social goals of the hero, as a way of immobilizing the hero, as when the hero is seduced by a spy or is held back from battle by a lover's pleas. (An example of this sort from Indian cinema may be found in Bedekar's *Rustom Sohrab.*) In contrast, the romantic plot almost invariably celebrates sexuality. The difference in emplotment is captured nicely by the 1960s slogan, "Make love, not war." Counter-cultural opponents of the Vietnam war tacitly emplotted their understanding of politics and society in romantic terms, while the proponents of the war relied on a heroic narrative.

Sivan takes up the romantic plot in just this contradictory way. First, he straightforwardly celebrates sexuality. He directly opposes the sexual relations between Malli and her dead lover, Chandran, to the violence of the LTTE. Indeed, he closely connects sexuality with fertility. Not only does he make Malli pregnant, he parallels the growth of the child in Malli's womb with the growth of seeds in the earth. In this way, he suggests that the true end of devastation, the true continuation of life for the Tamils of Sri Lanka, is not through suicide bombing, but through love and sexual union. Moreover, he connects this reproductive fertility with traditional Tamil culture. That culture has been denigrated by the Sri Lankan majority, but it is not preserved in the LTTE camps. Indeed, the camps have only alienated people from their culture. The point is brought out by the character, Vasudevan. Vasu is an old man who tells Malli agricultural fables, celebrates her pregnancy, and teaches her the customs of Tamil tradition—customs of which she is apparently ignorant.

These points in Sivan's film bear, not only on the narrative prototypes, but on the historical and political situation as well. Specifically, the LTTE follows the sacrificial plot quite strictly in its own official attitude toward sexuality, which is highly censorious. As Kennedy and Power explain, "love affairs are forbidden before the age of 25 for women and 28 for men," and adultery is punishable by death (23). (Malli and Chandran are well under the permissible age for sexual relations.) The lack of cultural tradition is also historically accurate. Again, the rebellion is a rebellion by a social group that is defined primarily by language, religion, and traditions related to religion. However, as Kennedy and Power explain, "organized religion is discouraged, and every morning, Tiger cadres salute an image of Prabhakaran while reciting the LTTE pledge" (23). In other words, LTTE militarism does not further traditional Tamil culture. Rather, it substitutes for that culture.

Sivan's use of the romantic plot contradicts the sacrificial emplotment of politics with respect to hierarchy as well, though here the contradiction is more complex than one might initially imagine. Sivan develops all the authority figures in the sacrificial plot in a way that is likely to inspire our antagonism. The Leader of the LTTE spouts meaningless slogans and sends young girls to their deaths. We never see his face, and thus are encouraged not to individualize and thus humanize him. But the Indian VIP is no better. He sends young boys to their deaths in Sri Lanka. We never see his face either. Perumal and his assistant are machine-like in their rehearsal of the assassination and in the heartless way they discuss Malli's death. Interestingly, the assistant wears red glasses that are identical with those worn by the VIP, as we see from a brief glimpse over the VIP's shoulder. This too suggests that the leadership on both sides is the same. In sum, Sivan undermines the usual celebration of social authority in sacrificial (and heroic) emplotments.

At the same time, Sivan revises the criticism of hierarchy in the romantic plot. He does this by creating a familial authority that is not a blocking figure. Specifically, Vasu is explicitly a substitute father for Malli, who has been orphaned. (Similarly, Malli is a substitute child for Vasu, whose only son has died.) Vasu is the one who first realizes that Malli is pregnant. But he does not condemn this unwed mother, as one would expect from a censorious representative of an oppressive social hierarchy. Rather, he and his assistant, Gopal, only celebrate this pregnancy and Malli's motherhood, supporting her in every way possible. His affirmation of life—including life that results from socially unsanctioned sexual union—is the antithesis of the puritanism and morbid politics of the Leader and the LTTE more generally.

Sivan not only particularizes the sacrificial and romantic plots by reference to historical and political conditions. Like Chakrabarty and Dutt, he also draws on paradigmatic cultural narratives. He uses these paradigms to develop his sacrificial and romantic stories, to enhance their (thematic) opposition, and to intensify the emotional impact of the stories on Indian (especially Tamil) viewers. For the sacrificial plot, Sivan takes up one of the great Tamil epics, *The Ankle Bracelet* of Ilangô Adigal. *The Ankle Bracelet* is a lengthy poem that culminates in what is, effectively, a suicide bombing. Kannaki is the devoted wife of Kôvalan. After years of philandering, Kôvalan finally returns to his devoted wife. They are reconciled and leave their city to begin a new life. They arrive in Madurai and stay with some gopīs or milkmaids—traditionally associated with Kṛṣṇa and romantic love—two of whom compare Kôvalan to Kṛṣṇa (Ilangô 106). Kôvalan takes Kannaki's ankle bracelet to sell in the city. When he enters the city, he is accused of stealing the ankle bracelet from the palace. The king orders his execution by the town guards. Meanwhile the gopīs have been dancing and singing in remembrance of Kṛṣṇa. When Kannaki learns of Kôvalan's death, she is first grief-stricken, then furious. According to ancient Tamil beliefs, true chastity in a woman involved "a sort of asceticism, the restraining of all impulses that were in any way immodest" (Hart 97). This chastity built up, and gave a woman control over, a fiery, spiritual power (aṇaṅku) that filled her body, particularly her breasts (see Hart 96–97, 102). Kannaki's years of chaste devotion to her husband had just this effect. Furious at her husband's death, Kannaki goes to the city and confronts the king, who dies in front of her. Subsequently, she rips off her left breast and throws it into the street, burning the city to cinders. In the course of avenging her husband's death, then, Kannaki causes the death of the king and also kills herself. Her death then becomes the excuse for another king to engage in extensive military conquest.

The parallels with the historical event depicted in the film and with Sivan's development of that event are striking. Prime Minister Gandhi (the VIP) is parallel to the king. Kannaki's husband, Kôvalan, killed by the King's guards, reappears in Malli's lover, Chandran, killed by Prime Minister Gandhi's soldiers. Malli plans to kill the VIP through an explosion much as Kannaki destroys the king's city in a fire (having already caused the king's death). Malli expects to die, like Kannaki, in the process—and to serve as an inspiration for military success. Finally, the explosives used by Malli are strapped directly over her womb, while the destructive force of Kannaki is released by tearing off her breast. In each case, the destructiveness is paired with a very pointed destruction of femininity, specifically aspects of femininity bound up with the bearing and nurturing of children.

Sivan's decision to manipulate this parallel is not purely aesthetic. Just as the *Rāmāyaṇa* is a crucial ethical and political paradigm for Hindus throughout India, *The Ankle Bracelet* is a crucial ethical and political paradigm for Tamils. In other words, this epic has political consequences in the real world. The film is in part undertaking a response to those consequences. Indeed, the importance of Tamil epics here is not simply a matter of inference. The LTTE Leader, Velupillai Prabhakaran, "devoured Tamil classics . . . glorifying the ancient Tamil kingdoms"; he "read Tamil classics over and over again" (Swamy 24, 69).

In keeping with common practices in Indian film, and Indian culture more generally, the romantic plot draws on Kṛṣṇa stories. Specifically, Chandran and Malli are a version of Kṛṣṇa and Rādhā. More generally, the positive characters in the film—including Vasu and Gopal—are in some way associated with Viṣṇu, most often with Kṛṣṇa in particular. (Again, Kṛṣṇa is one incarnation of Viṣṇu.) In setting up the opposition between these paradigms (i.e., the Tamil epic and the Kṛṣṇa stories), Sivan draws on a common opposition in Hindu thought between Viṣṇu, conceived of as the god of preservation, and Śiva, understood as the god of destruction. Kannaki is a version of the destructive Śaivite Goddess, similar to Kālī (destroyer of all things) or Durgā—who famously took the form of fire in defeating a dangerous demon (see O'Flaherty, *Hindu*, 247). Indeed, before they meet the Kṛṣṇa devotees, Kannaki and Kôvalan come upon a Kālī temple, a woman who incarnates the fierce Śaivite Goddess, and a group of devotees singing to Durgā and offering sacrifices (see Ilangô 76–85). The violent and destructive form of the Goddess is the divine model Malli initially imagines for herself. Chandran and Vasudevan, in contrast, stand for Viṣṇu, who becomes incarnate to save the world from destruction.

The film begins with Malli executing a traitor who betrayed the rebels to the Indian Peace Keeping Forces (IPKF). This betrayal led to seven deaths. We are told that one of those dead is Chandran, who took cyanide after being captured. We only learn much later that Chandran was Malli's lover.

After a scene showing Malli's bravery in combat, there is a scene in which the Leader explains that they need a suicide bomber to kill the VIP. A number of the girls volunteer. One takes up a nationalist version of the sacrificial myth, saying, "If today our flesh merges with the soil . . . tomorrow, this country can be ours." They all insist that they wish to die for the country, to be martyrs. It is important that Hinduism does not really have a concept of martyrdom. Martyrdom is found primarily in proselytizing religions, religions that advocate spreading doctrine and converting unbelievers. But, for the most part, one is born a Hindu or not. As such, dying as a witness to one's faith does not have a significant role in Hinduism. This emphasis on martyrdom further suggests the disconnectedness of the LTTE from the traditions it putatively represents. In any case, Malli is chosen. It is worth noting that Malli explains that her father was a nationalist poet. This stresses the importance of poetry for nationalism and for the specific act of suicide bombing. Moreover, as with the Tamil epics, this too is not merely Sivan's connection. Dhanu, the suicide bomber who carried out the assassination of Rajiv Gandhi, was the daughter of a nationalist poet (Swamy 232).

Following this, there is an interesting scene at night. Malli is alone, drenched in an obtrusively blue light. She removes the cyanide capsule that she wears around her neck, like all the militants. The significance of the scene—connecting the blue light with the removal of the cyanide—will become obvious only later on.

Malli goes to meet with the Leader. Camp number 1 is filled with young boys, roughly twelve years old, training for combat. Without shirts, their cyanide capsules are particularly prominent. The Leader announces, "We will shed our blood but not our tears." There is a flashback to Malli, a young girl, perhaps eight years old, weeping beside the coffin of her brother. The brother was a martyr for the cause. He was captured and took cyanide. This beloved brother was named "Ramu," suggesting the incarnation of Viṣṇu. The Leader explains, "We are fighting for the future of our people. We are sacrificing everything." Because people offer their lives, "our success is guaranteed."

Malli will be taken through IPKF territory by a boy of about twelve, Surya (the name of the sun god), nicknamed "Lotus." As she waits by the river, she remembers Chandran. (We do not learn that he is Chandran at this point; we infer this only later, when we learn that he, like Ramu, was captured and took cyanide.) This is the first flashback to her one night with him. She pulled him, wounded, from the water when Camp 7 was betrayed. The scene is bathed in the same blue light as we saw when Malli removed her cyanide. In both cases, it contrasts sharply with the brilliant reds of the fiery battle scenes and of the blood from their wounds. More important, in Hindu iconography, Kṛṣṇa is always represented as having deep blue skin. The blue light makes Chandran's skin blue in precisely the manner of Kṛṣṇa. This link between Chandran and Kṛṣṇa strongly suggests that the furtive relationship of Chandran and Malli parallels the furtive relationship of Kṛṣṇa and Rādhā. As the film progresses, it becomes clear that this forbidden love is profoundly opposed to all the ties that define Malli's militarism and violence. The meaning of the earlier blue scene becomes clear here as well. Remembering Chandran, bathed in the blue light that recalls Kṛṣṇa, she removed her cyanide, briefly refusing the death and self-destruction of the LTTE—a small gesture that prefigures the ending of the film.

This scene of Malli and Chandran introduces the Kṛṣṇa paradigm. The paradigmatic use of *The Ankle Bracelet* follows soon after. Lotus arrives and leads Malli into IPKF territory. Before proceeding, he has her change into traditional garb. For the most part, we do not see her change. But Sivan gives us a lingering close-up of one action—her attachment of her ankle bracelet (see Figures 1.8 and 1.9). The camera lingers on the ankle bracelet and Lotus calls verbal attention to it, saying, "the sound of anklets averts suspicion." The purpose, I take it, is to alert us to the relevance of the great Tamil epic.

The following scene gives us Lotus's back-story. He refers to a terrible communal riot in which many Tamils were killed. "They burnt the whole village," he says. Recalling the crucial experience that made Prabhakaran into a revolutionary, he explains, "My father was a priest. They immolated him." (Of course, the violence is not all on one side. The next day, a bomb kills or wounds a number of IPKF soldiers and Malli hacks another one to death with a machete when he discovers an LTTE weapons cache.)

Lotus and Malli finally make it to the shore, where Malli boards a boat to cross over to India. Before departing, she tells Lotus that she will not return. Again taking up the sacrificial motif, she explains, "My mission is for the future of our people." Lotus stares out across the water to Malli's boat. Behind him, out of focus, we see figures rushing toward Lotus. We

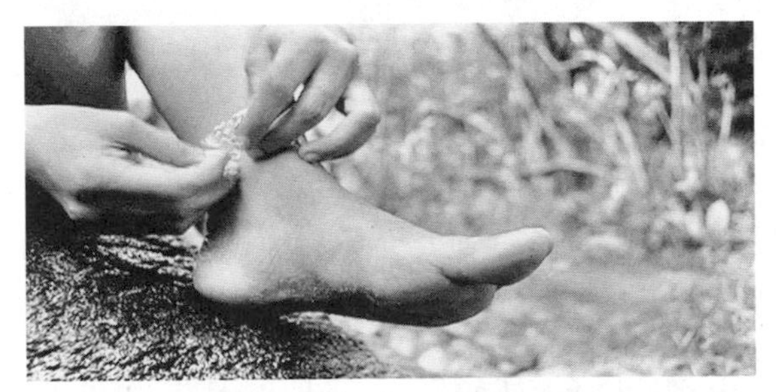

*1.8. Malli attaches her ankle bracelet . . .*

*1.9. . . . the camera lingers over the bracelet.*

recognize the red caps of the IPKF. Lotus turns. The camera cuts away, but we hear the sound of gunfire, and we know that Lotus does not have a gun. We only see Malli's horrified reaction from the boat.

On the mainland, Malli is greeted by Perumal and Thyagu. Here and subsequently, the round, red spectacles of Thyagu are very prominent. The reason will become clear at the end of the film. Perumal and Thyagu bring Malli to the house of Vasudevan, known as "Mad Vasu." The name "Vasudevan" derives from Kṛṣṇa's father. Kṛṣṇa's mother, Devakī, was the sister of King Kaṃsa. There was a prophecy that King Kaṃsa would be killed by his nephew, so Kaṃsa engaged in preventive murder of his nephews as they were born. When Kṛṣṇa was born, his father, Vasudeva, smuggled him out of the palace to the village of Brindavan, where he was raised by foster parents. (For a retelling of the story, see Prabhupāda I: 3, 30–32.) In this way, Vasudeva is the savior of the child Kṛṣṇa, who would otherwise have been killed at birth. The relevance of this story to Malli's unborn child is obvious. Mad Vasu is taking up the role of the mythological Vasudeva in saving the child from the political violence of a group's leader. It is also worth noting that Vasu's constant companion is the servant Gopal. Gopal is in some ways a male parallel to the female gopīs who play with Kṛṣṇa when he is a child and young man. Vasu's wife, Padmavathy, takes her name from the goddess Lakṣmī, Viṣṇu's consort, who is incarnated as Sītā and Rādhā (just as Viṣṇu is incarnated as Rāma and Kṛṣṇa). Finally, it is important to note that, when Vasu is introduced, we hear classical Indian music. Vasu is repeatedly associated with a long-standing, vigorous—and life-affirming—tradition. This is signaled in many ways, including the use of music.

As I have already noted, Malli's cover story is that she is doing agricultural research. Again, this bears directly on the sacrificial structure as it establishes the issue of whether her actions will contribute to feeding her people. From her room in Vasu's house, she sees a bird's nest, then young children, suggesting in an obvious way natural cycles of reproduction. The next flashback to Chandran begins with Chandran explaining that he gave up studying in order to take part in the revolution. This alludes to the discriminatory legislation that inhibited educational opportunities for Tamil speakers (see, for example, Pandit 95 and Swamy 15). After this, the physical interaction between the two increases, ending with a clear suggestion of sexual union. Following an ellipsis, Malli wakes up, then wakes Chandran. She whispers something to him, there is a cut to black, then a cut back to the lovers. She says that she will check to see if everything is clear. Sivan then cuts back to Malli in the present. He then cuts to another flashback, presumably after Malli has returned from checking the area. Now, Chandran has been discovered. He is being beaten by Indian soldiers. The traitor from the opening scene is there, with the soldiers. Chandran breaks open the vial of cyanide with his teeth.

Back in the present, Malli discusses the suicide/assassination with Perumal. Subsequently, she meets Vasu, who tells her and Gopal a parable about seeds and trees, then asks Malli to plant a seed. Through its clear contrast with the preceding scenes, this reinforces Sivan's thematic opposition between fertility and violence and thus, by implication, his invocation of the romantic narrative against the sacrificial emplotment of social life. The following scene once again connects these thematic concerns to mythological paradigms. Malli sleeps, bathed in blue light. In the background, we hear chanting from the nearby temple. The hymn is an appeal to Viṣṇu as preserver or savior: "O Lord of Seven Mountains, arise and save us all. O Lord with broad shoulders, wake up and save the world."

The next day, Malli is eating with Vasu and Gopal. Indian classical music is playing in the background. Around his neck, Gopal is wearing a very visible amulet. An amulet of this sort is worn traditionally to protect the wearer against misfortune. It bears a striking resemblance to the cyanide capsules worn by the LTTE militants. Indeed, it is difficult not to link and contrast the two. During this scene, Vasu notices that Malli does not know the mensal customs of Tamil tradition and has inadvertently insulted her host. Rather than berating her, he explains that one gesture signals the ending of a relationship while another signals bonding among those present. He gently alters her gesture to indicate bonding.

Following this, Sivan presents us with a highly ritualized rehearsal of the assassination, presided over by Perumal. During the rehearsal, Malli hesitates. When she does push the trigger, there is a brief flash of white. Interestingly, Sivan is reversing the cross-culturally standard association of white with good and black with evil. The white here is associated with death, while the black (as seen in the cut to black when Malli was with Chandran) is linked with new life. The inversion has mythological resonances.[14] Śiva, here the god of destruction, is covered with the white ashes of the cremation grounds. Kṛṣṇa, in contrast, is blue-black in color.

At this point, Malli discovers Padmavathy. They are in adjacent rooms. By a strange coincidence, there is a gap in the wall just across from the place where Padmavathy lies on her bed. Her face is turned toward the gap and it seems that she is observing Malli. This cannot literally be the case. She has been in a coma for seven years, since the time her son disappeared. Yet, despite her literal disability, Padmavathy is still a godlike figure, in some sense silently watching over Malli. Vasu makes this explicit when he analogizes her to God. He explains that we pray even though we do not know if God hears. Similarly, he speaks to her, even though he does not know whether she hears him or not.

Subsequently, Malli is exercising in good military fashion. She remembers how she buried Chandran's corpse with her own hands and how she vomited at the time. Back in the present, she vomits again. The scene is interesting for several reasons. For example, it seems to suggest Antigone's burial of her brother, thus pointing to the fratricidal nature of this war. More important, it again indicates that Malli is not following her own tradition. Rather than cremating Chandran, she has adopted the Christian and Muslim practice of burial. This cultural borrowing recalls the emphasis on martyrdom among the militants.

Some intrigue develops when Vasu tells Malli that he knows why she is there. This causes Malli to worry that he knows about the assassination.

Subsequently, he reveals that he knows she is pregnant. The suggestion is that he believes she is there either to have an abortion or to give birth discreetly, then return home as if nothing had happened. What is important here is that Vasu, despite being the representative of tradition, is not critical of Malli. He does not condemn sexuality and this illegitimate pregnancy. Rather, he sees it as something to celebrate. He urges her, "Don't hide anything," explaining, "Motherhood is to be revered. Be proud of it." Later, he tells her that he "will be the grandpa of the newborn." Again, Sivan changes the prototypical father figure here. Vasu is not the oppressive patriarch of standard romantic tragi-comedy. Rather, he is the precise opposite. What is most interesting is that he does not cease being a representative of society and tradition. Rather, he tacitly bases his own humane attitude on tradition. Indeed, he is right to do so. There is certainly a strain of Hindu tradition that is rigid and anti-sexual. However, there is another strain—represented most obviously by the stories of Rādhā and Kṛṣṇa—that celebrates sexuality. In addition, Vasu connects sexuality, not sacrifice, with agricultural fertility, explaining that "Earth is a mother, just like you."

In subsequent scenes, these themes are repeated and the emotional impact of Malli's dilemma is enhanced—for example, when Sivan presents us with extreme close-ups of Malli's tears as she remembers Chandran, or when he makes her agitated breathing prominent on the sound track. In the final rehearsal for the suicide/assassination, the viewer hears Malli's breath as if she were only inches away. It is clearly troubled as she tries to make herself press the trigger. There is a cut to black, recalling the scene of sexual intimacy with Chandran; a cut back to Malli; a cut to black again, then to Malli. In the end, she cannot press the trigger. Perumal tries to convince her, appealing to an implicit sacrificial narrative. He refers to martyrdom, explaining that "Your great sacrifice . . . your valiant death . . . will herald a new era for our people." She promises to go through with the suicide and murder.

But, just as Perumal is self-consciously working to make Malli follow the sacrificial narrative to its end, Vasu is working to help her follow through the romantic narrative to its culmination. He takes her to the temple, where he offers prayers for the delivery of her child. Outside, Malli holds the baby of another young woman. Both women are dressed in blue; the child has thick hair and a bright face, and is wearing purple. Particularly given the prominence of Kṛṣṇa elsewhere in the film, the child recalls popular paintings of the baby Kṛṣṇa.

Finally, it is the day of the assassination. At dinner, Vasu explains that he is fasting, an act done not only for one's own well-being, but for the well-being of one's spouse or children. Following the usual South Indian tradition, Malli is eating off a large leaf rather than a ceramic plate. Vasu puts aside his leaf using a traditional gesture explained earlier in the film, a gesture that signals the preservation of a bond with those present.

Later, Perumal stresses Malli's "sacrifice." Malli goes to Padmavathy and tells her, "I must sacrifice my future for that of the people." Though in a coma, Padmavathy grasps Malli's wrist and, for a time, will not let her go.

After freeing herself from Padmavathy, Malli makes her way to the site where the assassination will take place. In the distance, out of focus, we see the VIP approaching. The shot recalls the approach of the IPKF soldiers when they killed Lotus. Flower petals are falling everywhere. The motif is taken from classical Indian literature where miraculous events (such as Sītā's descent into the earth) are accompanied by showers of lotus petals. We cannot discern any distinguishing features of the VIP except the round, red frame of his glasses. It is precisely the frame worn by Thyagu.

After Malli places the garland around the neck of the VIP, she kneels. It is time to trigger the explosive. We see her hand on the trigger, there is a cut to black—here again recalling her night with Chandran—then back to Malli, then to black again, then to Malli. We hear her breathing as if she were as close to us as she was to Chandran that night. Finally, we see Malli open her hand and let go the trigger. There is a final cut to black. We hear only the musical motif of Malli's union with her Kṛṣṇa-like lover.

CHAPTER TWO

# The Film and the World

## Global Themes, Local Movies

### *Nishānt* and *Sholay*

Needless to say, films not only present us with characters and events. They present us with larger, intellectual issues, most often political or ethical issues. I use the word *theme* to refer to the development of such issues in the course of a work. The themes of a film are what give it social force, and mark it as having a purpose beyond aesthetic pleasure. In every tradition of literary theory—European, Middle Eastern, South Asian, and East Asian—there is at least some treatment of the ethical and political purposes of literature. In most, perhaps all, literary traditions, some people distrust the hedonistic qualities of entertainment and find literature justified by its moral message or political effect. Thus the first universal in this area is simply the presence of themes. Just as some aspects of European or American films make sense only in relation to thematic aims, so too some aspects of Indian movies are comprehensible only in relation to such aims. As the preceding chapter already makes clear, mainstream Hindi musicals, such as *Ardhangini* and *Baaz,* are not aimless entertainment. Despite clichés that oppose entertainment to seriousness of purpose, Hindi musicals—along with Tamil art films, and other genres of Indian cinema—are regularly pervaded by thematic commentary.

## Getting the Point: Stories and Their Morals

Theme is an area in which cultural and historical background are likely to be crucial for our understanding of particular works. As a result, we tend to think of themes as deeply culturally particular. Yet, to a remarkable degree, the same themes recur across different cultures. Here too cultural differences are little more than a matter of specification, conjunction, and emphasis. This is unsurprising once one realizes that themes are bound up with plots, and plots, as we saw in the preceding chapter, are commonly specifications of universal narrative prototypes—again, the prototypes of romantic, heroic, and sacrificial tragi-comedy.

Romantic narratives consider the limitations of social authority with respect to individual choice. The main narrative sequences of heroic tragi-comedy treat loyalty to one's society and its rightful leaders, as well as solidarity with one's compatriots and courage in the defense of that society, those leaders, and those compatriots. The sacrificial plot develops the theme of self-sacrifice for the good of the community. In keeping with this, *Ardhangini* takes up the romantic opposition to social authority, particularized as caste hierarchy. *Baaz* celebrates bravery, eschews disloyalty, and urges national unity behind an independent (i.e., non-collaborationist, anti-colonial) national leadership. *The Terrorist* is more complex in that it criticizes the usual themes of the sacrificial plot. However, those are the very themes it raises—the importance of self-denial and the necessity of individual sacrifice for the survival of the group. It then reconsiders those themes from the perspective of the romantic plot.

A further set of themes derives from an aspect of the heroic plot not treated in the preceding chapter. Specifically, there is a somewhat surprising epilogue to a number of heroic stories. In this epilogue, the victorious ruler or soldier does not rejoice in the national triumph. Rather, he or she feels remorse for the suffering he or she has inflicted. Thematically, the epilogue treats an ethical conflict—the conflict between an ethics of compassion and an ethics of defense.[1] The ethics of compassion involves aiding those who suffer, and certainly avoiding any infliction of suffering. The ethics of defense involves forcefully opposing anyone who would attack members of one's own group—family, nation, religion. The difficulty, of course, is that there are many cases in which one cannot simultaneously adhere to both forms of ethics. These to some extent contradictory ethical imperatives are codified in most explicit ethical systems. Their conflict is a recurrent thematic concern in literature across cultures.

Needless to say, the conflict between ethical imperatives is not purely intellectual. It is bound up with emotion, particularly empathy and remorse, on one side, and anger and fear on the other. The emotional intensity of this conflict is increased to the degree that the humanity and the suffering of the enemy are made salient. In keeping with this, the epilogue of suffering is commonly triggered by the killing of some innocent member of the enemy group, most often a child, sometimes a (non-combatant) woman (the effect of the latter may be intensified if the woman is a mother and her death causes a child to suffer). Conversely, if the enemy is dehumanized or his or her suffering is concealed, then remorse is an unlikely result of victory. There are crude ways in which an enemy may be dehumanized. Fascism provides obvious examples where the enemy (or, more generally, the out-group) is represented in animalistic or demonic terms. A more subtle version of dehumanization occurs when the enemy is presented as itself dehumanizing members of the home society. This is what we saw in *Baaz,* and it is the primary reason there is no epilogue of suffering in that film, despite some objectively heinous acts committed by Nisha (specifically, the massacre of prisoners by throwing them overboard). Again, the Portuguese are presented as thoroughly racist and entirely lacking in human feeling for Indians. This characterization effectively undermines any claims the Portuguese may have on our empathic identification. In connection with this, it is worth noting that Dutt ignores the fate of Rosita. I suspect that the ending of the film would have been different had the revolutionaries murdered her as well.

In any case, once the enemy is humanized and his or her suffering is made salient, empathy, remorse, and an epilogue of suffering become very likely. Most important for our purposes, that epilogue almost invariably presents some thematic treatment of the two varieties of ethics. It is often unable to resolve their conflict.

Since the preceding chapter included examples of the main themes from romantic, heroic, and sacrificial stories, I will concentrate here on themes derived from the epilogue of suffering, thus the conflict between the ethics of defense and the ethics of compassion. Specifically, I will consider *Nishānt* and *Sholay,* two heroic stories which are seemingly opposed in their treatment of conflicting ethics, but in fact have many points in common. As with the narrative prototypes per se, themes do not appear in their abstract, universal form. They appear in culturally specified ways. In keeping with this, we cannot understand the operation of these themes in individual films unless we understand both the universal concerns and their culturally particular articulations.

## Revolution and Remorse in Shyam Benegal's *Nishānt*

Since the death of Satyajit Ray, Shyam Benegal is arguably the most important director of alternative or, as it is called, "parallel" cinema in India. He is associated with a group of alternative filmmakers who came to prominence in the 1970's.[2] They rejected the conventions of Indian popular movies, most often adopting a realistic and self-consciously political style. They also rejected the economic structures of mainstream commercial cinema, in many cases relying on government sponsorship. Starting in the mid-1980's, the changing economics of Indian film—including the extension of video and television, as well as the increasing neoliberalism of Indian economic policy—contributed to the decline of the parallel cinema (see Datta 38–39). Nonetheless, directors associated with the movement continued to make films. Moreover, their work has had a lasting impact on mainstream cinema (see Datta 42). This is particularly true for Benegal.

*Nishānt* (*Night's End*) was Benegal's second film. It was highly praised by critics and won numerous accolades, including awards for best film and best screenplay. It is in many ways a paradigm of the parallel cinema. In this work, Benegal and Tendulkar (the screenwriter) take up the usurpation sequence from heroic tragi-comedy to present a revolutionary tale of peasant revolt against unjust rule. In doing this, they exploit an ambiguity in the heroic structure, by which a usurpation from one perspective may count as a restoration of legitimate rule from another perspective. For our purposes, the crucial part of the film is the conclusion. The entire film develops our sympathy with the rebels and our antipathy toward the feudal landlords. But the killing at the end is too brutal, and does not spare the guiltless. The organizers of the rebellion are clearly dumbfounded by the violence they have unleashed. Their response is precisely the remorse that routinely marks the epilogue of suffering, and it is triggered by the same killing of innocents. In connection with this, Benegal develops the two types of ethics. The ethics of defense is directly articulated in the film. Indeed, the leaders of the uprising appeal to this form of dharma or moral duty when rallying the people to rebel. For most of the film, this dharma of protecting one's family and community is not opposed to an ethics of compassion. It is, rather, opposed to fear and passivity. It is only at the end of the film that the ethics of compassion enters, and the terrible consequences of its prior absence become evident.

What is noteworthy about Benegal's film, however, is not only this universal theme, pitting the ethics of defense against the ethics of compassion. It is the culturally particular way Benegal develops this theme and gives it rhetorical force. In effect, Benegal marshals all the resources of Hindu tradition to represent the peasant revolution as a case of "justified violence." The end, therefore, functions as the strongest possible statement against violence, for even in this almost perfect instance, the violence goes beyond anything that can be considered permissible. First, the film presents us with two main heroes. They personify the two main professions of brahmins (the highest, priestly caste), and thereby the two main conduits of Hindu tradition. One is a teacher in the village school; the other performs rituals in the temple. These heroes, who arguably represent what is best in Hindu heritage, combine to urge the peasants to revolt.

Even more significantly, the narrative structure parallels the great paradigm of overthrowing unjust rule—Rāma's overthrow of Rāvaṇa. Like so many Indian films, *Nishānt* draws its plot in part from the *Rāmāyaṇa*. The main hero, the teacher, is clearly in the position of Rāma when his wife, Sushila, is abducted. As critics such as Prasad have indicated, the connections between Rāma's attack on Rāvaṇa's kingdom and the peasant rebellion are unmistakable (207). But, having noted this connection, these critics do not explain why Benegal and Tendulkar have developed the parallel. There are, I believe, two main reasons. First, the filmmakers aim to show us that violence is wrong, even when we have another Rāma battling another Rāvaṇa. It is wrong because it will always lead to excess and to the killing of the innocent. Second, this film not only criticizes violence; it also and equally criticizes the political use of the *Rāmāyaṇa* and other aspects of Hindu tradition to support violence—a practice that has been very common among Hindu nationalists. Indeed, Benegal stresses the motivational force of the *Rāmāyaṇa* story in propelling the villagers to violence.

The film takes place in a "feudal state" in 1945. It opens with chanting that invokes God as the protector of the poor,[3] thus perhaps preparing us for the subsequent alignment of the wealthy landlords with the demonic Rāvaṇa. The village priest enters the temple and discovers that it has been robbed. We learn quickly that the robbery was committed by three of the four brothers who are the landlords of the village. Two of the brothers had gambled on credit and needed a quick source of cash to pay their debts. It goes without saying that this crime—stealing from a temple—places them in direct opposition to everything good and holy, and prepares the way for their characterization as demonic (thus parallel to Rāvaṇa). The priest too knows who has committed the robbery, for he discovers a locket belonging to one of the brothers. However, he is too intimidated by the power of the landlords to say anything. A crowd gathers as news of the robbery spreads. The eldest of the brothers and chief landlord, "Anna," arrives. He abuses the police officer, who meekly accepts this mistreatment. Anna manipulates the situation until a homeless drunk is accused of the crime, chased by the villagers, and beaten cruelly.

We already discern a couple of thematically important points in this sequence. Most obviously, we have reason to distrust what is sometimes called the "spontaneous justice" of the villagers acting as a group. They decide too quickly who is guilty and who is innocent, and they act intemperately. Benegal also makes clear from this opening that the subservience of the villagers has nothing to do with some sort of Hindu fatalism, as some Orientalist commonplaces would have it. First, both the priest and the police officer clearly fear the landlords. That fear is undoubtedly the main cause of their acquiescence. Moreover, the police officer is Muslim. His religion encourages him to engage in a struggle for witnessing (i.e., jihād). But he is, if anything, more obsequious than the Hindu priest—unsurprisingly, as he is evidently part of a small religious minority in the village and thus has less security than the priest. Finally, there is nothing passive about the villagers who chase the poor scapegoat. They do not wait for God to punish him in the next life. They want to make sure he is punished now.

After these preliminaries, the teacher and his wife, Sushila, arrive in the village with their son, Munna. Early in their stay, the husband and wife bicker over whether he requested this transfer or whether it was forced on him. Clearly, Sushila sees this as a sort of exile. Though there is no reason at this point to link them with Rāma and Sītā exiled from Ayodhyā, subsequent connections make this clear in retrospect.

Over the course of several subsequent scenes, we learn more about the skullduggery of the landlords—particularly Prasad and Aanjaiya, and to a lesser extent Anna (Vishwam being the brother least involved or implicated in heinous acts). They pick out attractive young women from the village and have them sent up to the big house to service the brothers' sexual needs. They confiscate the entire harvest from one farmer. With no thought of payment, they take whatever they want from the market (while the police officer looks on). They heartlessly evict pathetic-looking tenants who beg not to be cast out. It is clear from these scenes that the landlords are, like Dutt's Portuguese, just the sort of heartless enemies that do not merit our empathy. As the story develops, Vishwam begins to notice Sushila. Benegal is carefully ambiguous about the degree to which Sushila's glances at Vishwam are glances of anger or a form of flirtation. Despite her name—*Sushila* means "good behavior"—it is not clear that Sushila's actions always preserve the chaste demeanor characteristic of that model of wifely chastity, Sītā. On the other hand, even Sītā does not seem to have preserved decorum entirely when she was approached by Rāvaṇa in the forest. She spoke with him, even though her husband was not home and his speech was highly sexual. For example, Rāvaṇa tells her, "Your breasts are high and round, resting close together and quivering, with the nipples firm and upstanding." Vālmīki explains, "Thus praised by the foul Rāvana," Sītā "honoured him with all attentions due to a guest" (II: 98). It is only after Rāvaṇa announces his name and directly propositions her that Sītā responds angrily—and, even then, she does respond (II: 101).

In any case, the result of this in the film is precisely the same as the result in the *Rāmāyaṇa,* for Sushila too is abducted. This puts Sushila clearly in the position of Sītā, and the brothers in the position of Rāvaṇa. Perhaps most important, it puts the teacher in the position of Rāma, with all that this implies about his exemplary relation to dharma. The teacher's first response is sorrow and despair; he weeps and cries out, not unlike Rāma after he discovered that Sītā was missing (see Vālmīki II: 127–140). He tries in vain to do something that will bring Sushila back, but he has no success. Initially, he goes to the police officer. The latter says that he cannot take any official action unless there is another witness to the crime. Though virtually the entire village did in fact see the abduction, no one is willing to give testimony. This stresses the ethically pernicious effects of the villagers' subservience. Even if Sushila was (like Sītā) a bit imprudent, she did nothing that justified the abduction—nor did her now abandoned husband and son do anything to deserve their loss. Moreover, the episode makes it clear again that the passivity of the villagers is self-destructive, whether it bears on the confiscation of their harvests, their eviction from the land, or the abuse of the women.

One of the most interesting points about the teacher's discussion with the police officer is that the officer finds it incomprehensible that the teacher would accept Sushila back after she had been taken by another man. This recalls a recurring theme in the *Rāmāyaṇa*. Rāma must deal repeatedly with the responses of "good souls" to Sītā's return (Vālmīki III: 342). These good souls, particularly his own subjects, do not view his acceptance of Sītā as reasonable, or as ethical. Indeed, they complain that Rāma is setting a bad example and suggesting to wives that they may run off with another man, then return to their husband with no repercussions (Vālmīki III: 516). This is why Rāma has Sītā pass through the fire before they are reunited (Vālmīki III: 342) and why he eventually exiles her (Vālmīki III: 518–519). Today, readers of the *Rāmāyaṇa* are likely to see this as a fault in Rāma. Such an attitude is not as uniquely modern as it may seem. Indeed, there is a long pre-modern history that shows considerable discomfort with Rāma's behavior toward Sītā. In this way, Benegal improves on Rāma's character by making the teacher not only state that he will accept his wife back, but express dismay that anyone would expect anything else.

Initially, the teacher takes a nonviolent approach to freeing his wife. He sees government officials, talks to newspaper editors, and generally follows through the usual means of pursuing justice. This takes a considerable amount of time and produces no result. Following repeated frustrations, he vents his impotent rage by destroying his umbrella and a small bush, then shouting at an innocent child. Though rather pathetic by cinematic standards of violence, even this suggests that violence is problematic. Once he allows himself to be violent, his aggression is not confined to proper objects. Indeed, in this case, it is confined entirely to improper objects.

This period of fruitless efforts is not entirely unlike Rāma's delay in rescuing Sītā, caused by his initial inability to discover her precise location. In both cases, the result is the same. Sushila, like Sītā, is imprisoned in the home of her abductor with no word that her husband has not simply given up all thought of her. Indeed, things are even worse for Sushila than they were for Sītā. In the landlords' home, Sushila is raped by Prasad and Aanjaiya. In contrast, Rāvaṇa gave Sītā a year to agree to sleep with him, after which he would not rape her, but have his cook prepare her for his breakfast (Vālmīki II: 122).

One small, but noteworthy link with the *Rāmāyaṇa* involves Vishwam's wife, Rukmani, who to some extent befriends Sushila. Rukmani is parallel to the demoness Trijatā who befriended and supported Sītā (see Vālmīki III:

117–118 and Tulasidasa 454). Moreover, Rukmani is repeatedly shown performing her morning ritual before the sacred tulasī plant. Though this is a common practice in many parts of India, it is strikingly emphasized here. I suspect the reason is twofold. First, it suggests that Rukmani is genuinely religious—thus unlike most of the people in the film, whether landlords or villagers. Second, Benegal may wish to call to our minds the author of the most widely read version of the *Rāmāyaṇa,* Tulasīdāsa, whose name could be rendered as "servant of the tulasī plant."

The landlords' employee, Pochamma, contrasts with Rukmani. Though she does help Sushila in certain ways, she is often rather malevolent, and thus like most women in Rāvaṇa's palace. For example, she tells Sushila right at the outset that her husband will never take her back. Later on, she reports that Munna is not allowed even to mention his mother. As far as the viewer can tell, the second statement is no less false than the first. But Sushila cannot possibly know this. Due to her despair over reunion with her family, and due to the relative kindness of Vishwam, she eventually accepts her situation and becomes a sort of second wife to Vishwam. It is worth pointing out that Benegal uses a striking stylistic technique when Pochamma tells Sushila that Munna is forbidden to speak about her. As Sushila becomes visibly angry, the dialogue sound is drowned by the music. We see Sushila and Pochamma talking, but we do not hear their words. This technique will recur later in the film.

Just as Rukmani shows compassion toward Sushila, Vishwam explicitly asserts Sushila's humanity and says that it is necessary to imagine what she is going through. The hypocrisy of this is obvious, given that he initiated the abduction and did nothing when his brothers raped her. However, even this minimal show of empathy serves to partially humanize Vishwam. Of course, Rukmani shows greater empathy, and thus is more thoroughly humanized. In addition, she is not guilty of any of the cruelty practiced by the brothers.

Meanwhile, when the teacher finally comes face to face with Anna, all he can muster is a timid, subservient greeting. The teacher then dreams of killing Anna. But when Anna looks at him in the dream, he cannot complete the act. The dream is a sort of inverted epilogue of suffering. The teacher cannot kill Anna in his dream for the same reason he would feel remorse if he did kill someone in reality. Evidently seeking some sort of comfort, the teacher goes to the temple. The priest tells him that we must all be oblivious to troubles in this life. He goes on to invoke a fatalistic ethics of trust in divine justice. Of course, we already know that he is motivated by fear, not by faith.

Subsequently, the teacher meets Sushila in the temple. (As she has accommodated herself to the situation with Vishwam, she has been granted certain privileges.) She berates him for abandoning her to the monsters who kidnapped her. He tries to explain that he did whatever he could, but she tells him, "You have to be a man first. You have to have dignity. You are a coward." Here we see a straightforward affirmation of the ethics of defense and its associated virtue of bravery. After this encounter, the teacher directly attacks fatalism and, by implication, the ethics of divine trust. Specifically, he refers to karma, the fundamental Hindu principle that all our acts have consequences for our well-being, if not in this life, then in a subsequent rebirth. The idea is commonly invoked to explain disaster or good fortune as the result of one's bad or good deeds in a former life. Thus it not only promises that the landlords will suffer for their current misdeeds in future lives. It also justifies the current misery of the villagers as the result of their own misdeeds in past lives. The teacher tells the priest that talk of karma amounts to nothing more than a mockery of people's suffering.

After this, everything changes. The priest and the teacher now devote themselves wholeheartedly to inspiring an active ethics of defense in the villagers. Indeed, even the style of the film changes, with the use of a hand-held camera giving the following scenes a documentary feel. Specifically, the priest and the teacher meet with different groups of villagers. We see them talking vehemently, but we do not actually hear the dialogue. Instead, we hear only ambient sounds and music. This recalls the dialogue between Pochamma and Sushila. It indicates that there is something common between the two scenes. In part, it is the anger of the speakers.

For our purposes, perhaps the most significant aspect of these scenes is the priest's clothing. From now until the end of the film, he wears a shawl which is imprinted, over and over, with one word: "Rāma." The obvious implication is that, in vigorously pursuing a violent ethics of defense, he and the teacher are following the example of the *Rāmāyaṇa.*

The talks by the priest and the teacher are clearly designed to excite the feelings of the villagers and spur them to action. In connection with this we witness a fight between bulls. The ordinary villagers are clearly excited by the spectacle of the battle. The teacher and the priest observe coolly. As the fight is going on, Prasad and Aanjaiya arrive on their motorcycle. No one pays any attention to them. As they leave, one of the bulls wins the fight and begins to chase the other out into the field. The editing of the scene suggests a parallel between the defeated bull and the brothers. When they arrive back at their home, the brothers find that the tires of their car have been punctured.

Now, we begin to hear the speeches by the priest and the teacher. They consistently oppose fatalism. Thus they seek to undermine the standard excuse for inaction that is due to fear. They urge, instead, an ethics of defense. The priest argues that "if one keeps bearing with injustice then it will be encouraged." Alluding to the *Rāmāyaṇa* and the *Mahābhārata,* he goes on to say that "in every age one has to fight against injustice." The teacher admonishes the villagers, "Why live in shame! It is better to die."

Then, as the culmination of this rallying for rebellion, the villagers stage a play about Rāma's defeat of Rāvaṇa. To the cry of "Victory [or Praise] to Lord Rama," they watch the battle. When the play ends, the priest berates the villagers, telling them that it is not only a sin to commit injustice. It is a sin to allow injustice. The point is in keeping with Hindu ethical principles. However, ironically, it is most famously invoked in connection with nonviolence. For example, in the *Yoga Sūtra,* Patañjali writes that "perverse ideas, such as the idea of violence, result in endless suffering and ignorance—whether the ideas are acted out, instigated, or sanctioned" (53).

Finally, the morning of the rebellion comes. A procession winds its way toward the landlords' mansion. The people cry out to Rāma. At the mansion, none of the servants has shown up for work that day. The brothers are bewildered. When the procession arrives, Anna goes out with an offering for the priest. After the offering is complete, the teacher attacks Anna. The priest, still wearing his Rāma shawl, urges the others to join in, and they beat Anna to death. However much we dislike Anna, it is disturbing to see a large crowd kill an unarmed man. It is also disturbing that he is killed just as he is making a religious offering. Luring him into a trap through a religious ceremony does not seem entirely right. Then there is the fact that the immediate incitement for the rebellion—at least for the teacher and the priest—is the abduction of Sushila. But Anna was not one of the abductors, and he is the only one of the brothers who did not rape Sushila. (Though her intercourse with Vishwam was not physically forced, the entire situation was so obviously coercive that it hardly makes sense to speak of Sushila's voluntary choice in that case.)

As this is going on, Prasad gets the family rifle and fires out into the crowd, badly wounding the teacher and one or two of the villagers. (A subsequent scene suggests that two villagers have died from the gunshots.) The crowd rushes toward the compound. Aanjaiya tries to shut the gates. As he struggles to hold the door against the furious villagers, he must be aware that he is going to die. But instead of thinking about himself, he remembers his youngest brother, Vishwam, and calls out to Vishwam that he should run. This moment of empathy and selflessness humanizes Aanjaiya, at least for me. Though he has arguably been the most sinister of the brothers, I respond ambivalently to his subsequent death for this reason.

Just as Aanjaiya thought of Vishwam, Vishwam thinks of Sushila, whom he tries to rescue. Sushila, in turn, thinks of Rukmani and repeatedly worries that she has been left behind. Here, too, we find the characters humanized by their empathy and selfless concern. Indeed, Vishwam's care about Sushila in some ways parallels him with the teacher and even with the viewer—for Sushila was, at least initially, part of "our" side. Sushila's empathy with Rukmani not only emphasizes Sushila's own humanity. It also recalls for the viewer that he or she should have empathy with Rukmani as well—for her innocence, for her kindness to Sushila, and indeed for her own suffering in this situation.

Rukmani, unable or unwilling to flee, observes the entire scene. The emotion on her face is complex and difficult to interpret. One has the sense that she, alone in the household, understands why the villagers are doing this, and why the landlords deserve this treatment. In contrast, as the villagers run through the house, we see Pochamma among them. It is not at all clear why Pochamma has the right to be with the rebels and Rukmani must remain with the landlords. Again, Rukmani had been humane to Sushila, despite her own pain at her husband's adultery. Pochamma had only led Sushila to despair.

Vishwam and Sushila run out into the wilderness. They stop, finally, behind a rock. Sushila caresses Vishwam's hair. It is clear that, after all, she has affection for him.

Now we see the teacher, covered with blood and dirt, holding his wounded arm. He enters the nearly deserted compound. He sees the dead brothers. He goes up the stairs, just where we saw Pochamma and other women running. He enters a room and sees something terrible. The priest is there, seated on the ground, devastated. The look on his face tells us he no longer believes that they did the right thing.

Outside, the villagers are chasing Vishwam and Sushila. The teacher hobbles after them, calling "Stop" and crying out for his wife. Then Benegal cuts the dialogue and ambient sound a third time. Now we see the teacher shouting, but we hear only the music. Drawing on the earlier instances, we tacitly connect this with anger. Just then the crowd surrounds Vishwam and Sushila. In the distance, we see the thick canes moving up and down and we know that the fleeing lovers have been killed. The other landlords may have been partially humanized, but they were still so evil that it is difficult to feel that their deaths were entirely wrong. Vishwam too is hardly guiltless. But Sushila was abducted and raped. Moreover, for the teacher—as for Rāma—the entire point of the violence was to retrieve his wife. Now he is in a worse state than before. Previously, he could hope that they would eventually be reunited. Now it is impossible, for she is dead. As is always the case in the epilogue of suffering, it seems in retrospect that the achievement of the heroic goal—here, vanquishing the landlords—was not worth the price. In this particular version, the heroic plot has been intertwined with a romantic plot. The utter loss of the romantic goal enhances the sense of futility regarding the achievement of the heroic goal.

But that is not all. We now return to the compound. A young boy enters. He reminds us of the boy abused by the teacher when he had his first violent outburst. The boy unknowingly retraces the teacher's steps, returning us to the room with the devastated priest. Now we see what has caused the priest's remorse—the dead body of Rukmani, perhaps killed by the women, including Pochamma. After the boy has left, the priest gets up and covers Rukmani's body with his shawl. The name "Rāma" appears in line after line across the screen (see Figure 2.1).

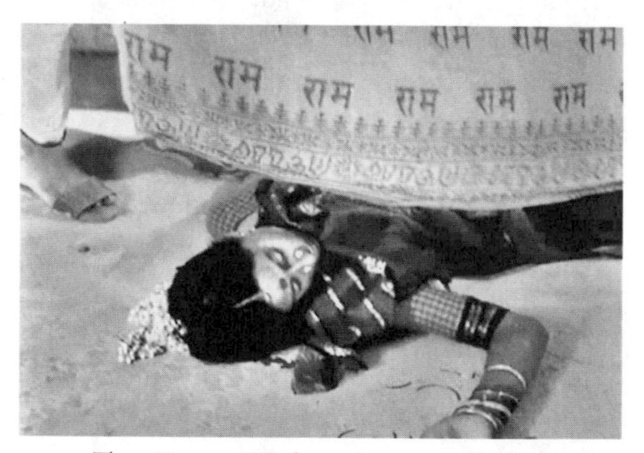


*2.1. The priest covers Rukmani's corpse with his shawl, which has line after line of the repeated name, "Rāma."*

*2.2. Munna and the other village children in the safety of the temple.*

The implication of all this is clear. The death of this innocent woman was caused by the preceding violence, violence inspired in part by the story of Rāma. However justified a violent ethics of defense may appear to be, it will inevitably catch up the innocent with the guilty. Moreover, it is likely to destroy the possibility of what it sought to achieve—as when the teacher's violent pursuit of reunion with Sushila makes it impossible for them ever to be reunited. The ethics of defense that should have protected his family has only destroyed it. Again, the criticism here is aimed not only at the ethics of defense in general, but at the *Rāmāyaṇa* in particular and at the use of that text for political purposes. This criticism was prescient on Benegal's part. In the years since the movie was made, the *Rāmāyaṇa* has become perhaps the central text in Hindu fundamentalist politics, underwriting violence against innocent Muslims, in supposed defense of Hindu tradition and as retribution for both real and imagined crimes committed by other Muslims in the past.

The final scene of the film shows the children of the village crowded into the temple (see Figure 2.2). Munna sits in front. Munna does not know what has happened. But we do. We know that now his mother has been killed. Moreover, his father has been wounded. Though he managed to follow the crowd, we cannot be certain that he will live. The teacher aimed not only to be reunited with his wife, but to reunite this son with his mother. The result may be that he has orphaned the child.

*Nishānt* is a politically disheartening film. It does not offer any positive solution to the problems it poses. But then, that is part of the dilemma that gives rise to the epilogue of suffering cross-culturally. It is never clear just how one should resolve the conflict between an ethics of defense, which opposes the cruelty of the powerful, and an ethics of compassion, which aids the powerless—particularly after one recognizes that there are powerful and powerless on both sides, and that it is virtually impossible to use violence against the former without it spilling over and destroying the latter as well. (It is also virtually impossible to calibrate violence against the powerful so that it ends oppression without being cruel itself.) Benegal faces this dilemma in a particular cultural and political context. Indeed, the historical urgency of the topic is shown by the fact that it is the central theme in the contemporaneous mega-blockbuster, *Sholay.* But it is also a universal problem and it is not clear that anyone has managed to give it a satisfactory solution.

## Ridding the Nation of Gandhi, or Why There Is No Epilogue of Suffering in *Sholay*

*Sholay* (*Flames*) was one of the most popularly successful Bombay movies ever made. If *Nishānt* epitomizes the Indian art film, *Sholay* may be said to epitomize the commercial cinema of its time. Appearing in 1975, the same year as *Nishānt, Sholay* also takes up aspects of the epilogue of suffering. In this case, it treats the death of an innocent young boy—perhaps the most common trigger for remorse in heroic plots. However, it treats this death not as an argument against violence, but explicitly as an argument *for* violence and against nonviolence.[4] It directly advocates a militant ethics of defense, and does whatever it can to work against an ethics of compassion.

One might argue that the political context for Benegal's film was communism. The film was made at a time when popular liberation movements seemed to be gaining success around the world. But they were also giving rise to violence. (Of course, the state-sponsored anti-communist violence was almost invariably far more destructive than the revolutionary violence. But this does not enter into Benegal's film.) In a sense, Benegal's film supports the aims of these movements, but suggests that they will be uncontrollably violent, that they will invariably lead to atrocities.

In contrast, the political context for *Sholay* is Gandhism. Gandhi had brought activism together with nonviolence, vigorously maintaining that the use of physical force was wrong. Moreover, he insisted on humanizing one's enemies. Put differently, he sought to combine an ethics of defense with an ethics of compassion so that one could struggle actively against injustice without harming the innocent—or even the guilty. That was all well and good for an independence movement struggling against a great empire. But India had recently begun to show itself to be a major military power. It had decisively defeated Pakistan in Bangladesh in 1971. It had exploded its first nuclear device in 1974 (see Wolpert, *A New History*, 395). The legacy of Gandhism was a potential impediment to the development and use of that power. Of course, Gandhism did not arise from nowhere. It had roots in Hindu and Buddhist traditions. Thus it was important to respond not only to Gandhi, but to the ideas that underlay Gandhian thought. To do this, the film's director, Ramesh Sippy, and the screenwriters, Javed Akhtar and Salim Khan, draw on a distinct strand of Hindu ethics, a strain prominently represented in the *Rāmāyaṇa,* as well as the Muslim concept of jihād.

Specifically, Hindu ethical theory involved a subtle analysis of different types of dharma or duty. Ancient Hindu ethicists distinguished, for example, different dharmas depending on one's stage of life (e.g., student versus householder) or family position. All the dharmas that distinguish one from other people are referred to as "swadharma" or "self dharma." Thus one has distinctive duties as a student, a son or daughter, a husband or wife, and so forth. One of the most crucial aspects of self dharma is one's caste dharma. Hindu society was divided into four large categories—priests or brahmins, rulers/warriors or kṣatriyas, farmers/merchants or vaiśyas, and servants or śūdras. Each of these categories was further divided into subgroups, giving hereditary occupations. Everyone had duties derived from their large caste category and from their sub-caste category. For example, cooks were often drawn from the priestly caste. They would have particular duties as cooks, as well as duties as brahmins. For our purposes, the most important caste duties were those of the kṣatriyas. The duty of the kṣatriya caste was to defend the society from outside threat and to preserve the internal order of society. In this way, kṣatriyadharma was a cultural particularization of the ethics of defense. Indeed, it was a development of the ethics of defense by way of heroic tragi-comedy. The duty of the kṣatriya was to prevent precisely the violations that initiate the heroic plot—usurpation and conquest. Moreover, in order to fulfill this dharma, the kṣatriya was allowed to use violence and deceit, as standard political texts, such as those of Kauṭilya and Nārāyaṇa, make clear. When the priest and the teacher lure Anna out of his compound with the procession, they are following the principles of kṣatriyadharma by using a simple method of deceit to accomplish their ends.

In Hindu tradition, the great exemplar of kṣatriyadharma is Rāma, who did not hesitate to use deceit, to attack people who were unarmed, to punish the innocent, or to behave in otherwise ethically problematic ways in order to preserve society and its hierarchies. For example, in an attempt to cement an advantageous alliance, Rama concealed himself and killed an enemy who was battling someone else (Vālmīki II: 200, 205; Tulasidasa 431; Narayan 104). In another incident, he learned that a member of the servant caste was engaging in spiritual austerities, a practice allowed only for the upper castes. Rāma dutifully went and beheaded him (Vālmīki III: 572–574). Then, of course, there is the exiling of Sītā, prompted by the patriarchal worries and disrespect of his subjects (Vālmīki III: 515–519). For Hindu advocates of the ethics of defense, Rāma stands as the perfect model, despite these moral blemishes. Or, rather, Rāma's standing as "Dharma incarnate" (Vālmīki I: 2) suggests that deceit, killing of the defenseless, and the abandonment of one's innocent wife (and unborn children) are not necessarily moral blemishes at all, but may be forms of duty.

Needless to say, there would be no point in naming swadharma if it were not opposed to something else. That something else is *sādhāraṇadharma*, universal duty, moral obligations that apply to everyone. The lists of these moral obligations vary somewhat. But they most commonly include two primary virtues—ahiṃsā and satya (see O'Flaherty, "The Clash," 96). *Satya* means "truth." *Ahiṃsā* is a little more difficult to translate. It is usually rendered as "nonviolence," though one might more properly say "refusal to cooperate with the infliction of harm." Advocates of ahiṃsā and truth were quite rigorous in their requirements. As Patañjali puts it, the "universal moral principles" are "unrestricted by conditions of birth, place, time, or circumstance." Moreover, as we have already seen, these moral principles constrain not only what one does oneself and what one urges others to do; they also constrain what one may simply allow others to do. Indeed, they cover not only actions and speech, but even ideas (53).

Generally speaking, sādhāraṇadharma should not come into conflict with other forms of dharma. For example, being a cook should not ordinarily face one with ethical dilemmas due to contradictions between swadharma and sādhāraṇadharma (at least not if one is a vegetarian cook).

However, there is one case in which such contradictions are virtually inevitable—when one's swadharma includes kṣatriyadharma. The centrality of violence to kṣatriyadharma obviously puts it at odds with ahiṃsā. The sanctioning of deceit in defense of one's society runs directly contrary to the imperative of truth. Ancient Hindu texts evidence a longstanding awareness of this conflict, and a history of attempts to deal with it. These are versions of the cross-cultural dilemma that gives rise to the epilogue of suffering. Of course, this dilemma is not confined to ancient texts, in India or elsewhere. Indeed, in modern India the dilemma assumed a particularly intense form because of a specific, political appropriation of sādhāraṇadharma—Gandhism.

Though more elaborate than an ethics of compassion, sādhāraṇadharma is a culturally specified instance of that general type. The basic principle of ahiṃsā in particular is a matter of not causing pain to anyone. One might think that this is, therefore, utterly irreconcilable with an ethics of defense. It is certainly irreconcilable with kṣatriyadharma. However, it is nonetheless possible to combine sādhāraṇadharma with another form of the ethics of defense, a nonviolent form. That is just what Mahatma Gandhi did. Gandhi drew on the fundamental virtues of sādhāraṇadharma as guiding principles, not for meditative withdrawal from the world (as was the case with Patañjali), but rather for active engagement with the world. Specifically, he used these principles to direct and organize his struggle for Indian independence. He made the notion of ahiṃsā renowned in political practice. He referred to his specific initiatives as "satyagraha" campaigns, campaigns of grasping (graha) the truth (satya). As a result of his efforts, ahiṃsā and satya were widely seen as both ethically right *and politically effective.* The latter point was crucial. It inhibited the efforts of anyone who wished to advocate strategic violence as a way of achieving political goals. As the strength of India's army grew, and as the middle classes became increasingly anxious about the security of their property and position, Gandhism became increasingly inconvenient. More exactly, it is all well and good to preach nonviolence to ordinary people, but surely the responsible officials of government—inheritors of the role, and dharma, of the kṣatriyas—must be able to exercise violence against the standard heroic dangers of invasion and usurpation, including social revolution.

In this social context, *Sholay* proved to be a brilliant and powerful intervention. The film directly addresses the conflict between compassionate ahiṃsā and "defensive" violence (i.e., political violence generally, for virtually every political group justifies its own violence as defensive). It explicitly and unequivocally supports violence. Moreover, it develops this support in a way that is likely to appeal to a broad range of Indians. First, primarily through parallels in plot, it recruits the *Rāmāyaṇa* to underwrite kṣatriyadharma in modern India. In this way, it suggests that genuine Hindu dharma—contrary to what we have come to believe due to Gandhism—not only permits, but requires violence. In addition, the film invokes Muslim ethics, specifically the notion of jihād or witnessing for truth. It directly and explicitly connects a militant ethics of defense with jihād. In this way, it joins Hindu and Muslim ethics in the service of "defensive" violence. This use of jihād appeals to two groups of viewers. It most obviously addresses Muslim viewers. But it also addresses secular viewers who are likely to respond favorably whenever Hindu/Muslim unity is stressed. Of course, as a matter of fact, advocates of ahiṃsā—though it is a concept drawn from the Hindu and Buddhist traditions—may be either Hindu or Muslim. Moreover, they are far less likely to be communalist than are advocates of violence. However, the rhetorical appeal here is to a sort of overlap between Hindu and Muslim traditions. Thus it appears to be more unifying than an (apparently Hindu-centric) appeal to ahiṃsā.

The film begins when a police officer arrives at a village to meet Thakur Baldev Singh. The opening clearly establishes that the film is modeled on American Westerns. This itself suggests thematic concerns—an advocacy of the values associated with the Old West and an advocacy of greater Americanization in Indian politics and culture.

The Thakur explains that he needs the help of two criminals, Veeru and Jai. The names "Veeru" and "Jai" refer, respectively, to heroism and victory. Veeru and Jai represent manly virtues, virtues of heroic action. In a flashback, we are introduced to them. Here and elsewhere, their clothing—particularly their preference for jeans and denim jackets—signals that they are not only manly, but American. The Thakur was formerly a police officer. He had arrested Veeru and Jai and was transporting them on a goods train. The train was attacked by bandits. For reasons that are not entirely clear, Veeru and Jai protect the train and the Thakur. (Perhaps it has something to do with the bandits having darker skin.) At the end of the flashback, the Thakur explains that Veeru and Jai are "dangerous, because they know how to fight back." The implication of the entire sequence is that Indian authorities need the help of people who "know how to fight back," people who do not feel constrained in the practice of violence or the use of modern weapons. These people prominently include the Americanized sector of the Indian population.

Of course, this does not mean that the film turns its back on Indian traditions. Quite the contrary. The Thakur's name, "Baldev," refers to Kṛṣṇa's elder brother, Bala-Rāma, meaning "Rāma-the-Strong." Among other things, the Thakur takes over Bala-Rāma's distinctive character trait, irascibility. More important, Bala-Rāma fought with his plough. The image of farmers becoming soldiers is a recurrent one in the film. Note that this is a different use of the Kṛṣṇa stories than we have met with up to now. In other films we have considered, Kṛṣṇa was invoked to oppose militarism, which was often associated with Rāma. Here, both Rāma and Kṛṣṇa stories are recruited to support militarism.

We now meet Veeru and Jai in the present. They are a couple of lovable madcaps who steal a motorcycle, then some fruit, and sing about how loyal they will be to one another. Unlike the thievery in *Baaz* and *Nishānt,* this is boyish mischief and wackiness, treated by the filmmakers with the same indulgence and even fondness. Since a reward is being offered for their arrest, they seek out the farcical Soorma Bhopali and arrange for him to turn them in, collect the reward, then share the reward with them when they get out of jail.

This leads us to the jail. The warden is a strange figure, evidently meant to imitate Hitler—or, perhaps more accurately, Chaplin's version of Hitler in *The Great Dictator*—along with Colonel Klink from the American television program, *Hogan's Heroes.* This continues the homage to American culture, perhaps reminding the viewer of America's role in the Second World War. It also increases our identification with Veeru and Jai. After all, who is going to identify with a character that combines characteristics of Hitler with blithering idiocy?

Ultimately, they escape from this prison, collect their money from Soorma Bhopali, are immediately re-arrested, break rocks for a while, and are released. Leaving prison, they are greeted by the stern figure of the Thakur. He explains that he wants to hire them to capture the notorious criminal Gabbar Singh. He needs to fight fire with fire, he tells them. Thus he needs criminals to fight a criminal. This furthers the theme of the necessity of violence.

From here, the scene shifts to the village—Ramgarh. The name of the village suggests that we should be sensitive to possible connections with the *Rāmāyaṇa.* This suggestion is reinforced by the name of the Thakur's servant, Ramlal, and by the standard greeting in the village, which invokes the name of Rāma.

Our heroes are driven to the Thakur's mansion by the female charioteer, Basanti. After an initial meeting, they are attacked by (dark-skinned) men, whom they repel. The Thakur explains that the attack was a test. Our heroes then decide to rob the Thakur and take off. When trying to crack the safe, they are surprised by the young widow, Radha, who lives with the Thakur in the mansion. She shames them into giving up their plan. Specifically, she gives them the key to the safe, explaining that they can take the jewels it contains. We know, and Jai and Veeru know, that, since she is a widow, tradition forbids her to wear jewelry. The exchange is the first hint that the film is opposed to restrictions on widows—an opposition that is unsurprising, given the film's embrace of Americanization. (Of course, the link with Americanization does not make this opposition any less admirable.)

Subsequently, we return to Basanti. She helps the blind Imam return from the mosque. This is part of the film's idyllic vision of village life. In this case, Hindus and Muslims live in harmony, with the majority Hindus helping their needy Muslim brothers. Even more important, other scenes show that the Thakur, the landlord of the village, is loved by everyone. As, for example, Kazmi suggests, one aim of the film is to present a view of Indian society in which problems are entirely the result of intrinsically evil outlaws, outsiders to the otherwise ideal community (98). In the world portrayed by Sippy, Akhtar, and Khan, there are no internal, structural problems in society, no problems of class, caste, or communal conflict. In the real world, however, despite the film's rosy picture of relations between the villagers and the police officer/landlord, Baldev Singh, this was "a time when the police officer–landlord nexus in India was considered the main curse in villages" (100).

The budding romance between Veeru and Basanti is taken up as Veeru teaches Basanti how to shoot, thus effectively extending the film's advocacy of kṣatriyadharma to women. Off to the side, Jai provides an ironic and somewhat mocking commentary. Most important for our purposes, he at one point says that Veeru is the grandson of Tantia Topi. Tantia Topi was one of the heroes of the 1857 uprising against the British. He fought along with the Rāṇī of Jhansi. In this context, Basanti's expertise with her horse might be seen as suggesting a link with the Rāṇī of Jhansi as well.

Now we finally meet some of Gabbar Singh's men. They burst into town demanding payment of their taxes or tribute. The Thakur refuses. The bandits reply that the villagers cannot resist because they are "hijras" (a third gender group including hermaphrodites, eunuchs, and others who are "neither male nor female" [see Nanda]). In other words, they are not real men. We saw a version of this accusation used by Sushila against her husband in *Nishānt.* In context, such an appeal to masculinity is tacitly an appeal to violence. The point is borne out when the Thakur reveals Veeru and Jai, two real men who use their skill at handling weapons to drive off the numerically superior bandits.

It is interesting that there is no question in the film as to whether the landlord and the state deserve their rent and tax. Indeed, Kazmi points out that, at the time, villagers commonly saw the landlord as the great exploiter and the bandits as their companions in a struggle against the landlord. (This is the point of view that Shekhar Kapur seeks to develop in *Bandit Queen,* which is in part a response to *Sholay.*) Here, however, the landlord is presented as the protector of the villagers against the bandits. Moreover, the director and script writers gesture toward Hindu myth in tacit support of this view. Most obviously, the main bandit is named Kāliya. This was the name of a serpent that threatened Brindavan, but was tamed by Kṛṣṇa. (In *Nishānt,* when preparing for the rebellion against the landlords, the teacher invokes this story, implicitly connecting the landlords with Kāliya.)

Needless to say, Gabbar Singh is not pleased with these events. He executes Kāliya and his assistants and plans retribution. Retribution comes on the festival of Holi, a day celebrating romantic love, prominently that of Kṛṣṇa and Rādhā (see Knappert 119–120). The villagers are celebrating happily when suddenly things begin to blow up and the bandits invade. Gabbar captures the heroes and explains to the village that his gang provides security in exchange for goods. He then demands that Veeru and Jai bow down before him. This is a recurrent motif in the film. Gabbar demands submission, but the heroic characters refuse to bow down and instead keep their heads held high with pride. This pride, the movie implies, is a good and manly thing and it is worth the price of quite a few deaths. At first, Jai seems to agree to prostrate himself. In fact, however, he is adopting the kṣatriya technique of fooling the enemy. Instead of bowing down, he creates a diversion. Then Basanti comes to the rescue, proving herself to be as brave as the men (not unlike the Rāṇī of Jhansi). The forces of good battle the forces of evil uncertainly until Jai gets hold of an automatic weapon (see Figure 2.3). Spraying bullets furiously—but miraculously managing

*2.3. Jai saves the village with an automatic weapon.*

to hit no innocent villagers—Jai chases the bandits away. The implication seems clear. If the forces of good are to defeat the forces of evil, they need the most advanced and technologically sophisticated weaponry. In the immediate historical context of the film, this almost necessarily points to nuclear weapons, such as the bomb tested by India only the year before.

At this point, we learn something startling. The Thakur has no arms. (This fact was concealed by a shawl from the beginning of the film.) He had arms when he was a police officer, so now we need to learn how he lost his arms. This gives rise to a flashback. The Thakur had captured Gabbar Singh. When Gabbar was sentenced, he swore revenge on the Thakur. Having escaped from prison, Gabbar went and murdered every member of the Thakur's family, except his daughter-in-law, Radha, and his servant, Ramlal, who were at the temple. The last person murdered was the Thakur's young grandson. This death is particularly emphasized. Moreover, when the Thakur arrives and discovers the massacre, he lingers over the dead boy. This focus on this child recalls what is probably the most common trigger of the epilogue of suffering cross-culturally—the death of a young boy. In this case, however, the death is used not to show the horrors of violence, but to show the horrors of nonviolence. It is precisely the humanistic liberality of the state that has given rise to the death of innocents. The Thakur captured Gabbar rather than killing him. The state locked him up, rather than executing him.

The Thakur rushes off to avenge the death of his grandson. He is captured. Rather than killing him, Gabbar cuts off his arms.

Back in the present, Veeru and Jai plan a response to Gabbar's attack.

Unfortunately, their plan goes awry and Jai is wounded. The wound is not serious and it serves primarily to allow Radha to express her concern for Jai. A fuller treatment of the romantic plot occurs with Veeru and Basanti. Basanti herself begins the talk of marriage, praying to Śiva that she will be made a rāṇī or queen. Subsequently, when she joins with Veeru, she will be made a sort of rāṇī—not a literal queen, but a version of the Rāṇī of Jhansi, joined with Tantia Topi. Unsurprisingly, this love affair does not proceed smoothly. In the usual manner of romantic tragi-comedy, Veeru wishes to marry Basanti, but Basanti's aunt forbids the marriage. Veeru threatens to kill himself. Finally, the aunt relents and allows the engagement.

After this romantic interlude, we return to the heroic plot. The blind Imam has a young son who must leave the village to find work. Riding alone through Gabbar Singh's territory, he is stopped by the bandits. Gabbar demands that he grovel. He refuses. Gabbar tortures him to death, then sends his corpse back to the village, slung over a horse. Thus we have the second death of an innocent. This brings us to the thematically crucial scene. Veeru and Jai take the boy off the horse. His father comes by. He is led to the boy and, touching him, recognizes his son (see Figure 2.4). He begins to weep and chant Muslim prayers. One of the villagers finds a note on the boy's body and reads it to the assembled community. It explains that Gabbar's antagonism toward the village results from their defiance. He demands that they hand over Veeru and Jai. Otherwise, there will be more killings.

The villagers initially blame the Thakur, saying that his defiance is what has resulted in the boy's death. The Thakur responds, "To lead an honor-

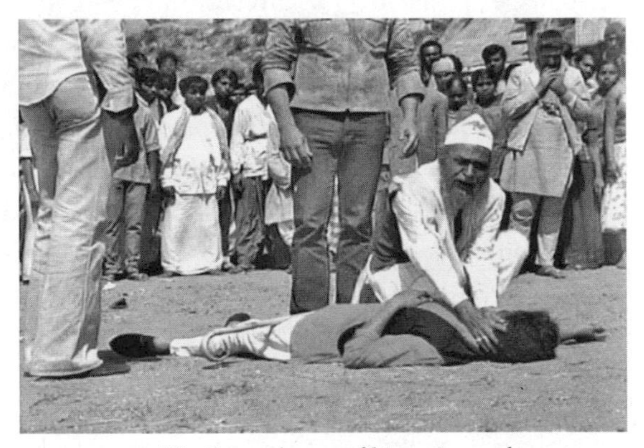

2.4. *The Imam learns of his son's murder.*

able life, we will have to pay a price." He goes on to cite the traditions of the village, insisting that "whenever someone evil has shown aggressive designs, by God, it was farmers who melted their sickles into swords!" The use of farm implements as weapons recalls the Thakur's namesake, Bala-Rāma, who fought with his plough. He continues, appealing to ancestry, "It's not the blood of cowards that flows in our veins!" The Thakur is indicating that this death is not the result of too much violence, as one might have thought. Rather, it is the result of too little violence, too little heroic manliness.

Here, the crucial exchange begins. One of the villagers—a very old man—asks, "But how is violence and bloodshed going to help?" He then broaches the topic of Gandhism, saying that "Ahiṃsā has its place too." He is implicitly suggesting that the proper response to destructive violence is not more destructive violence, but rather nonviolent resistance. The Thakur, however, has an immediate rejoinder: "I do believe in ahiṃsā. But it won't be an act of ahiṃsā to grovel before a wicked and evil man! It is nothing but cowardliness!" In this statement, the Thakur claims to support ahiṃsā. But he suggests that he supports ahiṃsā only in certain conditions. What are the conditions? It is not clear. Perhaps he supports ahiṃsā in cases where we are not provoked into violence. But, of course, that is not supporting ahiṃsā. Again, virtually every society, no matter how violent, justifies its own violence by claiming that it is defensive. Given this qualification, then, virtually every society can claim to follow ahiṃsā. Moreover, in the present case, the Thakur poses only two alternatives: groveling or violence. To commit oneself to ahiṃsā is, in the Thakur's account, to commit oneself to groveling. Of course, these are not, in fact, the only alternatives. But the Thakur manages to narrow the discussion in this way. He goes on to insist that he will never grovel, only die. The point is consistent with either violent or nonviolent resistance, as Gandhian practice shows. But the Thakur—and the filmmakers—clearly intend to communicate that only violent resistance is possible; nonviolence is, again, groveling.

Despite this, the villagers seem ready to turn over our heroes to Gabbar Singh. The implication, which is little short of bizarre, seems to be that ahiṃsā leads to this sort of betrayal, this acceptance of cruelty to others. In any case, the Imam now speaks. Standing over the corpse of his son, he berates the villagers, telling them that "an honorable death is any day better than a life of humiliation." The old man who invoked ahiṃsā now shakes his head, ashamed of whatever moral vice or ignorance had led to his error.

The Imam culminates his speech by crying out, "I will ask God today why He did not give me some more sons to offer them as *shahīds* [martyrs] to protect this village." Led by Basanti, he walks up the stairs to the mosque, presumably to ask just this question. Everyone is silenced. The father of the murdered child has himself indicated that this death did not result from too much violence, but from too little violence. The killing of the boy is not the signal for an epilogue of suffering, but for a renewed heroic effort to defeat the usurper and restore right order in society.

Of course, neither the Thakur nor the Imam makes his argument in a culturally neutral way. The Thakur tacitly appeals to kṣatriyadharma, now generalized to the entire community. He calls upon all the villagers to fight in defense of society, to take up this martial duty. The Imam is more explicit about the traditional sources of his argument. He directly invokes the notion of the shahīd, the martyr who has engaged in a struggle, a jihād, to bear witness for truth. Thus the film brings together the two major traditions of India, Hindu and Muslim, to argue that ahiṃsā leads to a loss of manliness, to suffering, to social disorder, while violence—the violence of the kṣatriya or of jihād—is the only way of preventing the death of innocents. Indeed, in an Islamic context, the issue of turning over the strangers recalls the evil of Sodom. According to the Qur'ān, God's messengers were sent to warn Lot of the city's destruction. When the people of the town demanded that Lot turn over the "strangers," he refused (see Dawood 15:51–15:77). Here, the Imam is established as parallel to Lot, while those advocating ahiṃsā (along with the bandits) are paralleled to the evil Sodomites, whose guilt led to the devastation of their city.

In sum, the scene plays out the issues that lead to the epilogue of suffering, the issues that often serve to support an ethics of compassion. But the filmmakers use the scene to argue still more vehemently for an ethics of defense, and for the necessity of violence in defense. (Of course, in the epilogue of suffering, it is a young boy on the *enemy* side that dies. Making the young boys part of "our" side is crucial to the use of their deaths in this film.) Here, then, we have a scene in which the main thematic points of the film are articulated and supported explicitly.

The next scene begins with Gabbar Singh's men discovering the motionless bodies of Veeru and Jai. It seems for a moment as if the villagers have retreated to cowardice (i.e., in the film's terms, "ahiṃsā") and have handed over the two for a gruesome death. However, in keeping with kṣatriyadharma, this is merely a ruse. Veeru and Jai spring into action, killing all but one of the men. They send the last fellow back to Gabbar with a note showing their high ethical sense—they will kill four of Gabbar's men for every person Gabbar kills.

Here, the heroic action is interrupted by the continuation of the romantic tragedy of Jai and Radha. Through a flashback, we learn how happy Radha was as a young girl. The contrast with her sorrowful widowhood is striking. Jai decides that he wishes to marry her. Here, the obstacle to the lovers' union comes in the form of a tradition that forbids widow remarriage. The Thakur takes a stand in favor of widow remarriage. Here, again, the film's attitude is in keeping with its broad, implicit advocacy of Americanization.

With Jai and Radha's future evidently set, we return to the heroic plot once more. This time the heroic and romantic plots intersect as Basanti is abducted by Gabbar Singh's men. Any such abduction is reminiscent of the *Rāmāyaṇa*.[5] Here, of course, the *Rāmāyaṇa* is invoked implicitly to support defensive violence, in this case, violence used to save one's family. In keeping with this, Veeru follows, determined to rescue his beloved. He is captured. Fortunately, Jai manages to rescue both Veeru and Basanti. Unfortunately, Jai is wounded. To make matters worse, his horse is killed. With only one horse, they cannot all escape. Jai convinces Veeru to take Basanti to safety, then to return with more ammunition. Jai bravely fights off the bandits, ultimately sacrificing his own life. He is clearly a shahīd or martyr of the sort invoked by the Imam earlier in the film. Veeru returns just as Jai is dying. Radha arrives as well, reminding us that Jai's death is not only part of the heroic plot, but also the tragic conclusion of a romantic story.

Furious with Gabbar for the death of his friend, Veeru rides off and kills all of Gabbar's men. He almost kills Gabbar himself, but the Thakur arrives and reminds him that he promised to capture Gabbar alive. Veeru agrees not to kill him. The first-time viewer of the film may wonder here if the Thakur is, in the end, advocating some form of ahiṃsā. In fact, nothing could be further from the truth. At this point, the film begins to draw on Kung Fu movies with their celebration of martial combat as the Thakur kicks Gabbar into a bloody pulp, eventually killing him. The scene is extremely violent, as a number of critics have noted (see, for example, Kazmi 109). The purpose seems to be, at least in part, to work against our spontaneous, empathic pain at witnessing others suffer, to habituate us to that suffering and thus to reduce or eliminate the usual emotional effects of seeing it. (Repetition of the eliciting conditions for an emotion tends to reduce the effects of those eliciting conditions. This is called "habituation" [see Frijda 318–321]. In commonsense terms, one might say that we become accustomed to the stimulus, so that we experience it as normal, rather than as emotion-producing.) Indeed, the filmmakers seem to encourage us to enjoy this spectacle of human misery, and thus to advocate its repetition outside the film, in the real world.

After Gabbar's death, we see Radha again, still a widow, and we are reminded of her romantic tragedy. However, the film ends with Veeru and Basanti leaving together on a train, the happy ending to their romantic tragi-comedy enabled by the final, comic resolution of the heroic plot—itself made possible only by the manly rejection of nonviolence.

As the preceding discussion suggests, *Sholay* is in many ways the precise opposite of *Nishānt*. *Sholay* is designed to advocate a violent ethics of defense, justified in part by reference to the *Rāmāyaṇa*. Narratively, it avoids the development of an epilogue of suffering, blaming innocent deaths on a lack of violence or, when they involve resistance, elevating them to the status of martyrdom. *Nishānt,* in contrast, is designed to repudiate a violent ethics of defense, justified by reference to the *Rāmāyaṇa*. Narratively, it culminates in the deaths of enemy innocents and the devastated response of the main protagonists, thus in an unresolved epilogue of suffering. (An epilogue is unresolved when the hero is never reconciled to the past violence.) So, it appears that we have two works that draw on many of the same materials—both universal and culturally particular—to make diametrically opposed points.

But, considering these works from the perspective of social structure and ideology, it turns out that there is a surprising degree of thematic convergence between them as well. *Nishānt* is addressed to the struggles of the oppressed. It suggests that revolutionary violence is unjustified. *Sholay,* in contrast, is addressed to the actions of those who have legal power. It suggests that violence used by those in authority may be necessary. In this way, the films may be seen as working together to preserve the hierarchical relations of Indian society.

CHAPTER THREE

# Once More, with Feeling

## Human Emotions and Cultural Imagination

### *Mother India, Bandit Queen,* and *Shree 420*

Arguably, the most important concept in traditional Indian aesthetic theory is rasa. Usually translated as "sentiment," *rasa* refers to the emotional impact of a work on viewers, listeners, or readers. The centrality of rasa theory in Indian tradition suggests the centrality of emotion to the Indian arts, including Indian cinema. In this chapter, I start out with a general account of emotion, treating its universal principles, but also considering how these principles entail a certain degree of individual and cultural variation. Such variation is, I believe, superficial. However, it can lead to serious misunderstandings and prevent emotional identification. In the second section, I take up cultural particularity by exploring Sanskrit aesthetic theory. This involves closer attention to particular emotions, such as fear, anger, and disgust, rather than the general structure of emotion treated in the first section. Moreover, it focuses on empathic emotion, clearly the sort of emotion crucial for aesthetic experience. In the third section, I return to universality, in this case considering the evolutionary background of emotion and the ways in which emotional functions (or, loosely speaking, "evolutionary purposes") may have biased our empathic feelings, especially in relation to children. The remaining sections consider the development of specific rasas in three films, giving particular attention to the ways in which these emotions bear on our relation to children.

Specifically, the fourth section treats sorrow or pathos in Mehboob Khan's renowned melodrama, *Mother India;* the fifth examines anger in Shekhar Kapur's film of social criticism, *Bandit Queen;* and the final section takes up mirth in Raj Kapoor's political satire, *Shree 420.*

## Feeling Your Way: How Emotions Work

Common sense and folk psychology lead us to consider emotions as relatively simple things—intense, often irrational feelings. However, cognitive neuroscientific accounts see emotions quite differently. Emotions are neither simple, nor simply irrational. The idea of irrationality is contradicted by the evolutionary function of emotion, which we will consider below. The simplicity is contradicted by the many components that constitute emotion. Specifically, we may distinguish the following constituents of an emotion: eliciting conditions, attentional focus, causal attribution, imaginative simulation of possible developments, processing strategies, physiological outcomes, phenomenological tone, expressive outcomes, and actional outcomes.

Eliciting conditions are what give rise to an emotion episode. For example, one might experience a sudden fright at an unexpected sound in a dark, deserted alley. In this case, the eliciting conditions include, not only the sound, but also the lack of distance visibility due to darkness, the lack of escape routes due to the nature of alleys, the absence of companions to whom one could appeal for aid, the contrast of the specific sound with what went before, and so on.

It appears that there are two "internal" sources for the efficacy of (external) eliciting conditions. The first comprises innate perceptual/emotional sensitivities. It may be that enclosed spaces, darkness, and unidentifiable motions trigger innate sensitivities for fear. An important set of innate sensitivities comes from the emotional expressions of other people. Though there are complications here, our basic or default response to someone else's weeping or someone else's look of fear is to experience some element of sorrow or fear ourselves (see Plantinga, "Scene" and citations).

The other internal source of emotion elicitation is what are called "emotional memories" (see LeDoux, *Emotional Brain,* 180–193; Schacter 171–172). These are implicit memories of particular experiences in which we felt some sort of emotion. Emotional memories are called "implicit" because, when they are activated, we may not have any self-conscious recollection of the actual events. When an emotional memory is activated, we experience the associated emotions, perhaps with no understanding of why we are experiencing those emotions. Thus emotional memories are distinct from "explicit" memories, specifically episodic representational memories, which bring to mind specific events from our past life. If Jones was once beaten to a pulp by fans of a rival soccer club, he may experience anxiety every time he sees someone wearing a jersey with the mascot of that club. This is clearly not the result of some innate fear sensitivity. Rather, it is the result of an emotional memory. Of course, in this case, Jones almost certainly remembers the incident explicitly as well. However, if Jones's brain has been damaged in a particular way during the episode, he may have no explicit memory of the beating, but nonetheless may experience the fear due to the emotional memory. (Emotional memories and episodic representational memories are stored differently in the brain. Thus damage affecting one system need not affect the other system.)

Clearly, the innate sensitivities are universal. The emotional memories, on the other hand, are not. This does not mean that the latter vary without any commonality or possibility of being shared. All memories are individual in the sense that they exist only in the brains of particular people. However, there are degrees to which memory-based emotion events are accessible to other people. Some memories are entirely idiosyncratic. For example, suppose Jones's beating took place in a flower shop. In that case, Jones might feel anxiety around flowers, which would seem rather odd both to people from other cultures and to people from Jones's own culture. Other emotional memories are more widely similar within a particular culture, but not outside that culture. For example, Jones's fear of soccer fans will be more readily shared within cultures where riots by soccer fans are a common occurrence. One function of cultural analysis is to provide information that will help viewers contextualize events or situations (e.g., in a film) that are otherwise culturally opaque. This information should further viewers' understanding of those events or situations. It should also facilitate emotional response, in part by providing links with the viewers' own emotional memories. Finally, there is a wide range of experiences, such as losing a parent or close friend, that are more or less directly accessible across cultures.

Attentional focus is just what it sounds like. Many things happen in our environment and our bodies, even in our minds. We cannot possibly take in all this information, nor would we want to. The most thoroughly assimilated set of information is the part on which we are concentrating at any given moment. For our purposes, the crucial thing is that we do not simply direct our attentional focus through some absolute free choice. Rather, emotions guide our attentional focus (see Ochsner and Schacter 174).

A crucial aspect of attentional focus is its close relation to causal attribution, our tacit inference regarding "responsibility" for a particular emotion. In most cases, when I feel something, I immediately and tacitly blame or praise some putative cause for that feeling. I say "putative" because I am not always correct. As Gilbert and Wilson explain, "Feelings do not say where they came from, and thus it is all too easy for us to attribute them to the wrong source" (183). This causal attribution is largely a matter of attentional focus. As Clore and Ortony put it, "people tend to experience their affective feelings as reactions to whatever happens to be in focus at the time" (27). Our attentional focus and causal attribution are guided by several factors. The first is simply salience. Salience is in part a matter of objective properties and in part a matter of our own sensitivities. In general, an object or event is salient if it has some degree of sensory intensity (e.g., in the case of a sound, if it is loud) and if it involves a significant change from our ongoing, usually prototypical expectations. Thus the continuous buzz during an airplane flight is loud, but not salient. In a library, however, it would be salient, at least initially. Usually, salience is a good clue to causality. I hear a loud noise and jump. The sound was highly salient. I tacitly and rightly attribute my fright to the noise. However, in some cases, salience is a bad choice. For example, diffuse environmental factors, such as weather, have a great deal of effect on one's emotions. However, people often attribute their weather-dependent mood to some recent event (see Gilbert and Wilson 183 and citations). The point is hardly confined to weather. We are all familiar with cases where we falsely blame someone close to us (e.g., a spouse) for feelings of anger for which they are, in fact, guiltless.

The second factor guiding attentional focus and causal attribution is a set of innate propensities to scan for certain environmental or bodily features when experiencing a particular emotion. For example, when angry, I tend to look for malevolent agents, though my anger may be due to frustration at ill-fitting clothes or an excessively hectic schedule. These innate propensities are often elaborated culturally into prototypes. In relation to anger or fear, for instance, cultures often specify the sorts of people on whom we focus our attention and thus our blame. John feels diffuse anger and focuses attention on his wife. This is in part because his culture represents one's wife as a restraint, a "ball and chain." Jane feels diffuse anxiety and remembers the suspicious look of the Black man on the subway. This is bound up with the cultural association of criminality with Black men.

The third factor guiding attentional focus is episodic memories. When I have experienced a particular emotion in the past, that memory is activated when I experience that emotion in the present. It then helps to guide my attention and causal attribution, focusing them on what is common to the memory and the current experience. If I am repeatedly angered when I am with Jones, I may focus attention on and blame Jones, even if the proximate causes are unrelated to Jones in each case.

While attentional focus is in part guided by emotional factors (as well as salience), attentional focus may also guide our emotions. At one level, this is obvious. If attentional focus had no bearing on the development of emotion episodes there would be no point in activating it. But the effects of attentional focus are much deeper than merely helping us to determine just where a danger is and where we might flee to escape it. Indeed, this is an area in which cultural ideas and social practices may be surprisingly consequential. This point has been indicated by writers in cognitive sociology and related areas. Consider, for example, romantic love. As Zerubavel explains, "our erotic sentiments" involve both universal and culturally specific elements. The latter are "manifested in the way we tacitly refrain from even considering certain objects as potential sexual partners because we basically regard them as erotically irrelevant. If we do not usually perceive . . . our best friends' spouses as sexually attractive, it is mainly because they 'belong' in social categories that, given our society's norms of erotic focusing, are excluded from the universe of objects that we consider erotically relevant" (52).

The effects of attentional focus are clearly related to the imaginative simulation of possible developments. Part of our emotional concentration on some object involves projecting what to expect from that object in the near future. In speaking of imaginative simulation, I am not referring to self-conscious inference, but to the unself-conscious, spontaneous imagination that accompanies virtually everything we do. As Boyer notes, "we cannot operate normally without a keen sense of the possible dangers that might result from intervening circumstances as we are performing an action. . . . Opening the car door before the car has come to a complete stop may be" taken up by one cognitive "system and rejected by running a quick scenario of what might happen and giving it a negative emotional valence before it is considered" self-consciously (239). In Chapter Four, we will consider the emotional operation of such imagination in more detail. It is important to note here that the brain treats imagined events in much the same way that it treats perceived events (see Kosslyn 295, 301, 325 and Rubin 41–46, 57–59). In consequence, imagined events may have emotional consequences precisely in the manner of actual perceptions (as Boyer indicates). There are, of course, differences in the degree of emotional effect, but not in its existence or kind.

The remaining components of an emotion episode may be treated relatively quickly. By "processing strategies," I mean two things. First, the general reasoning principles or the way we draw inferences in processing information may change with our emotions. For example, Clore and Ortony explain that "there is a reliable association between positive moods and inclusive, integrative, category-level processing and between negative moods and piecemeal, analytic, and item-level processing" (51).[1] Beyond reasoning, our selection of information itself changes with our emotions. This, in turn, affects our inferences about that information. For example, it is well established that emotion tends to give rise to "emotion congruent" thinking. Being sad leads us to recall sad memories and sad ideas. It thereby inclines us to understand events or conditions in a sad way.[2]

The physiological outcomes of an emotion are the bodily changes in, for example, respiration and heart rate that mark different emotions. Many writers argue that our experience of emotion—called "phenomenological tone"—is nothing other than our subjective experience of these physiological changes.

Actional outcomes are the behaviors that respond to the emotion in such a way as to alter (or, in certain cases, sustain) one's current experience. The actional outcome of fear may be flight, which distances one from the danger. In contrast, expressive outcomes are the behaviors that serve to signal the emotion without necessarily serving to change (or preserve) the situation. Weeping is an expressive outcome of sorrow. An important aspect of expressive outcomes is that, as already noted, they are contagious. Other things being equal, weeping and sorrowful faces make us sad while laughter and happy faces perk us up.

In all these cases, there are possibilities for inhibition or, indeed, enhancement. An emotion may foster a particular actional or expressive outcome, but we are often able to modify that outcome, constraining or intensifying it. Here as elsewhere, there are personal idiosyncrasies and cultural patterns. For example, many cultures ritualize mourning, exaggerating the spontaneous gestures and natural cries. Many cultures inhibit negative emotional expression, training people from childhood to limit their frowns, at least around other people. Indeed, all societies inhibit emotional expression in some degree in certain contexts. Moreover, many actional outcomes vary culturally. As Gainotti puts it, "Behavioral patterns included under the heading of 'emotion' span, accordingly, from a small set of hard-wired survival-related behavioral schemata, mainly related to social interactions, to a large number of learned complex behavioral patterns, highly integrated with the cognitive system" (225).

One result of cultural variation here is that we may misunderstand the significance of expressive or actional outcomes if we are unfamiliar with cultural practices. If a given culture strongly suppresses the expression of grief, then even the slightest hint of sorrow may be more revealing than a flood of tears from someone in a culture that encourages flamboyant display. This is particularly true in art, where cultural conventions may be followed more rigorously than in real life. (For example, with real people, grief has a tendency to break through, even when strongly discouraged by the culture.)

More technically, we may require cultural knowledge to "encode" emotional information in relevant ways. Encoding is a process by which we tacitly select pieces of information from our environment, group these into sets, and assign structure to them by connecting them with already organized mental entities, such as prototypes. For instance, if we are unaware that a particular culture minimizes the facial expression of negative emotions, we may simply not encode a slight trembling of a character's lip. In other words, we may not select that piece of information from what we see on the screen (i.e., roughly, we may not notice it). If we do select it, we may not group it with other aspects of emotional expression (e.g., we may see it as an isolated twitch) and we may not organize it in causal relations with the preceding events (understood as, say, eliciting conditions for anger). The point holds even more obviously for more arbitrary (thus more culturally determined) actions, such as a woman removing the bindi from her forehead when she is widowed. A viewer unfamiliar with this culturally specific practice is unlikely to encode the action appropriately.

There are many sorts of information that may bear significantly on our encoding of and response to events and actions in another culture. In the case of literature and film, one of the most important sets of information is found in the culture's aesthetic theories. As I have already noted, all major literary traditions developed explicit sub-traditions of literary and aesthetic theory. These influenced the production of literary works and, subsequently, films. This is perhaps particularly true in the case of India, where the early theories were preserved in living traditions of music and dance. Moreover, in India, these theories directly addressed emotional response. Thus they are singularly consequential for our present concerns.

## The Cultural Elaboration of Empathy: Rasadhvani Theory

Like some reader response critics today, ancient Indian aestheticians saw the emotional response of an audience as crucial to art. For this reason, the centerpiece of most classical Indian aesthetic theories is the notion of rasa, aesthetic emotion (for the classic treatment of rasa, see Chapter Six of Bharatamuni). Aestheticians developed this theory in relation to a range of arts, prominently including drama, dance, and music. For millennia, the notion of rasa has retained its importance in dance and music particularly. As writers such as Valicha (27) and Thoraval (54–58) have pointed out, these performance traditions have contributed powerfully to the formation of Indian film. However, this acknowledgment has not led to any more detailed understanding of Indian cinema in relation to rasa theory. Occasionally, critics remark on its relevance (e.g., Mishra 25, 50, 100). However, with only rare exceptions (see Cooper, *Between,* and Joshi), this does not lead to a developed analysis of Indian films in terms of rasa. Perhaps this is why writers such as Dwyer and Patel feel that rasa theory is "ill-defined" (28).

The first principle of rasa theory is that rasa, usually translated as "sentiment," is distinct from *bhāva,* usually translated as "emotion." Simply put, bhāva is what the characters in a play feel, while rasa is what we in the audience feel (see Richmond 82). Sītā feels fear of Rāvaṇa. We are not afraid of Rāvaṇa. But we feel something akin to fear; we feel empathic fear for Sītā. Thus the difference between bhāva and rasa is, in part, a difference between egocentric emotion and empathic emotion. Perhaps the greatest theorist of rasa, Abhinavagupta, refers to this by saying that rasa is a "generalized" emotion (see *Aesthetic,* 87). Among other things, this means that it is extended beyond egocentric concerns to the feelings of others (see ibid., 96–97). It is important to note that the rasa of a viewer need not directly parallel the bhāva of a character. The hero may be walking about his or her home quite happily, unaware that a bomb is set to blow up that home any minute. If we are aware of the bomb, our experience of rasa will be one of empathic fear (i.e., fear for the character), not empathic joy.

Of course, rasa is not identical with empathy. Specifically, rasa is a type of empathic emotion, but not all empathic emotion is properly referred to as rasa. There are two main characteristics that distinguish rasa from other sorts of empathic emotion. The first characteristic is universal and spontaneous; it results from the nature of human emotional response. Rasa bears on fictions. As such, it involves constraints on actional and expressive outcomes. This does not simply mean that we feel like running up on stage and punching the bad guy, but refrain from doing so. It means that we inhibit our own imagination of actional outcomes from the outset. In watching a film or reading a book, our imagination of ourselves is different from our imagination of ourselves in a real situation (a point stressed by Abhinavagupta, and bound up with his idea of rasa as generalized emotion; see *Aesthetic,* 96). If someone has just suffered a bloody accident, my imagination of myself in a real situation will probably involve thoughts about where to find a telephone, so that I can call an ambulance. In contrast, if I am watching a film, my imagination of myself may involve finding my way to an exit, should I find the image too painful. But it will not involve telephoning for help.

The second crucial distinguishing characteristic of rasa derives in part from the theorization of aesthetic response. Thus it is to some extent culturally defined. Specifically, rasa is systematically developed in the course of a work and in the context of a particular system. Our emotional experience of a play or film necessarily involves emotional spikes or moments of distinct intensity (as Greg Smith would emphasize). But, according to rasa theory, a successful work incorporates these spikes into a deliberately elaborated, relatively continuous emotion episode. When an artist is following rasa theory, he or she extends one "dominant" rasa throughout the course of the work (see, for example, Raghavan 7).[3] This does not mean that other rasas do not enter. Indeed, they necessarily do enter. However, they are subordinate to the main rasa. Their function is to contribute to the main rasa, the ongoing emotion episode.

For example, a work might have pathos—corresponding to the bhāva of sorrow—as its primary rasa. Indeed, works of pathetic rasa are quite common in Indian cinema. The inclination of most westerners is to immediately assimilate this genre to tragedy. However, works of pathetic rasa are not tragedies, at least not in the European sense. They are "tragic" in involving a great deal of sorrow. However, they do not commonly involve the sort of culminating reversal we associate with tragedy. Aristotle characterizes tragedy as involving two main emotions, fear and pity. Pity is roughly equivalent to the Sanskrit *karuṇarasa* (usually translated as "pathetic rasa"). However, the standard structure of an Aristotelian play involves pity only at the end of the work. The paradigmatic Aristotelian tragedy, *Oedipus the King,* builds up to its tragic conclusion slowly. The bulk of the play is designed to inspire Aristotelian fear, not pity, as we worry about the result of Oedipus's investigations. In contrast, a work of pathetic rasa is more directly parallel to what is called "melodrama" in the west, for it consistently develops pathos throughout the course of the story. It does not confine that pathos to the ending.

An important part of rasa theory, and Sanskrit dramatic practice, is that the audience should be aware of the rasa of the work from the beginning. Tarla Mehta explains that "in the ancient stages the colours of the curtain were suggestive of the rasa-bhāva presentation of a play." This use of signal colors, as well as other practices indicating the rasa, were "necessary for aiding the process of rasa realisation of the spectator" (210). This is fully in keeping with cognitive accounts of emotional response.[4] Emotions, again, develop through attention, encoding, imagination, and so on. We attend to different details depending on our emotional orientation in a given context. Jane may be doing everything she can to indicate her romantic interest to John. But if John has categorized Jane as only a colleague, he may be oblivious to her signals. He will not attend to relevant nuances of expression, encode actions appropriately, and so forth. The same point holds for plays or movies. As Noël Carroll has argued in his influential work, our attention to films is "criterially prefocused" by emotional expectations (see, for example, "Art," 202). In a horror film (which involves a version of the terrible rasa, corresponding to the bhāva of fear or terror), we are particularly sensitive to any dark place from which something might jump out and attack the vulnerable heroine. In a romantic comedy (which involves a version of the erotic or romantic rasa, corresponding to the bhāva of romantic love or eros), we may ignore dark places, or we may encode them as possible nooks for lovers seeking privacy, rather than as hiding places for ghouls and vampires. A virtually identical scene may inspire empathic fear in the case of a horror film, but a sort of romantic hope in the case of a love story. Of course, this is not solely a matter of genre labels. Staging may make a threat particularly salient even in works without a well-defined genre. Music is commonly used in this way as well (e.g., when it operates to give a particular emotional valence to otherwise ambiguous scenes, as discussed by Jeff Smith). Moreover, once we begin to experience the relevant emotion, mood-congruent processing enhances the effect. On the other hand, that emotional experience may never reach a sufficient threshold if our attentional orientation is wrong or there is some other problem with our criterial prefocusing.

To some extent, the signals for criterial prefocusing are universal. This is obvious in the case of staging that involves dark places and sudden movements. It is true even in less obvious areas, such as music. For example, as far as I am aware, no culture standardly uses fast tempi to suggest sorrow or slow tempi to suggest joy. On the other hand, most signals will be, to some extent, culturally particular as well. Different pieces of music and different types of music have different, emotionally relevant histories and cultural associations. The case of colors in rasa theory is a striking instance of this sort. For the most part, the link between colors and rasas is apparently arbitrary (e.g., what links mirth with white [see Bharatamuni 75]?). The only evident exception to this is the association of red with the furious rasa, the correlate of anger.

Of course, the most important part of rasa theory is the rasas themselves. The early rasa theorists named eight primary rasas. These are most readily understood by reference to their corresponding bhāvas: romantic love, mirth, sorrow, fear, anger, disgust, wonder, and "heroic energy." Heroic energy is roughly what drives one in athletic competition or battle. It is sometimes confused with anger, but it is not precisely anger. If someone is "pumped up" for the big game, he or she is not necessarily angry with the opponent. He or she is in a distinctive emotional state. Subsequent theorists add two further rasas, corresponding to affection—specifically, parent/child affection ("vātsalya" in Sanskrit)—and peace, śānta, the ideal resolving rasa, according to writers such as Abhinavagupta (see his *Locana,* 521). While this list may seem culturally idiosyncratic—and has sometimes been characterized as culturally idiosyncratic (see, for example, Hjort and Laver 15)—it is, in fact, very close to being universal. Standard lists of universal, biologically innate, "basic emotions" commonly include happiness, sadness, fear, anger, and disgust (see, for example, Oatley and Johnson-Laird, and Johnson-Laird and Oatley), which clearly parallel mirth, sorrow, fear, anger, and disgust respectively. Ekman includes surprise on his list—in effect a pale shadow of wonder. "Attachment," the equivalent of vātsalya, is widely accepted as universal as well. Romantic love, heroic energy, and peace remain. Romantic love is the emotion depicted in the most common universal plot structure, romantic tragi-comedy. Heroic energy is central to one of the other two universal plot structures. These emotions are clearly as universal as the narrative genres they animate. This leaves only peace. My hope is that this is not unique to the Indian tradition.

The romantic is almost certainly the most common rasa in the Indian literary tradition and elsewhere. Indeed, every film we have discussed thus far makes some use of the romantic rasa, whether or not it is the dominant rasa in that work. The heroic is quite common as well. In keeping with this, most of the films we have discussed include some use of the heroic rasa also. This is unsurprising, given the obvious relation of these rasas to romantic and heroic tragi-comedy. In the following pages, however, I wish to discuss three other dominant rasas. Two are standard cross-culturally—pathos and mirth. The third, anger, is somewhat unusual as the dominant rasa, though of course it appears frequently as an ancillary rasa.

In order to explore these rasas, I will consider one exemplary instance of each type—*Mother India* for pathos, *Bandit Queen* for anger, and *Shree 420* for mirth. On reconsidering these films in relation to rasa theory, I was surprised to see that, in addition to the primary rasas, the first and second feature vātsalya directly, while the third takes up vātsalya implicitly or indirectly. Upon reflection, however, I decided that this conjunction makes sense. Specifically, I believe that there is a close evolutionary relation between our affection for children, on the one hand, and empathic anger and empathic sorrow, on the other. Moreover, I believe that the origins of mirth are bound up with our relations to children. It is worth saying a few words about these connections before going on to the films themselves.

## How Emotions Became Universal: Evolutionary Backgrounds

In recent years, the evolutionary study of psychology has become increasingly important in cognitive science. This importance has been pronounced in the study of literature and in the study of emotion. For example, Gainotti has maintained that emotion "must be considered as a nonhomogeneous, hierarchically organized, multicomponent adaptive system" (224). Thus it is particularly relevant to take up evolutionary themes in this chapter.

Before considering the evolution of emotions, however, we need to recall a number of preliminary points. First, the most basic principle of evolutionary theory is that evolution is driven by the enhancement of reproductive success. Changes in individual organisms occur by mutations that are largely random (i.e., random within the constraints imposed by laws of biology, physics, and so forth). Due to complex interactions with the environment, some of these mutations end up increasing the reproductive capacities of the mutated organisms. This is what makes those properties "adaptive."[5] When a mutation is adaptive, it tends to spread throughout the population. Generally, evolutionary psychologists explain adaptation by reference to functions. A particular mutation increases reproduction because it functions in a certain way. For example, there are obvious human sexual preferences for some physical qualities over others. These preferences are commonly explained by an argument that they lead us to prefer healthy mates over sickly ones.

This brings us to the second point, a point often ignored by evolutionary psychologists, but one that is crucial for an evolutionary account of anything. Evolution does not produce functions per se. Rather, it produces mechanisms that approximate functions (and it does so in a context that is enormously complex). The distinction is crucial because the mechanisms may serve certain functions only in limited circumstances. For example, if we have an innate preference for the taste of certain high-calorie foods, this may be adaptive in a context where food is scarce and we need to find sources of calories so that we do not starve. Thus, in the environment of adaptation, this preference approximates a function—the function of consuming enough calories. But no mutation produced that function as such. Rather, mutation produced a mechanism—in this case, a mechanism of preferring certain tastes. In a context of caloric plenty, that preference can become non-adaptive.

A third point about evolutionary explanations is important as well. Evolutionary accounts of a given phenomenon become redundant when these phenomena are fully accounted for by otherwise undeniable, non-evolutionary factors. For example, if our emotion system explains cross-cultural patterns in narrative development, then we do not need a further, evolutionary account of narrative. We can—indeed, should—stop our evolutionary account with the emotion system. The converse of this holds as well. If we have a good evolutionary account of a certain phenomenon, we do not need to posit further, non-evolutionary factors. Specifically, when we explain psychological universals (e.g., universals of emotion), we usually want some intuitive fit between the mechanism and the function. We want the link to make intuitive sense. But, if a given evolutionary account works, the intuitive fit becomes irrelevant. Put differently, we often want an intuitively compelling *reason* for a particular trait or tendency. But a good evolutionary account may not give us such a reason.

Consider, for example, "recreational fear," our enjoyment of artificially induced feelings of fright, as in horror movies. Accounts of recreational fear commonly involve attempts to relate fear to experiences that we find pleasurable for more intuitively obvious reasons. For example, a theorist might posit that recreational fear satisfies an urge to control or dominate fearful events. We feel that accounts of this sort "make sense." However, there is a fairly obvious evolutionary account for the genesis of recreational fear, and it renders further accounts unnecessary. Specifically, consider the following scenario. Our ancient ancestors responded negatively to the imagination of fear-inducing situations in just the way they responded negatively to the actual experience of such situations. As a result, they avoided imagining such situations. Due to some mutation or complex series of mutations, Glug experienced a more complex emotion when imagining such situations. On the one hand, Glug experienced fear, but on the other hand, he or she experienced a sort of pleasure as well. As a result, Glug was more likely to imagine such situations. Imagining such situations has well-known adaptive advantages (see, for example, Carroll, "Paradox," 86). Specifically, Glug could more readily anticipate possible outcomes of his actions, recognizing when those actions were likely to result in danger. Thus he or she was more able to avoid the dangerous actions. This account does not make recreational fear intuitively plausible in that it does not relate recreational fear to anything that we ordinarily see as a reason for pleasure. In other words, it does not give an intuitively satisfying answer to the question that must have plagued Glug's contemporaries: "Why does Glug keep thinking about such awful things?" However, it does give a plausibly sufficient explanatory account of the phenomenon. Additional, intuitively meaningful accounts are, therefore, redundant. (Of course, this account could be entirely wrong. In any case, it is greatly oversimplified. My point is not to give a final, complete explanation of recreational fear, but simply to illustrate the nature of evolutionary explanation in such cases.)

Finally, we need to distinguish the ways in which adaptation may occur. Obviously, one way is through increasing sexual activity or increasing fertility. Evolutionary psychologists tend to stress sexual activity to the virtual exclusion of everything else (hence such strange theses as the claim that rape is an innate tendency produced by adaptation). Arguably, the most important factor in enhancing reproductive fitness, however, is staying alive, increasing longevity. If Glug dies at age seven, it does not matter how potent or promiscuous he would have been after puberty. Thus the most crucial factor in determining adaptation is probably whether a given mutation increases an organism's likelihood of survival (as in the preceding account of recreational fear, which makes no reference to increasing sexual activity). A final factor is crucial as well. In order for Glug's mutation to spread throughout the population, it is not sufficient for Glug to survive and reproduce. It is no less necessary for Glug's children to survive and reproduce. That survival is not simply a matter of the children's genetic endowment. It is equally bound up with the behavior of caregivers. In consequence, evolutionary accounts should make frequent reference to mutations that foster parent/child bonding and related phenomena.

One area in which this emphasis on offspring becomes particularly important is empathic feeling. In evolutionary terms, one obvious function approximated by evolutionary mechanisms of empathy would be an aspect of offspring preservation. Indeed, the obvious evolutionary place where it becomes crucial to become angry or sad on behalf of another person—specifically, the obvious evolutionary place where the actional outcomes of protection and comfort become centrally important—is in the treatment of one's children. But, again, this is a function. Evolution produces mechanisms, not functions. What is the relevant mechanism here? It is now commonplace to assert that our genes are selfish and that this leads to altruism in the service of kin. I am unconvinced by these arguments, which tend to assume a remarkable level of discrimination on the part of genes (e.g., they must be very good at picking out just who is a relative and who is not). This "selfishness" is undoubtedly the function approximated by the mechanism in question. But it is not the mechanism itself—or, rather, the mechanisms themselves. I suspect there are at least two relevant mechanisms. First, empathy increases with an object's increasing familiarity. This is well established empirically. We prefer people that we have seen before even if we don't know them (see Zajonc). The second mechanism, I would suggest, is that empathy decreases with the object's increasing autonomy. Put in a more intuitively plausible way, our empathy decreases as the object is increasingly capable of taking care of himself or herself and particularly of harming us. If this is correct, then we should show increased empathy for familiar children. As a general rule, our own children will be more familiar than other people's children. Thus we should have maximum empathy with our own children.

This account suggests that particularly intense forms of empathic anger—thus particularly intense forms of protective response—should result from physical threats to children. Along the same lines, particularly intense forms of empathic suffering should bear on a child's loss of protection and nurturance. More exactly, due to their limited autonomy, children require one or more adults who serve to guarantee their well-being. When the child's physical or emotional security is threatened, we respond with anger and protective behavior. When he or she lacks the physical and emotional support of a caregiver—for example, when he or she is lost or abandoned—we respond with compassion. Just as empathic anger drives us to protect children, empathic sorrow makes us wish to mother them.

One implication of this analysis is that filmmakers who aim to inspire empathic anger or sorrow might make productive use of our empathic propensities regarding children. This is just what Shekhar Kapur and Mehboob Khan do. They use childhood suffering to inspire our anger and compassion, in both cases toward political ends.

This analysis is, perhaps, intuitively plausible for anger and sorrow. After all, few crimes inspire such public fury as cruelty to children, and charitable agencies rely heavily on children's suffering to inspire our compassion and, thus, our generosity. But what about mirth, such as that employed in Raj Kapoor's film, also toward political ends? Mirth may seem very different, and unrelated to childhood. However, in my view, the crucial evolutionary function of mirth is, roughly, that it contributes to bonding with children, while simultaneously limiting some potentially excessive or counteradaptive consequences of such bonding. Thus my account of mirth differs radically from other evolutionary accounts. For example, Eitzen has sought to formulate a theory of comedy by conjecturing adaptive functions for smiling and laughter. This is a problematic approach for several reasons. Perhaps most important is that smiling and laughter do not invariably express one emotion. In other words, laughter coincides with mirth or humor only partially. (On the separability of laughter and humor, see, for example, Provine 195.) Consider, by way of illustration, running. Running is a primary outcome of fear, but it hardly follows that the adaptive function of fear is best approached by considering the possible adaptive functions of running.

More exactly, I would argue that mirth is first of all a response to children who are neither threatened nor lost. It is triggered particularly when children do something that is distinctively childlike, but that also involves striving toward adult behavior, thus adult autonomy. The evolutionary function of this is fairly straightforward. Rather than panicking the child with excessive concern when he or she wobbles, then falls awkwardly on his or her backside, we chuckle, encouraging him or her to try again. Rather than chastising or insulting the child for his or her peculiar use of language, we enjoy it, making the hard work of speech development into play. Mirth, then, promotes adult/child bonding, while at the same time encouraging the child's development of his or her autonomy.[6]

One theorist who came close to this general view was Desiderius Erasmus, when he asked, "Who can deny that everyone finds the first age of man most charming and delightful? What is it about babies that makes us hug and kiss and coddle them, so that even an enemy would assist them at that age. Nothing but the allurement of folly, which Nature in her wisdom purposely provided to newborn babes so that by giving a recompense (as it were) of pleasure they might lighten the burden of rearing them and wheedle their way into the good graces of their guardians" (20). There are also some close connections with Freud's analysis of humor, which he links directly to childhood, though for different reasons.

Developing this idea a bit further, we may distinguish physical and verbal aspects of humor. Physical humor is most obviously involved with lack of physical control. But only certain sorts of physical inability are humorous. These include pratfalls and strange manners of walking or eating. However, they do not generally include tremors of the limbs. Another aspect of physical humor is a matter of imitation or mimicry. In both cases, the relation to childhood behavior—and, specifically, to striving beyond childhood capacities—seems clear.

Verbal humor may be divided into wordplay and narrative development. Wordplay has at least one source in childhood malapropisms. Specifically, there is a great deal of research showing that the activation of meanings in the right hemisphere is far less constrained than that in the left hemisphere. Chiarello explains that "a wider range of meanings is activated within the [right hemisphere] than within the [left hemisphere]." Moreover, "the [left hemisphere], but not the [right hemisphere], can supplement meaning activation with selection and integration processes that modulate and restrict the scope of available meanings to those that are closely related to current context." In consequence, the right hemisphere "maintains a broader range of related meanings" (145). Faust connects this directly to humor (180). In keeping with this, right hemisphere damage inhibits one's ability to "comprehend jokes and humor" (Beeman 272; see also Brownell and Martino 315). What does this have to do with children? As Kane explains, "Young children . . . do *not* exhibit the left-hemispheric dominance for language." In consequence, their speech is "marked by . . . 'poetic' (i.e., right-hemispheric) devices" (43), including those that are crucial to verbal humor.

Turning to stories, I am not sure anyone has a very good descriptive account of what constitutes narrative humor. On the other hand, the sorts of childhood narrative error described by Gardner are clearly funny—as when a child tells a story in which the resolution makes the hero taller rather than happier (175). This at least suggests possibilities for future research on childhood narrative and mirth.

In sum, I am suggesting that mirth has its initial adaptive advantage in promoting the enjoyment of children. Put simply, people who find children's wobbling and babbling to be delightful are more likely to hang around, keeping an eye on them, but not overprotecting or frightening them. Of course, this does not explain everything. For example, it does not fully explain the humor of puns. We do not laugh at near mistakes made by children. The mistake has to involve some degree of distance between the normative usage and the child's use—much like metaphors. Suppose a child sees many dogs, learns the word "doggy," then sees a cat and calls it "doggy." We probably would not laugh at this. However, if the child sees, say, a canister vacuum cleaner and says "doggy," we might laugh, or at least smile. If he or she sees a relative with shaggy hair and a scraggly beard and says "doggy," we are probably still more likely to laugh. This difference is not explained by the current proposal.

On the other hand, this account does at least point toward partial explanations for certain aspects of humor that have been emphasized by other writers. For example, it indicates why laughter is sometimes viewed as an assertion of dominance or superiority (see Eitzen 95 on the "superiority theory"; see also Plantinga, "Gender," 161). Specifically, humor is bound up with adults' relations to children. When aimed at an adult, mirth can be insulting if the target is unwilling to be put in the place of a child. (This is often the case when the target lacks a sense of trust in this person laughing; the point applies even to children.) At the same time, this account preserves the insight that laughter—when it is an expression of mirth—is related to social bonding (see, for example, Eitzen 94).

Of course, Raj Kapoor had no sense of this evolutionary account. However, he drew intuitively on the model of children's movement and speech in fashioning the comedy of *Shree 420.* I will turn to this after considering compassion in *Mother India* and empathic anger in *Bandit Queen.*

## Maternal Care, Abandonment, and Compassion in Mehboob Khan's *Mother India*

Many writers have noted the prominent place of melodrama in Indian cinema. More often than not, their evaluation of this prominence is negative. For instance, Valicha refers to the "juvenile melodrama" of Hindi cinema (7), and Bahadur seems to have melodrama in mind when he characterizes the "aesthetics of Indian film" as "kitsch par excellence" (188). In part, this negative judgment results from an expectation that sorrowful Indian films should fit the Aristotelian definition of tragedy. But, again, these films are not tragedies. They are, in fact, based on a different aesthetic, that of rasa, and are primarily works of pathos.[7] Of course, the denigration of Indian melodramas is bound up with the denigration of western melodramas. But nearly the same point applies in both cases. Western melodramas too tend to be judged by Aristotelian criteria. Though not based on rasa theory, they are, I believe, better judged by the criteria of rasa theory.

This is not to say that rasa theory provides the only valid and valuable way of approaching melodrama. In fact, western melodrama has received some serious analytic attention in recent years, particularly from cognitive theorists. Just as rasa theory has bearing on western melodramas, this cognitive work has bearing on Indian films.

Perhaps the finest cognitive work on melodrama has been done by Noël Carroll, Ed Tan, and Nico Frijda. Carroll argues that melodrama combines pity and admiration, often admiration for a sacrifice (see "Film," 36). Tan and Frijda argue that the related category of sentimental narratives is bound up with a sense of helplessness. In my view, each account is partially correct. A more complete account emerges from their integration with one another and with rasa theory. This can be seen more clearly when we approach melodrama in terms of prototypes. A prototypical case of melodrama involves our ongoing empathic sorrow for characters who are suffering but who are caught in a situation in which they are helpless to effect a fully positive outcome. In other words, there is no option that resolves the problems of all the characters we care about. As a result, one of these characters has to make a personal sacrifice for the benefit of another. This sacrifice is motivated by the close bond between the characters. However, the bond also makes the sacrifice all the more tragic, for it usually leads to the irreversible separation of these characters. Perhaps the most prototypical form of this is the sacrifice of a parent for a child, as when a disgraced parent disappears from a child's life in order to prevent the stigma of his or her disgrace from being passed on to the child. In this way, melodrama is bound up with childhood, particularly with parent/child relations. This is due in part to the enhancement of pathos with respect to lost or abandoned children, as discussed earlier. It is also due in part to our related sense of admiration regarding the self-sacrifice of adults for children.

*Mother India* is probably the best-known Indian melodrama. As a work of pathetic rasa, it is fairly straightforward. The first part of the film has more joy than sorrow. However, the eventual suffering is suggested from early on. Moreover, the initial joy serves primarily to enhance the later suffering, which is set out for the viewer in a series of catastrophes that span most of the film. As a melodramatic narrative (i.e., as a work that invokes the prototypical plot structure of a melodrama), it is somewhat more complex. Specifically, it repeatedly develops the theme of mother/child bonding and attachment, preparing us for the ultimate self-sacrifice that separates the mother and child. However, it transforms the standard scenario in two ways. First, the child feeds and protects the mother as often as the mother feeds and protects the child. In this way, the relation of dependency and helplessness is much less clear than in most melodramas. Second, in this case, the mother's sacrifice is a matter of killing her son. This ending is even more painful than the usual sorts of separation, for the sacrifice gives no compensation either to the mother or to the child. This transformation of the prototypical structure is further complicated by Khan's use of Hindu myth—specifically, Kṛṣṇa stories—to characterize the son. All this has both emotional and thematic consequences.

The film begins with the logo of Mehboob Khan's production company—a hammer and sickle on a large "M." The "M" stands most obviously for "Mehboob." But, with the hammer and sickle, it necessarily suggests

"Marx" as well. It is crucial here that Khan has as his logo, not, say, an image of India (such as we find in *Mughal-e-Azam*) or some other nationalist symbol, but a hammer and sickle. This image begins the film and already suggests that, despite its title, the film is not, first of all, a nationalist work. It is, rather, most centrally a socialist work. In keeping with this, Chatterjee notes that "Turkey banned *Mother India* as a 'communist film'" and "Mehboob's insignia was excised from the print sent for Oscar nomination." Moreover, Chatterjee explains that "many" members of the "film team . . . belonged to the Progressive Writers Association" (41–42).

The All-India Progressive Writers Association (AIPWA) was a Marxist organization that advocated a specific social program for authors to pursue in their writing. The program was articulated in their 1936 Lucknow Manifesto, which set out a series of economic and political aims, insisting that "the new literature of India must deal with the basic problems of our existence today—the problems of hunger and poverty, social backwardness and political subjugation" (Coppola 41). These aims guided a range of stories and novels, plays and films, over the following decades. *Mother India* follows not only the thematic concerns of the movement, but many of the narrative conventions of AIPWA writers as well (e.g., setting up the village moneylender as a central villain).

The opening shots establish some of the primary thematic concerns of the film. An old woman ("Mother India," the character Radha) holds a piece of earth to her lips. She is one with the soil—like the Goddess Sītā, who was born from the earth, but also like the nation, which is, in one sense, a particular expanse of land. It is no accident that she is dressed in red, the color of communism. A tractor, also red, passes behind her. The scene makes no literal sense. It is a sort of allegory. Mother India is inseparable from the land. Both require the advances of industry. As Chatterjee points out, many scenes in the film suggest links with "Soviet-style cooperative farming" (41). Except for Mother India herself, the scenes of the tractors, power lines, a crane, a bridge, a dam, all suggest a Soviet newsreel. After this, we see a group of men dressed in the white outfits associated with the Congress party and particularly with Prime Minister Jawaharlal Nehru, a socialist and a leader of the Non-Aligned Movement. They approach Radha and explain, "Ma, the water canal has reached our village." Since she is mother of the whole village, she must inaugurate it. She refuses at first, but ultimately agrees.

This opening involves a certain degree of optimism, with its emphasis on the advancement of the countryside through the development of industry—a standard Marxist idea, shared by Nehru in principle and in practice (see Spear 248–250). However, Radha is not only old and decrepit; she shows no joy over this achievement. The Congress men too—including her one surviving son, Ramu—seem to be undertaking some difficult business. The tone of the opening is somber. It suggests that the main rasa of the film will be somber too.

As she is about to inaugurate the canal, Radha remembers the events that led to this moment, beginning with her marriage to Shamu, which brought her to this place. The scene is a wedding, and thus to some extent joyful. However, here as in so many Indian films, the departure of the bride from her parental home is marked by sadness. A chorus of women sings a song of parting. We see an older couple, presumably Radha's parents. The man daubs the tears from his eyes. By the end of the film, we know that what makes Radha initially refuse to inaugurate the canal is her separation from her own son. Here, the film begins to suggest that its narrative will be marked not only by pathos, but specifically by the pathos of severed parent/child attachments.

The sorrowful tone is subsequently qualified by the affection and joy of the married couple. But the governing rasa of pathos is brought home to us again soon enough as we learn that Shamu's mother mortgaged their land for the wedding. This serves to suggest the cause of the sorrow that will follow—the economic system. The crucial aspect of this system is that the rich are in a position to become richer simply because they have money, for they can invest that money (e.g., in loans). In contrast, the poor will almost invariably become poorer, simply because they have no money by which to advance themselves. Indeed, they must mortgage what little they have, whether it is land or, in wage labor or prostitution, their own bodies.

The concrete, visible symbols of this condition are the bangles that adorn Radha's wrists as a new bride. When she hears of the mortgage, she removes the bangles to sell them. The scene is very poignant in an Indian context. First, they are the symbol of her happiness as a new bride, a happiness cut short by poverty. Second, jewelry was a woman's own property. It served as security for her in times of disaster. When a woman gives up her jewelry in Indian film or literature, it is a great sacrifice on her part. It is also potentially a great humiliation for her husband, for it suggests that he cannot fulfill his obligations as a householder. Here already we see part of the standard melodramatic structure. One person offers a sacrifice that is necessary for the well-being of the other person, but also terribly painful for that other person. In this case, the sacrifice is refused. Shamu slips the bangles back on his wife's arms. The gesture is imbued with tenderness and Radha says that she wants him to repeat the act again and again.

Shamu tells Radha that he needs four strong sons to help him with work. She will, in fact, bear him four sons. Three will die. None will ever help him with work.

After Shamu announces this, Khan gives us a joyous song of communal farming. The color red is ubiquitous—here, again, a symbol of communism. Soon we will see the joy and productivity of communal farming contrasted with the loneliness and futility of private farming. The thematic point is obvious.

At the end of the song, we learn that Radha is pregnant. After she gives birth to Ramu, Shamu wants to hand out grain to everyone in the village. But the moneylender, Sukhi, comes to claim his share. He takes three-fourths of the grain. If it was not clear before, it is clear now that the joy of Shamu and Radha—and, specifically, the joy of parent/child affection—will be undermined by an economy that the film subsequently characterizes as thievery. The next scene shows us the village council meeting to determine the ownership of the grain. Sukhi produces a contract which Shamu's mother accepted with her thumbprint, though she could not read its contents. The council accepts Sukhi's claim. This scene suggests that the economic structure may be the fundamental source of oppression, but it is not the only cause of social misery. The legal system too is at fault, for it serves to support the economic structure, even in cases where that structure is plainly unjust.

To repay the loan, Shamu and Radha must engage in constant, backbreaking labor. In the following sequence, we see the two working alone, paying Sukhi, working alone again, paying more to Sukhi, and so on. The injustice of the system is evident, as is the painful contrast between this miserable, alienating, private drudgery and the fulfilling communal work we saw earlier in the film. This sequence also serves to collapse the passage of time. At the end, Shamu and Radha have three children, a point that suggests the enduring nature of their debt. The second child, Birju, is now perhaps four years old. We are again at the end of a harvest. The tiny Birju sits on the heap of grain (see Figure 3.1). He refuses to allow Sukhi to take it, insisting, "You didn't plow the field." He then articulates a view that will recur throughout the film: "You're a thief."

The precociousness of Birju is related to his mythological prototype. The name refers to Kṛṣṇa, and Birju is (like so many young boys in Indian cinema) a version of Kṛṣṇa. While some writers have connected his brother Ramu with Rāma (see, for example, Chatterjee 44), it is in fact more reasonable to connect him with Kṛṣṇa's brother Bala-Rāma, who both worked with Kṛṣṇa and quarreled with him. Kṛṣṇa is notorious for his childhood exploits, and particularly his defiance. Chatterjee maintains that "Krishna stealing cream and butter from the adoptive father's larder and distributing them to poor peasant boys has been seen as a benevolent as well as a political act" (84n.21). Given this, it is clear that the choice of Kṛṣṇa has thematic significance. However, the link is perhaps more important emotionally than thematically. Many non-Indian viewers may find Birju's pranks irritating or even contemptible. But their connection with the pranks of Kṛṣṇa can make them not only acceptable, but even charming to an Indian viewer.[8]

Another connection here is with romantic Satanism, the celebration of Satanic rebels that achieved prominence with the Romantic movement. In connection with this, Birju's grandmother calls him "Shaitan" (i.e., Satan) after he taunts Sukhi. Later, Birju sings a song claiming that he is neither God nor Satan. In a sense, he is both.

Subsequent scenes develop both the mother/child bond—thus vātsalya—and Birju's mischievous and rebellious character. In one scene, the schoolmaster punishes Ramu unfairly. Birju takes out his slingshot and punishes the schoolmaster in turn. As a result, his grandmother has him tied up. The scene refers to a famous incident when the child Kṛṣṇa was

*3.1. Birju protects the harvest from the moneylender.*

*3.2. Birju sacrifices his plate so that his mother can eat.*

bound as a punishment (see Prabhupāda I, 66; cf. Chatterjee 46). The bond between mother and child, Radha and Birju, is shown when Radha unties and feeds him secretly.

Given the connection between melodrama and sacrificial narratives, it is unsurprising that much of the pathos and sacrifice in the story surround food. Difficulties with food are first introduced at this point in the film. Specifically, there is a problem with the harvest. There is nothing for Shamu's family to eat. Shamu's mother goes to Sukhi, who refuses to lend them money. He will only buy from them. He will take Radha's jewels, or their copper and bronze pots and plates. The grandmother agrees, but at home, Birju tries to prevent the sale, explaining once more that Sukhi is nothing other than "a thief." First Birju gathers all the pots together. Failing to protect them, he grabs hold of his own plate, one of the few things in the world that was his alone. This is a crucial point in the film and provides one of its most intense spikes of pathos. Radha explains, "If you don't give this plate, your father will sleep hungry. Ramu will be hungry. Your Grandma will be hungry." A tear rolls down her cheek. Birju's face is contorted with emotion, but he does not cry. This already suggests that he is the older one; he is the one controlling his emotions. He then asks the crucial question, "My mother will also starve?" He holds her chin like a parent holding the face of a child (see Figure 3.2). "Will you also starve?" he asks. She never answers. Her silence is crucial. Both the parent and the child wish to sacrifice for the other. Radha does not wish to appeal to her own well-being, thus forcing Birju to sacrifice. But Birju too does not wish to obligate his mother. He does not wish to indicate that he is making a sacrifice at all. He sets down the plate, saying, "I don't want it." It is a gesture of great magnanimity, rendered even more powerful by the tiny size of the person making the gesture.

Faced with the repeated frustration of having to grovel before Sukhi, and driven to near distraction by the death of one of their oxen, Shamu threatens to burn the food they have gotten from selling their pots and dishes. Radha tries to protect the food, saying that her children are hungry. Shamu strikes her and breaks the pot with the food. She covers the food with her body, to preserve something for her children. Birju throws his tiny body over hers to protect her. He caresses her hair comfortingly, lifting her face in his hand. Radha then tries to give Shamu her bracelets once again. She tells him to buy a new ox. He slips one of the bangles back on her wrist. Birju, once more reversing the roles of parent and child, takes food and feeds both his parents with his hand (see Figures 3.3 and 3.4).

*3.3. Birju feeds his mother . . .*

*3.4. . . . and his father with his own hand.*

In the next scene, Shamu suffers a terrible accident while trying to clear the land with Radha. Through the collective efforts of the entire community, he is saved, but both his arms must be amputated. Now he must be cared for as a child. Birju particularly stresses that he will take good care of his father. Sukhi comes upon him one day in the village, abuses him, calling him a burden on his wife, and has his men humiliate him. While the family is asleep that night, Shamu leaves. Before going, he tries to wipe the bindi off his wife's forehead. He is setting her free, saying that she is no longer married. Many viewers might think that the pathos of this sequence derives from the accident. In fact, it derives most importantly from the sacrifice. Shamu feels that the only way he can give Radha and their children a decent life is to leave them, so that he will not be a burden. However, he cannot tell her this, because he knows that she would never accept this sacrifice from him. Indeed, his departure is a terrible thing for her. Moreover, the pathos of abandonment bears, not only on the children and Radha, but on Shamu himself, for he has become like a child to his wife and children; he has lost his power to be autonomous. Finally, it is crucial that he leaves, that he does not simply die. For her entire life, Radha maintains the hope that he will return, and the deep worry that he will suffer and die alone. This lack of resolution is a common characteristic of melodrama, for it enhances and prolongs the characters' suffering.

When Radha wakes up and realizes what has happened, she runs after Shamu. As she moves to the door, we hear her bangles striking against one another. Birju runs after her, calling, "Ma! Ma!" Finally she collapses. Birju and Ramu try to pick her up, as if they were the parents and she were the child. Learning that his father has left, Birju asks the question of a parent as well: "Who will feed him?"

From this point on, the development of pathos is even more consistent and intense. Birju finds his grandmother dead. Radha gives birth to her fourth child. When we see this, we can hardly forget the joy of Shamu as a new father. But he knows nothing of this child, who is also another mouth to feed. Sukhi comes to try to seduce Radha. Radha is defiant, but her life has now become almost unbearable. In the following scene, we see her pulling the plow as if she were an ox. Then there is a natural disaster—torrential rain at just the wrong time. There is flooding everywhere. One of Radha's children is swept away in a flash flood. Their home is destroyed. Radha struggles to prop up a ledge where the children can sit above the water. Wading through the flood, she encounters a large snake. Tiny Birju, again taking on the parental role, reaches into the water, pulls out the snake, and tosses it away, ordering it, "Go away from my mother!" This alludes to a famous incident in Kṛṣṇa's youth, when he defeated the water serpent Kāliya (see Dowson 144 and Prabhupāda I: 119ff.). Eventually, the baby dies as well. Here, too, Birju is the one who discovers the death.

In the middle of their misery, Sukhi comes with his old offer. Radha remains firm. But after he leaves, Birju collapses from hunger. Radha decides that she has no choice but to turn over her body to Sukhi in exchange for food for her children. Again, we have the melodrama of concealed sacrifice generating pathos. Radha will sacrifice herself in a way Birju would reject, and she will do so for the benefit of Birju. She arrives at Sukhi's home covered in mud—again, a sort of Sītā, born from the earth. Sukhi is like Rāvaṇa, doing everything he can to seduce Sītā. Sukhi says he will adorn her and compares her to Lakṣmī, the goddess incarnated as Sītā—and, of course, as Rādhā. There is an icon of Lakṣmī in the room and Radha chastises the goddess, saying, "You won't be able to carry the burden of motherhood." If Radha here is similar to the mythic Sītā and Sukhi parallels Rāvaṇa, there is also a difference. Sītā had no suffering children. That is what makes Radha desperate. However, Radha is suddenly reminded of her husband. She realizes that she cannot go through with what she had planned, and she leaves Sukhi's home.

Now Radha joins with the other villagers again. They all wish to leave, but Radha convinces them to stay. They work together to reclaim the land. The culmination of the collective work is a huge harvest, suggesting the value of socialized labor. Moreover, the grain forms itself into a vast map of India (see Figure 3.5)—indicating how fertile India could become through socialized labor.

This is another sequence in which a great deal of time passes. At one point, Radha falls when pulling the plow. Once again, the boys run to lift her, like parents running to a fallen child. But when they stand, Ramu and Birju are no longer little boys. They are grown men. Now we see something curious. Even when he is covered with mud, it is clear that Birju's skin is bright red. Kṛṣṇa is well known as having blue skin (clearly depicted in paintings, such as those in Prabhupāda). The unusual color in part operates to link Birju once again with Kṛṣṇa. But why is it red, rather than blue? There are at least three reasons. First, he is red like some versions of the rebellious Satan. Second, Birju's rebellion is driven by anger, which, again, was signaled by the color red in the rasa system. Finally, and most impor-

*3.5. Social labor unites with national well-being as the grain and workers form a map of India.*

tant, the red of Birju's skin is an allegorical symbol for communism, and the revolutionary tendency that Birju will come to represent. As the sequence continues, Birju and Ramu now pull the plow. Radha feeds Ramu. But when she tries to feed Birju, he refuses, taking the food from her hand and trying to feed her instead—once more reversing the parent/child roles. The sequence also introduces the village girls on swings. Because the swing is traditionally associated with Rādhā and Kṛṣṇa, this almost necessarily leads the viewer to associate the girls with the gopīs or milkmaids who were Kṛṣṇa's companions as a youth, the girls that he would tease endlessly.

With the harvest complete, this grown Birju reprises the rebellious role of his childhood. He says that he will not allow Sukhi to have a single grain. Ramu insists. Even redder than usual, Ramu threatens to set fire to the grain.

At this point, Khan begins to develop love interests for the brothers. Birju has romantic feelings for the young teacher, Chandra. But he also has a practical interest in her. He asks to learn the "vidyā" or knowledge that will allow him to understand Sukhi's accounts. Punning on the word *vidyā,* which can mean knowledge of any sort, but is often used to refer to spiritually elevating knowledge, she says that there is no "vidyā" in Sukhi's books. The suggestion, of course, is that his books are all deceit and thievery. She then explains, both for Birju and for the audience, how the system will leave Birju and his family perpetually in debt and perpetually controlled by Sukhi. "This cycle . . . will continue forever," she tells him. Though she is speaking of a particular case, the idea is in keeping with the Marxist analysis of the cycle of capital—except, of course, that, according to Marx, contradictions in capitalism will eventually lead to the overthrow of the entire system. Birju is ready for revolutionary action now. He tells Chandra that the land "is my mother. Nobody can snatch it from me."

Birju's first act of rebellion is to steal cotton from Sukhi and exchange it for bangles for his mother. He is caught and Radha has to remove the bangles and hand them over to Sukhi. In Sanskrit aesthetics, the rasa of a scene is communicated most powerfully, not by the literal references of the language, but by the dhvani or suggestions of the scene—the memories and ideas that a word, a phrase, an object, or an act brings to the reader's or viewer's mind.[9] The removal of the bangles recalls earlier events in this film, in other films, in life. No less important, it suggests ideas as well—here, Radha's rights and, through her, the rights of all the poor villagers who are repeatedly deprived of what should be theirs. Much of Birju's subsequent behavior is aimed at retrieving those bangles, along with the rights that they suggest.

One seemingly irrelevant aspect of Birju's behavior is teasing the village girls. But this is part of his characterization as Kṛṣṇa. For example, he continually shatters their water pots, recalling Kṛṣṇa's treatment of the gopīs. (A number of critics have recognized the relation of this to Kṛṣṇa stories; see, for example, Sumita Chakravarty 154 and Chatterjee 63.) It is clear that, just as Birju parallels Kṛṣṇa in this respect, one girl parallels Rādhā. That girl is not Chandra. It is, rather, Rupa, the daughter of Sukhi. Birju's relation with her is peculiar. Sometimes it seems to be a matter of genuine flirtation. (A point that fits the notorious philandering of Kṛṣṇa.) At other times, however, it is opportunistic. Rupa wears the bangles Birju got for his mother, and he intends to get them back. The ambiguity continues when Ramu marries another girl from the village, Champa. At the wedding, there is a surprising degree of flirtation between Birju and Rupa. Later, Champa teases Birju, suggesting indirectly that he might marry Rupa.

This sequence of events reaches a culmination at the festival of Holi. Sometimes Birju plays with Chandra, sometimes with Rupa. Again, this seems appropriate to his role as Kṛṣṇa. As Knappert explains, "Holi celebrates the dalliance of Krishna . . . with the Gopis." Moreover, in keeping with the thematic concerns of the film, it is a festival that permits the "reversal of relationships" such that "the lowly can abuse the high-born" (120). Eventually, Birju grabs Rupa and tries to take her bangles. This results in a terrible fight in which Birju stands against virtually the entire village. Even Radha comes and beats him viciously. Everyone agrees that Birju should apologize to Sukhi. Unrepentant, Birju refuses and demands the bangles that, he says, rightfully belong to his mother—the very mother who has just beaten him in defense of Rupa. Here, we begin to see the allegorical significance of Birju's character. He is the socialist activism that works to end the class system of Indian society. It is Mother India herself that gave birth to that activism, that nurtured and was nurtured by it. Moreover, that activism is itself motivated by love of Mother India. And yet, India herself abuses just those socialists who wish to free the ordinary people from an otherwise endless cycle of poverty and exploitation. The new nation has not protected the weak. It has protected the strong, despite its own inclinations and interests.

Ultimately, Birju is evicted from the village. Now Radha pleads desperately that he should remain. She promises that he will never do anything amiss again. He will be the perfect citizen. But it is no use.

Driven out of society, Birju takes up the revolutionary option. He steals a gun and vows to kill Sukhi. Following the standard structure of sacrificial tragi-comedy, he swears, "My dying will bring back the ornaments of the women in the village. Grain will come to their homes." Here it becomes particularly clear that this red Birju is a socialist revolutionary. But, having made this choice, he has to struggle with his own family. He strikes the very mother he is acting to protect, and he wounds his brother with an ax. In one scene, Khan has Radha and Ramu struggle with Birju over a rifle. It is an action sequence and one expects the standard, fast-paced action music that one finds in comparable scenes elsewhere in the film. Instead, Khan gives us slow and dolorous music. The scene is violent. But it is pathetic rather than heroic or furious. It is painful to see the members of the family hurting one another in their disagreements over how to help one another. It suggests the sad and self-destructive conflicts among communist revolutionaries, their fellow citizens or "brothers," and the nation, Mother India, that gave birth to them.

Birju does finally attack Sukhi, but ends up being shot himself. He runs away, hiding in a field of haystacks. Sukhi comes with a huge mob to burn the field. Radha runs madly through the haystacks trying to find and save Birju. Ultimately, she collapses amid the flames. Birju, though wounded, saves her. This too recalls a famous incident from Kṛṣṇa's life when he protected his companions from being burned in the forest by a fire demon (see Knappert 144).

Ultimately, Birju escapes and becomes a bandit leader. Now, though his face is still red, he dresses in blue. His uniform recalls Kṛṣṇa's skin. His position as commander recalls Kṛṣṇa's eventual assumption of a military position in the *Mahābhārata* war. Time passes and Rupa is to be married. Birju warns Sukhi that he and his gang will abduct her from the wedding. This too has a precedent. This too recalls an act of Kṛṣṇa. Rukmini was in love with Kṛṣṇa. Similarly, it seems that Rupa was in love with Birju. Rukmini's evil brother was forcing her to marry. Similarly, the evil Sukhi was having Rupa marry a man of his choosing, though she made it clear that she did not wish to get married. Kṛṣṇa abducted Rukmini from the wedding, killing many demons and sparing Rukmini's brother only because Rukmini pleaded for his life. (On the story of Kṛṣṇa and Rukmini, see Prabhupāda II: 121–136.)

Of course, the sequence of events is not precisely the same in the two stories. First, Kṛṣṇa did not have to battle his mother. When Sukhi receives word of Birju's intent he goes to Radha. Radha forgives him for what he did to her and promises to protect Rupa, for the honor of Radha herself and the honor of the village both depend on defending the girl. At one level, the sentiment is admirable, and as such it contributes to the profound pathos of the ending. But, at another level, Mother India's speech here recalls the insistence of government leaders after independence—in India or elsewhere—that the stability of the new nation rests on guaranteeing law and order, prominently including security of property, thus on preventing any radical and violent attempts at redistributing wealth. Allegorically, the forgiveness of Sukhi and the vow to protect Rupa represent the suppression of socialist revolutionary struggle in independent India.

Further differences from the Kṛṣṇa story come with Birju's precise relation to Sukhi. When Birju encounters Sukhi, he first demands that Sukhi give him the bangles. He places them in his vest to give to Radha. He then gathers the account books to burn them. Finally, he does not consider Rupa's feelings, but kills Sukhi and throws his body into the courtyard where the wedding is to take place. Before he does this, however, he explains that he knows perfectly well that the law will not spare him. This too suggests the anti-revolutionary stance of the Indian government. Again, the law does not serve justice, the uplifting of the poor and weak, but the protection of the strong and rich. After all, what Sukhi did was perfectly legal, even though it contributed to a number of deaths in Birju's family, as well as Shamu's dismemberment. The only criminal here, legally speaking, is Birju.

After a fight with Ramu, Birju manages to take Rupa. Radha has gotten hold of a gun and she stands before Birju telling him to return the girl. Birju refuses. Radha explains, "I can give up a son, but not my honor." Again, the statement echoes the attitudes of the independent Indian government. It can sacrifice even a patriot—a "son of the nation"—but it must retain its "honor," its international respect, which requires that it protect the social order. As Birju rides away with Rupa, Radha shoots him. The scene is implausible at a literal level. Radha cannot possibly be so proficient with a rifle as to shoot Birju at such a distance, and to spare Rupa. Allegorically, however, it makes perfect sense. India, through its system of legal punishment, would kill the revolutionary while sparing the children of the rich.

Needless to say, the themes of the film would not be well served if this ending were positive and triumphal. Indeed, it is crucial that this is the culminating moment of pathos. After shooting Birju, Radha cries out and runs to him, weeping. This is the reverse of the usual melodramatic sacrifice. The mother has sacrificed her own happiness, but she has not done this for the happiness of her child. Rather, she has sacrificed her own happiness by destroying her child. On the other hand, this is also a version of the standard sacrifice, if one in which the positions of mother and son are reversed. In some sense, Birju has sacrificed himself for the material well-being of his mother, and of Mother India. The final moment of pathos comes now. As Radha runs toward him, Birju pulls the bangles out from his vest. He is staggering. We know he will die soon. But he has a look of pathetic happiness, for his sacrifice is allowing him to return to her what has always been rightfully hers. When Radha reaches him, he embraces her, dying in her arms. The camera is behind Radha's back, facing Birju. We see the bangles slip from his hands and fall to the ground, unseen by Radha. Again, it is crucial to the melodramatic sacrifice and to the pathetic rasa that the beneficiary of the sacrifice not want the benefits. Radha does not care about the bangles. Now, she wants only Birju.

The point is generalized in the next scene, which finally returns us to the present. Radha is inaugurating the canal. As Chatterjee has pointed out, the water flowing through the canal to irrigate the fields is blood red (see Chatterjee 71). In keeping with the structure and themes of sacrificial tragi-comedy, this indicates that the sacrifice of Birju—thus the sacrifices of socialist revolutionaries, including those killed by Mother India—has produced this economic development. (As Chatterjee rightly notes, the ending "evokes . . . human sacrifice—conducted with the belief that it would help to contain or release water for the benefit of the community" [71].) But, remembering the cost, Radha cannot be happy. The culmination of the film is emotionally powerful. It is also thematically effective. It draws on the compassion developed by the preceding events to move viewers to reconsider their attitude toward class hierarchy and toward the men and women who would eradicate that hierarchy. Khan suggests that, even when misguided, these revolutionaries are not the enemies of the nation who should be gunned down. They are, rather, its true children.

## Child Abuse and the Politics of Anger: Shekhar Kapur's *Bandit Queen*

It is no accident that *Mother India,* the paradigmatic Indian melodrama, focuses to such an extent on hunger. As Chatterjee explains, "India's food problem had not improved much with independence and India had seen the government's inability to compel hoarders to release hoarded food grain, a bungling and corrupt public food-distribution system" (54). Given this situation, one would expect hunger to become a central topic for progressive writers and filmmakers. Moreover, this topic fits particularly well into the prototypical structure of melodrama, for feeding is central to the parent/child relationship. In many ways, hunger is the ideal topic for a work treating the pathos of parent/child separation. It is, of course, also the standard concern in sacrificial tragi-comedies. In this way, one might expect a political treatment of hunger to be linked with melodrama, sacrificial tragedy, and the pathetic rasa.

In addition to hunger, the poor in India suffered more direct forms of violence as well. There was physical abuse of peasants by the landlords' goons, as suggested, somewhat mildly, by the humiliation of Shamu after he loses his arms. There was sexual exploitation of peasant women, also present in mild form in *Mother India.* There was brutality by the police, only hinted at in Radha's law enforcement role at the end of the film. (Again, as Kazmi remarked, at a certain point, "the police officer–landlord nexus in India" came to be "considered the main curse in villages" [100].) These concerns of direct violence were taken up by Shekhar Kapur in *Bandit Queen.* Just as we might expect a treatment of hunger to develop as melodrama, we might expect a treatment of direct repressive violence to develop as a work of the furious rasa, which is to say, empathic anger. Given the preceding analysis, we might expect the intensity of our empathic anger to be enhanced insofar as that violence is directed against children. This is precisely what we find in *Bandit Queen*.

*Bandit Queen* is the story of Phoolan Devi, a low-caste woman who became a bandit leader in the Indian state of Uttar Pradesh and was celebrated as a hero by low-caste people throughout the region. In many ways, the film is a response to *Sholay*. Though I will not concentrate on this aspect of the film, it seems clear that Kapur had *Sholay* in mind during a number of scenes. Sippy's film presents Gabbar Singh as a villain with no past and no motive for his actions beyond a crazed demand for submission. In contrast, Kapur sets out to explore the background of Phoolan Devi's banditry, which was almost exactly contemporary with that of Gabbar Singh. Kapur does share one purpose with Sippy. He is apparently sympathetic with the use of violence in the pursuit of social justice. However, at another level, his goals are the precise opposite of Sippy's, for a primary aim of *Bandit Queen*, it seems, is to encourage viewers to support rebels against established order, especially against caste and class stratification. (In this way, the film may be contrasted with *Nishānt* as well as *Sholay*.)

Here, rasa enters importantly. Like many filmmakers treating political topics, Kapur works to create a sense of empathic anger in viewers. In other words, in order to accomplish his political aims, he systematically cultivates the furious rasa. Indeed, Kapur's development of the furious rasa is consistent, systematic, and very much in keeping with the principles of Sanskrit aesthetics. There is only one way in which his use of rasa differs from that of the classical writers. He clearly hopes that the viewer will carry that empathic anger out of the theater and that it will motivate his or her actions in the real world.

Intuitively drawing on the close relation between empathic anger and adult/child relations, Kapur consistently develops the furious rasa by reference to the physical abuse of Phoolan as a child. Since that physical abuse took place in the past (i.e., the abuse is not a current crisis, but a painful memory), and since it involved a sort of abandonment by her parents, there is a strong secondary rasa of pathos in the film. However, Kapur is careful to stress the anger over the sorrow so that the film does not become melodrama. The risk of melodrama is that it will provoke compassion for individual suffering in the past, but will not motivate action for the future. Sorrow, even empathic sorrow, tends to immobilize, inhibiting our action, except in private expressions of sympathy and comfort. Anger has the opposite effect. The difficulty, then, is to use pathos in such a way as to enhance anger without allowing the pathos to overwhelm the anger and inhibit its actional outcomes.

The film begins by announcing that it recounts "a true story." The function of this is twofold. First, it serves to enhance our feelings through the awareness that a real person experienced these events. Second, it encourages us to extend our response to the real world after leaving the theater. If we feel empathic anger, this should not be confined to the world of the film, for the world of the film is the real world.

Kapur goes on to suggest the film's attitude toward its subject by translating Phoolan Devi's name as "Goddess of Flowers." In fact, worship of the goddess pervades the film, as does the identification of Phoolan Devi with the goddess, particularly in the form of Durgā, who uses violent means to protect the world.

The first scene of the film clearly serves to set the rasa, fully in keeping with the principles of Sanskrit aesthetic theory. The adult Phoolan faces the camera and announces who she is, cursing her addressees as "sisterfuckers." The anger is palpable (see Figure 3.6). It is clear that this will not be a film that deals primarily with, say, pathos or romantic love. This short scene establishes the rasa genre, the criterial prefocusing. But who are the addressees here? Phoolan's face is partially obscured by bars. She is presumably in prison. (Most Indians going to see the film would know that Phoolan Devi was eventually imprisoned.) Thus her addressees are jailers. But they are also everyone in the audience. A recurring theme in the film is that

*3.6. Phoolan addresses the camera in the opening shot of the film.*

great injustices occur because ordinary people stand by and let them occur. The film seeks to inspire action on our part by causing us to recognize our own complicity in injustice. This curse from Phoolan—which does not distinguish between the often brutal jailers and ordinary viewers of the film—suggests that complicity.

From here, the film moves backward in time. It is 1968. The use of actual years in this 1994 film serves to reinforce our sense, not only of the historicity of the events, but of their recentness, their relevance to the present. Phoolan is eleven. She is swimming with a group of other girls. The scene shows us her prepubescent body. Meanwhile, a grown man with a full moustache is talking with her parents. He has come to take Phoolan as his wife. He explains, "I've paid for her." Undoubtedly, there is some pathos in this. But I suspect that the response of most viewers is closer to anger at the very thought of this young girl being bought and sold like an animal. Our emotional response to the scene is enhanced by her father's comment, "A daughter is always a burden." Since this statement suggests a sort of parental rejection, it may incline some viewers to compassion more than anger. Compassion, however, is partially mitigated when we hear little Phoolan talking about her future husband with a degree of comic bravado, reporting how women at the well and in the fields consider all men to be "motherfuckers."

What follows is an obscene wedding, a tiny girl and a towering man who looks more like a father than a husband. Despite the esteemed place of wifely devotion in Indian tradition, most viewers are likely to be grinding their teeth when Phoolan's father has her touch this man's feet. The tone changes to pathos when Phoolan's father notices that Phoolan is holding something in her hand. He pries back her tiny fingers to discover a pair of earrings, a token from her mother. This was not part of the deal, he explains, again indicating that this marriage is not a human relationship, but a business arrangement. Phoolan weeps and tries to hold on to her mother as her new husband looks on, indifferent to her misery. She is separated from her mother in a scene that is virtually the prototype for empathic sorrow. Even at this point there is some qualification of our feeling because the attitude of the husband is so inhuman. We blame both the father and the husband for Phoolan's pain and thus, combined with the empathic sorrow, we feel anger as well. But here the anger is not central to our response. Indeed, the pathos of the events is enhanced when the women begin to sing a song that marks the departure of the girl from her parental home. The

*3.7. Young Phoolan leaves home with her new husband.*

song is in the voice of the girl, who pleads with her mother—you raised me with such love, why are you separating us in such a cruel way; what was my sin, that you are making me a stranger at such a young age? Personally, I find the scene almost unbearably sorrowful.

But the problem with sorrow and compassion is already suggested by the song itself. As Phoolan and her husband descend to enter the boat and leave, the women of the village look on. They are singing about how terribly sad all this is. But no one does anything to oppose the obscene spectacle. Everyone expresses sorrow. But that is all they do.

Kapur then qualifies our compassion more fully, pushing it in the direction of anger. On the boat, as the new couple is being ferried to the husband's home, we have a shot of Phoolan. She is not weeping. She has a hard and angry look on her face (see Figure 3.7). The first scene in her new home extends this. Phoolan carries a large clay jar to the village well. Better dressed and much older women are pouring water into their brass pots. They are thakurs, upper-caste women. They tell Phoolan that, as a "mallah," a person of low caste, she cannot use the upper-caste well. She struggles with the rope and bucket at the other well. Kapur emphasizes the squeaking of the pulleys. One reason for this is probably to create a sort of irritation in the spectators, an irritation that will contribute to anger, rather than compassion—for at this point, the scene is ambiguous between the two. After much effort, the tiny Phoolan finally manages to place the jar on her head and to walk away. Three young boys taunt her, then break the jar. This is an unmistakable allusion to the childhood pranks of Kṛṣṇa. But here those pranks are not cute. They are a form of harassment. Kapur is implicitly criticizing, not only actual behavior, but the religious stories that serve as justifications for that behavior. Here we have a crucial point in the development of rasa. We might expect the young girl to begin weeping, a response that would inspire our compassion. In fact, she turns and curses the boys. In this case, the response may not inspire anger so much as conspiratorial laughter. However, it orients us toward empathic anger. This continues when Phoolan, berated by her mother-in-law, tells her that they should have brass pots that do not break.

The conflict with her mother-in-law leads to what is perhaps the most crucial scene in the film, a scene that definitively directs us toward the furious rasa, that does so through extreme physical threat to a child, and that extends this feeling of anger to our own possible actions in the real world. Phoolan's husband begins to beat her. First, we merely glimpse the action through windows and doors. Kapur uses these shots that suggest a point of view, someone (us) watching the brutality from outside. Kapur then cuts to inside the room. We are more intimately involved with the scene as the husband's slaps change to caresses. "You have to do this after marriage," he says; "You're my wife. You have to do this with me." Phoolan holds her hand up to fend him off. She pushes something below the frame of the camera, presumably his hand moving up between her legs. There are elements of both fear and compassion in the viewer's reaction. However, I suspect that most viewers feel shock and anger more strongly, along with disgust. Rape is perhaps the most intense sort of physical threat to a child. This not because it is the most physically damaging to the girl (e.g., Phoolan's life is never in danger), but because it makes the discrepancy in age and status so salient.

The theme of complicity—prominently including the complicity of other women—is brought back into focus when Kapur cuts to a shot of Phoolan's mother-in-law in the next room. While Phoolan screams and struggles, the mother-in-law sits quietly, moving her prayer beads. This too conduces toward anger. In this case, the anger is directed toward two salient causes—not only the man perpetrating the rape, but all those who stand by and allow it. It is intensified in this case by the fact that the person permitting the crime is in the position of a mother. This is followed by a stunning sequence in which the viewer is directly involved in the sequence as well. As Phoolan screams, Kapur cuts to an outside shot. The camera dollies swiftly through a herd of goats, through two sets of doors, through a courtyard, to another set of doors, half-closed. The movement of the camera imitates someone hurrying toward the source of the scream—precisely the actional outcome that should result from empathic anger and the associated desire to protect the victim. Moreover, we are the ones who have the point of view; we are the ones who seem to be moving toward the room where Phoolan is being violated. But we are too late. Phoolan sits, weeping, her hand between her legs. Here, we have a moment of pathos. But the sorrow is quickly broken by anger again when the husband reappears and orders Phoolan to feed the goats. "It hurts here," she explains. The complete inhumanity of the husband is communicated by the fact that he has no compassion, but merely threatens her.

This rape is in effect repeated several times in the course of the film. Even when Kapur is depicting events many years later, parallels with these early scenes serve to link Phoolan's adult suffering with her childhood experiences. This, in turn, enhances the emotional impact of those later events.

After her rape, Phoolan manages to escape from her husband and return to her family where she grows into young adulthood. The upper-caste youths in her village begin to eye her and make vulgar comments. Eventually the son of the village headman tries to rape her. When he first approaches her, she puts her hands up before her face to fend him off. The teenage Phoolan repeats the gestures and expressions used by Phoolan at eleven. The second, attempted rape is designed to remind the viewer directly of the first. The difference is that Phoolan has grown. Now she fights back. But a group comes to her attacker's "rescue" and they beat her. The scene would give rise to anger in any case. That anger is intensified by the connection with her earlier rape as a child. The feeling is further enhanced when the ruling council of the village judges Phoolan guilty in the incident and evicts her from the village.

Of course, there is pathos here as well. However, the pathos of this eviction is mitigated in the following scene. Phoolan is helped by her cousin, Kailash. She does not express self-pity. Nor does she show herself terribly grateful to Kailash. Rather, she makes fun of him, in a good-humored way, and takes charge of his bicycle. She is subsequently evicted from Kailash's house by Kailash's wife. This too could be pathetic or angering. However, Phoolan's proud and defiant response pushes us in the direction of the furious rasa.

Our accumulating experience of this rasa is intensified when Phoolan is arrested, raped, and beaten. As the police officers approach to violate

Phoolan, Seema Biswas once again uses gestures and expressions that recall the initial rape of Phoolan as a little girl. Here too the anger is enhanced by the connection with the physical abuse of a child. Upon her release, Phoolan alternately weeps and shouts about her mistreatment in prison. Once more, we see a partial balance between pity and anger, but a balance leaning in the direction of anger, particularly due to Phoolan's shouted accusations. (The effect would have been quite different had she pleaded for compassion.) Kapur again tacitly links these feelings with our sense of Phoolan's suffering and rage as a child—here in part by stressing the father/daughter relationship, for her father, Devideen, comes to collect her at the police station.

When Phoolan returns to her village, the headman's son hires a group of bandits to kidnap her. The gang is directed by Baba Gujjar, himself a thakur. When they do not find Phoolan, Baba Gujjar threatens to cut off the nose and ears of Phoolan's brother. The detail is suggestive. Rāvaṇa's sister, Śūrpaṇakhā, propositioned Rāma and Lakṣmaṇa, then threatened Sītā. In response, Lakṣmaṇa cut off Śūrpaṇakhā's nose and ears as Rāma looked on (Vālmīki II: 39). This act was what initially prompted Rāvaṇa's antipathy toward Rāma. Kapur is implicitly setting up a parallel between Phoolan Devi and Rāvaṇa. He is doing this, however, not in the mainstream tradition of Rāma worship, but in the alternative tradition of "oppositional" retellings of the *Rāmāyaṇa*. Such retellings, discussed by Paula Richman, change the heroes and the villains, sometimes celebrating Rāvaṇa and demeaning Rāma. In this case, the parallel is aided by the fact that the ultimate boss of Baba Gujjar's gang is a high-caste thakur named Sri Ram, who is accompanied by his faithful brother, Lala Ram.

Baba Gujjar subsequently rapes Phoolan and, once again, everyone—including members of her own caste—do nothing. However, when Baba Gujjar continues this abuse and rapes her once again, Vikram—a mallah, from the same caste as Phoolan—cannot control his anger and takes action. He shoots Baba Gujjar and leads a sort of uprising of the lower castes. This, I take it, provides a positive example of how we should move our anger from the film out into the world, acting on it in response to injustice. It also introduces a mythological alternative. The rebels do not cry out to the god Viṣṇu or to his incarnation, Rāma. Rather, they call out to the Goddess. Subsequently, they make offerings to Śiva and the Goddess. Moreover, Vikram speaks to a village of mallahs, introducing Phoolan Devi as the militant, protector goddess, Durgā. In connection with this, and in keeping with the color scheme of the *Nāṭyaśāstra,* he gives her a red bandana.

The next section of the film focuses primarily on the developing relationship between Vikram and Phoolan. Though sexual and romantic, the relationship is presented primarily in terms of comradeship in battle. Standard Hindi films often include a sequence of playful romance—lovers running through fields, frolicking on hillsides, splashing water, and the like. In this case, Kapur has the lovers running through ravines (in training), trying to crawl up steep hillsides, shooting guns. Even their love-play is rough and almost violent. I take it that Kapur wants to give us a sense of their intimacy and affection without softening the main rasa of the piece.

After a series of incidents in which Phoolan becomes an enemy of Sri Ram, she returns briefly to her parents' home, accompanied by Vikram. The scene builds tension through several means, primarily her father's insistence that she should return to her husband and by the loud crying of a child. Kapur brilliantly uses incidental sources of irritation, such as this child's screaming, to remind us of the earlier rape and simply to enhance anger by grating on our nerves (as in the case of the squeaking pulleys at the well). The scene intensifies Phoolan's anger, as well as our empathic anger, and crystallizes her resolve to act on that anger. She explains that she will do what her father should have done many years ago. Phoolan and Vikram then go to her husband's village. A bird caws loudly on the soundtrack. In a stunning sequence, Kapur repeats the dolly shot from the first rape scene, swiftly moving us into the courtyard of the husband's home and toward the room where she was raped. Now, however, we are faced with the scene that should have occurred much earlier—the husband, Puttilal, being pulled from the room and dragged in humiliation out of the village. In an iconic repetition of the rape, Phoolan repeatedly rams him with her rifle, announcing that she will kill any man who marries a little girl. At one point, Kapur cuts briefly to a flashback, tiny Phoolan screaming at the rape. After the adult Phoolan finishes beating Puttilal, she explains, "I feel at peace, like after a pilgrimage."

Though this judgment fits Abhinavagupta's view of how a narrative sequence of emotions ideally resolves (see his *Locana,* 521), this is not the end of Phoolan's story. Vikram is shot and Phoolan is abducted by Sri Ram. They go to Behmai village. Sri Ram rapes her, then all his goons rape her as well. The soundtrack uses a flute, often reminiscent of Kṛṣṇa's love-play with the milkmaids in Brindavan. But here the scene has no element of the erotic rasa. It is entirely a matter of disgust—and, of course, anger. Moreover, Phoolan's makeup is designed to make her look, not like Rādhā, but like the terrible Goddess, Kālī. Though she is helpless and suffering now, the suggestion is that destruction will follow. After three days of rape, Phoolan is taken out and sent naked to draw water from the well. Carrying the pot, she recalls the milkmaids of the Kṛṣṇa stories. Indeed, in one famous story, Kṛṣṇa stole the milkmaids' clothing and they had to come naked before him to ask for its return (see Prabhupāda, vol. 1 153–154). The description of the gopīs—"completely naked," trying "to cover their nakedness" with their hands (154)—bears on Phoolan as well. But, again, there is nothing romantic or erotic here. The scene, like the earlier scene where the boys broke her water pot, serves to make us angry at her humiliation, and at the Kṛṣṇa stories that seem to justify such treatment. Our anger is enhanced by the fact that, once again, the villagers stand about, observing this cruelty, and do nothing.

At this point, Phoolan goes to a Muslim bandit, Baba Mushtaquim, for help. He tells her that Sri Ram and Lala Ram will be attending a wedding—in Behmai village. Phoolan, like the Goddess in her destructive form, goes to the village to fight.

This is another crucial scene. Phoolan has her gang pull out all the men in the village. She explicitly orders them not to touch the women and children. When the men are lined up, she tries to ascertain the location of Sri Ram and Lala Ram, but no one tells her anything. We recognize two of the men as part of Sri Ram's gang. We saw both of them in the earlier scene when Phoolan was raped, beaten, and humiliated. Phoolan strikes, then shoots these two men. She curses the entire group as "sisterfucking thakurs." Eventually, she massacres all twenty-four of them.

In many ways, this is a straightforward scene of anger. It may repulse viewers, but I believe Kapur tries to give us empathic access to Phoolan's fury. One technique he uses for this is particularly powerful and unexpected. At the start of the scene, word arrives that Phoolan Devi is coming. The marriage ceremony stops quickly and everyone runs off to hide. But they leave a tiny, naked girl, less than two years old, walking about and crying on the platform of the well. I imagine that most viewers simply take this to show that some father or mother was so caught up in the events that he or she forgot about the child. However, it seems to me enormously unlikely that this is what is going on. In the course of the entire scene, no one in the film even notices the child. This clearly indicates that the child is not, in fact, a literal presence in the story world. Rather, she is a sort of metaphor. To put it crudely, she is the screaming child inside Phoolan Devi that is motivating her violence. The fact that the child is naked and standing on the ledge of the well serves to recall Phoolan's humiliating walk to the well after three days of rape by Sri Ram and his men. It also serves to connect that humiliation with the violence suffered by the child Phoolan. All this enhances the furious rasa of the scene. Then, in a final shot, we see the white earth of the courtyard stained red with pools of blood, the color of anger. The girl, still naked, walks through the pools. After this act of revenge, she is no longer crying.

This massacre is, in effect, the beginning of the end for Phoolan. The state government determines that it must use any means necessary to secure her arrest. Much of what follows serves to show the terrible brutality of the police and to foster our empathic anger toward them. They capture Baba Mushtaquim and shoot him in the back, then present the murder as if he were trying to escape. They shoot Phoolan's men when they are unarmed and have surrendered. We are told that some of them were "stripped naked and killed in front of their families." They join together with Sri Ram to hunt down Phoolan Devi and her companion, Man Singh. (The alliance recalls the cooperation between the police and the noble bandits pursuing Gabbar Singh in *Sholay*—but, of course, Kapur exactly reverses the ethical judgments of that film.) They poison the water so that Phoolan Devi nearly dies of thirst.

Though there is no direct relation to childhood in this sequence, there is considerable imagery of childhood and protection by parents. Fleeing from the police, Phoolan declares that the ravines will hide her in their womb. The image is not only general, it also recalls Sītā's final rejection of Rāma. Rāma demands a second fire ordeal, after having abandoned her in the wilderness many years earlier. Sītā refuses. Instead, she calls upon her mother, the earth, to take her back. The earth opens; a chariot appears; and Sītā descends into the earth in a rain of lotus petals. Needless to say, there is no comparable maternal intervention protecting Phoolan from the fiery heat of the wasteland where she has been driven by the police and Sri Ram. Subsequently, in one of the saddest moments of the film, Phoolan expresses complete despair over her situation, saying, "The goddess is angry with me." The statement suggests that she is a child whose protector has abandoned her. It is deeply pathetic. The connection with childhood is made explicit when she goes on to call out for her mother and for her father. However, here as elsewhere, Kapur deftly distances us from the pathos, presenting us with diffuse irritants, and reintroducing Phoolan's anger—all to support the furious rasa. Phoolan is beside a train track. The train rushes past, swiftly and loudly. Kapur cuts to the other side of the track, so that we see Phoolan only through the gaps between the cars. Moreover, she is struggling angrily against Man Singh, who tries to calm her.

This scene prepares us for the conclusion, the resolution through the peaceful rasa, in keeping with Abhinavagupta's views. Phoolan is surrendering. The terms of the surrender are not harsh. They include a guarantee that all their children will be given free education. The emphasis on the protection of the children is obviously crucial to the sense of peace. There is a great crowd gathered to watch the surrender. They shout, "Long live Phoolan Devi!" Just as the film began with the adult Phoolan cursing her addressee and announcing her identity, the film ends with the child Phoolan doing the same. Now it is a cry of defiance, a final triumph of the abused girl over all of her abusers. "I am Phoolan Devi, you sisterfuckers!" But it is still angry. And it is still aimed at us. It is a way of qualifying the final peace so that it does not overwhelm our accumulated anger. Again, Kapur almost certainly wishes us to take our anger outside the film, so that we no longer look at injustice and do nothing.

The final shot is the glimmering, red surface of a river. A brief account of subsequent history scrolls across the screen. It furthers the sense of peace, but also points toward real political activism. The text explains that, in 1993, a government of the lower castes was elected in Uttar Pradesh. It withdrew all charges against Phoolan Devi and she was released from prison on 18 February 1994. As we read this, we hear once again the song of the new bride leaving her home. But this time, it is not sung by the adult women. It is sung by a young girl, an amateur, who repeatedly clears her throat, interrupting the song, grating against its pathos. We are once again reminded of the first source of our empathic anger—Phoolan's child marriage (or sale) to Puttilal—and of the complicity of all those who let this story begin as it did.

Though it goes outside the film, viewers familiar with what happened in the following years are likely to find the feeling of peace disrupted, but the feeling of anger enhanced. After being released from prison, Phoolan Devi left banditry and entered politics as part of the democratic socialist Samajwadi Party. Though illiterate, she was elected to parliament to work for the interests of socially and economically oppressed groups. This work was cut short when she was assassinated in July 2001.

## Mirth and Cuteness in Raj Kapoor's *Shree 420*

The pathetic and the furious are the most obvious rasas for inspiring an audience's positive response to appeals for social transformation. However, this does not mean that a political filmmaker is confined to compassion and anger. Raj Kapur's *Shree 420,* like *Mother India,* has a political orientation that is fully in keeping with the principles of the AIPWA. Indeed, the wealthy Seth Sonachand Dharmanand parallels Sukhi; Vidya recalls Chandra; and Maya is not unrelated to Rupa. However, Raj, the hero of Kapoor's film, is very different from Birju. Indeed, he is almost the reverse of Birju. Even as a child, Birju is the nurturing, self-sacrificing adult. In a sense, he is never truly a child. That is both his fault and his strength, for it is what drives him to challenge unjust authority, despite the palpable limitations on his autonomy and power. In contrast, Raj is almost all child. For a large part of the film, there is hardly anything adult about him. In connection with this, rather than making his political points through pathos (or anger), Kapoor does so, first of all, through the childlike cuteness and humor of his main character.

More exactly, Raj Kapoor's *Shree 420* is a Chaplinesque comedy that consistently develops the rasa of mirth.[10] As in Chaplin's films, much of its humor results from the hero's childlike behavior—ranging, in this case, from his wobbly walk to his "ill-fitting clothing," as emphasized by Dissanayake and Sahai (*Raj* 106). As I have already mentioned, one standard variety of mirth-provoking action, a variety with a clear relation to children's behavior, is mimicry. Referring to Henri Bergson, Dissanayake and Sahai treat the importance of imitating or repeating other people's behavior as a source of humor. As Dissanayake and Sahai indicate, this is very important in Kapoor's film. Indeed, Kapoor's use of imitation suggests another cultural particularization of a literary universal. Dissanayake and Sahai point out that Kapoor began his career as a stage actor. Among other roles, he played the standard Sanskrit clown character at that time (see *Raj* 17). According to the great Sanskrit dramaturgical text, the *Nāṭyaśāstra,* this character, the Vidūṣaka, "is eager to amuse and humour people." His comic success is aided by the fact that he "can mimic people and imitate others easily" (Bharatamuni 528, altered).

Despite its largely light-hearted tone, filled with instances of harmless mirth, *Shree 420* involves complex political and social commentary, combined with some recurring Indian philosophical concerns as well. Indeed, it is a national and ethical allegory, which draws on Hindu metaphysical principles to develop and give greater force (and humor) to its political ideas.

The hero, Raj (or rule), is homeless and unemployed. He must choose between Vidya, whose name means *knowledge,* and Maya, whose name means *illusion.* Vidya is a teacher and the daughter of a man named "Shastri," indicating that spiritual knowledge is the child of expertise in the sacred scriptures or śāstras. Maya is a westernized expert at fraud. The opposition between Vidya/vidyā and Maya/māyā has deep historical roots in Hindu metaphysics (e.g., in the opposition between vidyāśakti, the power of knowledge, and māyāśakti, the power of illusion, in Śaivite philosophy [see book three of Utpaladeva]). Specifically, the film draws on the metaphysical doctrines of Vedāntism.

Very briefly, Vedāntic principles derive from a set of sacred texts of ancient Hinduism. Advaita (or non-dual) Vedānta is the most prominent school of Vedāntism. It includes a number of principles familiar to anyone who has even passing acquaintance with Hinduism. First, the material world is not real, but an illusion, "māyā." Māyā is characterized by continual change. The material world is not stable, but ephemeral. In contrast, the truly real—brahman, "godhead"—is unchanging, eternal. Our mistaken belief in the reality of the material world is bound up with desire. We are attached to the material world. Desire drives our actions in this life, leading us to pursue sensory delight, position, and prosperity. Moreover, desire affects us after death, keeping us bound in a cycle of rebirth through the effects of karma. What is perhaps most crucial about desire, in this view, is that desire or attachment leads invariably to suffering. The ephemeral nature of the material world prevents any happiness from being permanent. We achieve peace, śānta, and liberation from rebirth, mokṣa, only when we no longer fall prey to the illusions of māyā, but acquire true knowledge, vidyā, and realize in experience that our individual souls or ātmans are all one and no different from brahman.

But, again, the film is not only metaphysical. It recruits metaphysical ideas to political purposes. In the end, Raj unites with Vidya and calls on the impoverished masses to join together and change India, to build themselves new homes, literally and figuratively. In this way, the film develops

Kapoor's and (story-writer) K. A. Abbas's "critique of the unfulfilled promises of Independence" (Bakshi 108; see also 103). The fundamental political point of the film is that independent India—our "raj" or rule, represented by the character named "Raj"—has been bought by the wealthy, so that it is little more than a fraud. Our raj/Raj arrived, but it did almost nothing for the ordinary people. It got caught up with māyā/Maya and the seductions of wealth, ignoring true vidyā/Vidya. Moreover, it never inspired a recognition among the poor of their collective identity, parallel perhaps to the identity of individual souls in brahman. Had Kapoor chosen to present this in a less comic format, it is likely to have seemed ponderously didactic. Had he chosen to present it in the furious or pathetic rasa, it may have led to an excessively negative evaluation of the independent Indian raj. Kapoor and Abbas wished to characterize Indian self-government or swa-raj in a generally positive way, while still criticizing its mistakes. One obvious way of doing this was by tacitly attributing those mistakes to the "youth" of the government (only eight years old at the time of the film). Making Raj childish thus serves, not only the humor, but the implicit allegory as well.

It is worth noting that all this is in keeping with the prescriptions of the AIPWA manifesto. The manifesto explains the goals of AIPWA writers in the following terms: "Preserving the best traditions of India [hence vidyā/Vidya], we will comment pitilessly on the decadent aspects of our country [hence māyā/Maya and the wealthy classes] and will depict in a critical and creative manner all those things with which we may arrive at our destination. It is our belief that the new literature of India must respect the basic realities of our present-day life," such as "hunger and poverty" (Coppola 10–11),[11] here represented by Raj's inability to buy food and the widespread homelessness depicted in the film. The end of the film fits the activist orientation of the AIPWA as well. The manifesto states that the new literature must "help us to understand these problems and through such understanding help us act" (Coppola 11). Kapoor and Abbas take this up in the concluding call for the solidarity and collective effort of the homeless and unemployed.

The film begins with Kapoor's tramp, Raj, moving in fast motion. The peculiar walk and the speed indicate (in keeping with the prescriptions of rasa theory) that this is going to be a work of mirthful rasa. In other words, they begin to establish our criterial prefocusing. The confused look on Raj's face also begins to suggest his childlike character. In keeping with the right-hemisphere language processing that is more prominent among children, his first words are a pun. Interestingly, they are a pun on the word *car*, clearly borrowed from English. After failing to secure a ride, he pretends to pass out in the middle of the road following a wobbly walk that could appear sick, drunk, or infantile. When he is picked up by Seth Sonachand Dharmanand, he peeks about in a manner that cannot help but recall a child's game of playing dead.

As it turns out, Dharmanand—whose name means "bliss of dharma" (dharma being duty, ethics, or law)—is the villain of the piece, the inveterate breaker of law or dharma. He introduces the theme of the "420." A 420 is a fraud. (The number refers to the section of the Indian penal code covering fraud.) Raj has committed a small fraud in pretending to pass out. Dharmanand, however, commits grand fraud all the time. Indeed, Raj says, grand fraud is precisely what makes someone rich.

Evicted from the car, Raj sets out on his way to Bombay, the film capital of India, thus in one sense the capital of fraud. It is 420 kilometers away. As he goes, Raj sings one of the most famous songs of the film, explaining that his shoes are Japanese; his pants are English; his red cap is Russian; but his heart is Indian (Hindustani). The correlations are suggestive. It is particularly important that the cap is Russian. It is not so much that the object on his head comes from the USSR as that the ideas in his head are connected with Russia. The link is stressed by telling us the color of the hat (not visible in black and white)—red. The ideas, in short, are socialist. On the other hand, Raj's loyalty is not to Russia or even to the international proletariat. This is a socialist film, but it is also a nationalist film. Hence the importance of the fact that Raj's heart is Hindustani. The nationalism is also indicated by the different aspects of India treated in Raj's trip to Bombay. He passes several village girls on the path; he rides a camel with travelers in the desert; he sits on an elephant beside two wandering ascetics in the countryside. Moreover, in each case, there is something mirthful in his action. The village girls smile with delight as he passes. He sits before a camel driver like a boy on his father's lap, and the camel driver imitates his movements (see Figure 3.8). First we see a Raja or prince on an ornate elephant; then we see the ragged Raj beside his spindly ascetics, in effect imitating the Raja.

When he gets to the city, Raj is the archetypal bumpkin. More fast motion emphasizes the comic tone. However, the thematic development begins in earnest now. Raj meets a beggar on crutches who insists that, in Bombay, "Only one thing is sacred; that's money." Raj absurdly shows the

*3.8. Raj takes a ride toward Bombay from a fatherly camel driver.*

beggar his college diploma. This suggests his adult age and his intellectual development. But, at the same time, he exhibits a gold medal that he received for honesty. The medal suggests the sorts of awards children are given in grammar school. The fact that he still prizes the medal serves to link him with that honest, orphaned child. We subsequently learn that he received it from the "Rashtriya Orphanage" (*rashtriya* meaning "national"). This operates allegorically. The newly independent India has no national "parents." This is presumably because it was cut off from its own forebears by being subjected to foreign rule.

Hungry, Raj goes to Ganga Ma to buy some bananas. This is allegorical in several ways. Most importantly, "Ganga Ma" is not only some mother ("ma"), but specifically Mother India, the land of the sacred river Ganges (or Ganga). Raj has a goofy argument with her where he confuses the math and tries to haggle her up to a higher price rather than down to a lower price. She finally agrees, but he has no money at all. Laughing, she gives him two bananas, then says that, if he never pays her, she will just think that her son ate them. He leaves her by making a complimentary pun. The entire sequence is both amusing and endearing. In keeping with the preceding analysis, it combines mirth with vātsalya (parent/child affection).

When Raj walks off, he comes upon a destitute street urchin. He gives the urchin one banana. In a comic imitation of a parent, he tells the urchin that he should not throw the banana peel—then illustrates what the child should not do by throwing the peel himself. This sets up a round of slipping-on-the-banana-peel jokes, with several characters all landing on their rumps. Kapoor not only manages to make this hoary joke amusing, he recruits it to his thematic purposes. First, it turns out that everyone laughs—but only when someone else is falling. Second, it turns out that the person who started the sequence (Raj) ultimately falls himself, and by his own banana peel. It is part of the mirthful optimism of the film that a sort of karma will lead ultimately to justice—and it will do so within this life, within this society.

The exposition of political and metaphysical concerns continues when Raj goes to a pawn shop. Vidya is there, trying to sell her bangles in order to get money for her school. While Vidya is trying to do something noble (in keeping with her name), Raj's first action in the big city is to pawn his medal. This is explicitly presented as Raj selling his honesty. It suggests that the new raj of India was forced to sell its truthfulness right at the outset. Unfortunately, if unsurprisingly, Raj's money is stolen immediately when he leaves the pawn shop.

Hungry and homeless, Raj comes upon a group of street people sharing the pavement. At first, they attack him. But Ganga Ma intervenes and they welcome him. One explains that "Ganga Ma's children are like brothers." The statement has obvious allegorical significance. The children of India are all one family. Hearing that he is Raj, the others quickly celebrate that their raj/Raj has come, thus spelling out part of the film's allegory. Raj sings them a song about poverty and police repression. In the end, the police attack and disperse them.

We next see Raj waking up on the beach. A policeman stands over him. Like his fellows the night before, this officer is devoted to protecting the property of the wealthy against the infiltration of the homeless and destitute. In the course of their exchange, Raj stands on his head. He explains that "to see this wretched world, you have to look at it upside down. All the leaders of the country do the same thing." The comment alludes to Marx's repeated analyses of the upside-down nature of capitalism and bourgeois political thought. First, it suggests his analysis that capitalism inverts human economic and social life by making relations between people subordinate to relations between commodities (relations of exchange that sustain capitalist economy), by impoverishing those who produce goods (the workers) while enriching those who do not (the capitalists), and so forth. A viewer might particularly recall Marx's striking image of an object that, by virtue of its status as a commodity, "stands on its head, and evolves out of its wooden brain grotesque ideas" (71). Second, it recalls his insistence that bourgeois thinkers invert our understanding of the world—perhaps most crucially in presenting ideas, rather than material conditions, as the driving force of history. Indeed, one of Marx's most famous (and most widely misquoted) statements concerns this. Speaking of dialectic in Hegel, Marx wrote that "with him it is standing on its head. It must be turned right side up again, if you would discover the rational kernel within the mystical shell" (20). Politically consequential inversions form a recurrent motif in the film, where, for example, being homeless subjects one to police harassment, while bilking people out of millions gets one respect and high position.

Leaving the police officer, Raj accidentally ruins a sand castle being built by two children with Vidya. Angry, Vidya tells Raj that he should go drown himself. When he goes and falls into the water (after some giddy wobbling), a distressed Vidya jumps in to save him. As she drags him out of the water, he makes no effort to help himself. On the beach, she stands over him as he puffs and makes faces. The whole scene makes her into a sort of mother saving her babe from his tumble into the water. Raj acts like a child who is threatening to hold his breath or to eat worms until he dies. The sequence is hilariously funny. When the police officer returns, he asks them, "Why bicker like children?" Then Raj begins to playact that he is Vidya's husband, convincing the officer to give her a talking-to about the virtues of a good wife. Raj then follows Vidya home, in this case less like her son than like an irritating younger brother who tags along with an older sibling. Vidya's father invites him in and he keeps falling off the chair. He also shows misunderstandings that go along with being a child, not a college-educated man. For example, he is startled when Pandit Shastri (Vidya's father) says that Vidya has to see to her children, explaining that there are fifty of them. It is implausible for an adult not to understand that her fifty children are her students. This confusion serves once again to link Raj with childhood. When Vidya goes out to teach her class, he joins in, making childish faces and playing the games just like the children. The entire sequence is sometimes very funny, sometimes cute, sometimes both.

Yet the sequence is also very serious. Pandit Shastri is in a wheelchair. This suggests that traditional learning has been crippled. Moreover, Vidya—knowledge—has no financial support. Yet, at the same time, Vidya continues to act haughtily toward Raj, perhaps suggesting the sense of superiority fostered by the caste system. (Her patronymic indicates that she is a Brahmin, a member of the highest caste, the caste of priests and teachers.) Raj gently rebukes her, saying, "It's shameful that the poor forget the poor." Yet he himself seems concerned only with gaining position and respect.

The following scene is one of the most brilliant in the film, and a direct attack on the politics of the time. Dharmanand is about to give a political speech on swadeshi or the use of home-manufactured goods. The fact that he is giving a speech suggests that, allegorically, he is not one person, but an entire complex of businessmen and politicians who continually defraud the people. Dressed like Prime Minister Jawaharlal Nehru or the Congress Party officials of the time, Dharmanand begins his speech by stressing the importance of dharma (duty) and nation. He then explains that all his clothes are swadeshi. Raj has set himself up on a soapbox across from Dharmanand's stage. He calls out that his shoes are Japanese; his pants are English; his red cap is Russian—but his heart is Hindustani. The suggestion, of course, is that the reverse is true of Dharmanand. His clothes are Indian, but not his heart. Dharmanand then begins a grand statement. "Our greatest problem," he announces, "is . . ." But Raj interrupts him, shouting that the greatest problem is bread. Specifically, he names a variety of breads, covering different regions of India and different personal preferences. The scene is funny as Raj engages in a sort of childlike imitation of nationalist rhetoricians, taking us through a wacky sequence of reasoning. He is able to win the people over with his reference to bread. At first, he seems to be a communist agitator. He then asks, "What is required to eat bread?" Members of the crowd, reasonably, guess "money." But he explains that the crucial thing is not money, but teeth. (The Indian breads to which he refers are generally chewier than baked European bread.) He then insists that bad teeth lead to bad nutrition and thus "will end up by weakening the entire nation. Then enemies can invade and conquer us, making us slaves. If you want to keep India free and the nation stronger, preserve your teeth."

The sequence is side-splitting (at least for me). But it is also very serious. Marxists will recognize Raj's doctrine as a form of materialism—biological materialism, or physicalism—a form rejected by Marxists, who advocate historical materialism. But Kapoor is not using the speech to criticize physicalism. He is using it to criticize cultural nationalism. His argument for the importance of teeth is precisely the cultural nationalist's argument for the preservation of tradition. We must preserve tradition or our nation will be weakened. The loss of tradition, in this view, is the weakness that allowed enemies to invade and make Indians slaves. The argument was commonplace at the time and continues to this day. (For example, Yash Chopra's *Dharmaputra,* made a little after Kapoor's film, puts a version of this argument into the mouth of one of the main characters.) Moreover, Raj ends his speech by arguing that the strong nation can be preserved only if everyone buys the tooth powder he has manufactured. The suggestion is that the advocates of cultural nationalism are also making their arguments for direct profit. Unlike the cultural nationalists, however, Raj is found out, and thrashed by the crowd.

Fortunately, Raj manages to find honest work at the Jai Bharat ("Victory to India") laundry. The new government/raj is thus reduced to, so to speak, cleaning dirty laundry under the rubric of "Victory to India." During this time, Raj's relationship with Vidya develops. While courting, Raj often tries, with comic incompetence, to imitate a wealthy man (e.g., he borrows fancy clothes from the laundry, but he fails to replace his disintegrating shoes).

One evening, Vidya visits Raj at the laundry. He goes out to meet her, thoughtlessly leaving his iron face down. The following scene is exquisitely romantic, as Raj and Vidya play two very shy people in love, neither of whom is accustomed to physical contact. Raj moves around the topic of marriage very delicately. Vidya makes it clear that she loves him as much as he loves her. But the entire dialogue is very elliptical. He explains that he will see her father the next day. Rain begins to fall—as is standard in the romantic scenes of Indian literature. (The association of romance with rain extends back through the Sanskrit tradition.) Hesitant to huddle under the umbrella together, each tries to give the umbrella to the other, and each ends up soaked. Then they sing. Raj plays the flute, like Kṛṣṇa for his Rādhā. Vidya refers to their future children. We see three children passing by, the youngest walking in the funny way small children walk.

At the end of the song, they meet the same police officer from the beach. Remembering their previous encounter, the officer asks Raj if his wife is no longer overheated or angry. As it happens, due to puns across Hindi and Urdu, the very same sentence can also be understood as a question about whether his iron is still hot. Raj rushes back to the laundry in fast motion. What follows is uproarious slapstick. His forgotten iron has started a fire. Raj runs for the fire hose, but he is unable to handle its force (see Figure 3.9). Though the stream does not appear that powerful, Raj is

*3.9. Raj finds himself unable to control the fire hose, or his hat.*

spun around by the pressure as if he were one-quarter his actual size. The result is that he drenches everyone and propels himself down, backside first, into a barrel of water.

Despite having sold his honesty, Raj owns up to the error. In punishment, he is required to do extra work. This includes delivering clothes to a wealthy woman named "Maya." As already noted, māyā or illusion is the opposite of vidyā or knowledge in some versions of Hindu metaphysics. Moreover, māyā is inseparable from desire, from attachment to the material world. While waiting in Maya's rooms, Raj reveals his talent as a card sharp. Seeing possible profit in Raj's skill, Maya takes him to a nightclub and casino, what she calls "a dreamland—the world of wealth." The world of Maya/ māyā is, of course, the world of fraud par excellence. Occupied in this world, Raj is unable to fulfill his promise and visit Vidya and her father. We see the national allegory operating here as Independent India is seduced by the illusory world of wealth. As a result, it leaves behind both the ordinary people and vidyā /knowledge. The sequence ends when Dharmanand pays Raj a huge advance to be his partner. The allegorical significance regarding government/business partnerships is obvious.

Of course, Raj does not entirely leave Vidya behind, just as Independent India does not abandon traditional knowledge completely. However, his relation to her changes radically. In a subsequent scene, it is the Hindu festival, Dīpāvalī, which celebrates Lakṣmī, the consort of Viṣṇu and the goddess of wealth. Raj tells Pandit Shastri that he is taking Vidya to the temple of Lakṣmī. In a sense, he is telling the truth, for he takes her to a place where wealth is worshiped—not a temple, but the nightclub and casino. In keeping with the allegory, Vidya/knowledge has no place in this world of dreams; she is insulted by Maya/illusion, and flees. Dharmanand explains to Raj that he does not need Vidya/vidyā, but Maya/māyā—which is, of course, consistent with his new occupation of fraud. The point fits the nation as well. It too needs illusion (e.g., in the form of propaganda), not knowledge (in the sense of wisdom). In the following song interlude, Raj is clearly caught up in illusion, appearing to play the trumpet, gliding along the dance floor evidently without moving his legs. There are some moments of wit in this sequence. For example, I at least find it funny that Illusion dances to the rhythms of the "Rhumba Boys." Indeed, the diminutiveness of "boys" is important. I would not find it so funny if they were the "Rhumba Musicians" or the "Rhumba Orchestra." Nonetheless, despite these moments, the sequence as a whole is not funny. This is not, I believe, unrelated to the fact that, in the palace of illusion, Raj is an adult, not a child.

At the end of the evening, Raj visits Vidya. In this scene, he is more an adult than perhaps anywhere else in the film, and the entire episode is mirthless. Indeed, it is pathetic. Raj tells Vidya that he can gain position and respect only through wealth. Vidya, following standard Vedāntic thought, tells him that his material possessions will all blow away. In Vedāntism, that ephemeral character is precisely what makes the material world illusory. As she tells him this, a wind comes and scatters the bills he has pulled from his pockets.

Mirth returns in subsequent scenes, however, as Raj and Dharmanand hatch another scam. In this one, Raj is selling shares in an illusory mining operation. When credulous customers enter, Raj takes phone calls from his assistant, claiming that they are calls from around the world. In one case, he has to pretend that he is speaking with a Japanese client. His mimicry of Japanese speech is very funny, and very much in keeping with the behavior of children. (I know from having been the object of such mimicry by tiny, Hindi-speaking nieces and nephews, who could imitate the sounds of American English with remarkable accuracy, while saying nothing whatsoever.)

However, pathos returns as well. In fact, the sorrowful rasa is somewhat more common in this middle section, where Kapoor and Abbas develop the main themes of the film. In one scene, Raj returns to the pawn shop and meets Vidya, who is selling her books. He asks how things are at her school, where she raises little "dharmātmas," children whose very soul is governed by dharma. Vidya tells him that the school is closed and that the children are on their way to becoming 420s. Later, they meet again at the tea stall where they first expressed their love and spoke of marriage. She tells him, "You've been tempted by a false world." She also tells him that he has shattered their hopes for a home. The image is particularly resonant in light of the national allegory.

The last point is developed when Raj, wandering the streets, returns to the pavement dwellers. He is greeted with joy. One of them says, "Didn't I tell you, one day Raj will be back? Then we'll have our own homes." Again, this is the promise of independence. "Our own homes" means two things here. First, we will all have India as "our home." Second, the new India will end poverty and homelessness. As it turns out, this is not merely the people's fancy. It is a scheme drawn up and advertised by Dharmanand. Like a politician promising whatever it takes to be elected, Dharmanand has circulated an advertisement, in the name of Raj, claiming that the "People's Colony" will provide homes for 100 rupees each. Raj is angered and panicked by this news. He approaches Dharmanand, saying that he will not cheat the poor. He insists that Dharmanand take back his money and whatever they have gained through their collaboration. Now, Raj no longer wants wealth and position. He wants only "śānti," peace. Again, according to Vedāntic thought, śānti is the only true goal of human existence, and it can be achieved only through spiritual knowledge or vidyā. But Seth reminds him that he has already set out on the path of māyā, not that of vidyā. Suddenly, Maya is revealed behind a pillar in Dharmanand's home. Evidently, Maya/māyā had been there all along.

From here, it seems that Raj has decided to go along with the swindle. He accepts money from crowds of destitute people, promising to build them homes. In a deeply pathetic scene, his homeless friends come to purchase homes. The beggar on crutches is no longer cynical. He has been filled with hope and a sense of humanity by Raj's actions. Ganga Ma tells him, "In jest, you called me a goddess. You turned out to be a dharmātma." Again, the allegory only enhances the effect. The nationalist leaders called India a goddess. Indians came to believe that those leaders were dharmātmas. Indeed, this statement suggests a more specific connection, for there was one nationalist leader with a very similar title. Though he was not known as "Dharmātma," Gandhi was known by the related title, "Mahātma" (great/mahā soul/ātma). In this way, the statement suggests that Indians came to believe that all their leaders were like Gandhi, when, of course, they were not. Ganga Ma has 225 rupees and wants three houses for her three children—one of whom seems to be Muslim (roughly in keeping with the proportion of Muslims in South Asia). She is 75 rupees short. To make up the difference, she turns over a marriage necklace. The value of such a necklace obviously goes well beyond its price. Indeed, the marriage necklace is an object of great sentimental attachment in Indian culture. Its use here reminds us that the fraud perpetrated by the rich against the poor is not only monetary, but affects the most important human bonds and the deepest human emotions as well. In keeping with this emphasis on human relations, Ganga Ma explains that she herself will not need a home as she will stay with her three children. The allegory is fitting, for one might reasonably say that India resides everywhere in the homes of her children.

Raj evidently packs up the money, in preparation for his escape; then Vidya enters and hands him back his pawned medal. True knowledge returns honesty to government. It is fitting that this follows Raj's meeting with Ganga Ma.

Mirth recurs at this point as Dharmanand and his incompetent goons try to get the money from Raj. There is a great deal of very funny running about, falling, jumping, throwing, and general hijinks. At the climax, Dharmanand finds no money in Raj's case, but he does find a gun and shoots Raj. The scene is a little peculiar. Kapoor seems to wildly overact Raj's pain and death on being shot. At least in my experience, audience members are unsure of how to react. On the one hand, the event itself is tragic. On the other hand, it seems playfully comic. Our reaction is tipped in the direction of pathos as Vidya runs back and Ganga Ma cries out, "Who shot my son?" Faced with an angry crowd and Vidya's accusations, Dharmanand claims that Raj was perpetrating fraud on all of them. He says, "You all know my first dharma is to serve the people." He then argues that "for their sake, I shot him. If that makes me a criminal, then hang me. For the sake of the people, I'll give my life." The effect of the speech is almost horrifying, for it closely recalls the perverse justification of the assassins who shot Mahatma Gandhi. This is a moment when, the rasa theorists would say, the dominant rasa risks being entirely broken—for how can anyone retain mirth when recalling that murder.

However, before we really have time to assimilate the implications of the speech, Raj sits up. He had filled the gun with blanks. Retrospectively,

*3.10. Vidya leads Raj to a vision of a new India.*

we realize that Kapoor was not overacting pain and death. Rather, he was acting Raj's overacting of pain and death. Thus, we were right to find it comic to begin with.

Raj uses the fake murder to expose Dharmanand as not only an ordinary 420 but as "Shree 420"—Mister 420 himself. He then delivers a speech to the crowd, which is in effect Kapoor's and Abbas's speech to the audience. He calls on them to "unite." "Don't disperse your strength," he tells them. "Go to the government," he continues; "say we are a million people, we will build our own homes." Through "work," we will produce "prosperity" for the land and the people.

The scene is remarkable. It calls on a million people to go to the government. But it was not censored (unlike a much milder scene in *Mother India* where a crowd demands that a food hoarder release his stored grain [see Chatterjee 53–55]). I suspect this is, at least in part, due to the mirthful rasa of the piece and the general cuteness of Raj. By developing the film's themes through mirth, rather than anger or even pathos, Kapoor manages to communicate, without appearing didactic or threatening, a message that is in many ways radical. There is also a certain slyness in the phrasing of Raj's speech. Kapoor calls on the masses to go to the government. But this is only to say that they will make homes with their own money and hard work. How dangerous could that be? The masses are pledging to spend their own money, and to work hard. That seems just what business wants. In fact, the radical and threatening part of the message here is not explicit, but implied. The people cannot make homes with their own money and their own hard work if they are harassed by the police, if they are evicted from the land. They must be supported by the government. Indeed, their project requires a fundamental change in government. Specifically, the government must—like the new Raj—ally itself, not with the wealthy, but with the ordinary people; not with business, but with labor and the unemployed. In short, the project articulated by Kapoor and Abbas (through the character of a transformed Raj) requires a sort of revolution.

At the end of the film, Raj is once again dressed as a tramp. Dharmanand and his cronies are being hauled away by the police. Raj begins to walk out onto the open road, singing that his shoes are Japanese, his red cap is Russian. It seems that we are simply back where we began. But then Vidya calls to him. They sing together that their heart is Hindustani. She takes him back toward the city, to the top of a hill. They look down into the valley, the future, a sort of promised land. They see a gleaming city filled with new housing for the poor—what the government and the people, what wisdom and self-rule, can do together (see Figure 3.10). The music stops and, resolving (as Abhinavagupta suggested) on peace, Vidya sings a cappella: "My heart is Hindustani."

CHAPTER FOUR

# "So, What's the Deal with All the Singing?"

## The Cognitive Universality of the Hindi Musical

### *Kabhi Khushi Kabhie Gham . . .*

The first thing non-Indians say when they see a mainstream Bollywood movie is often something along the following lines: "So, what's the deal with all the singing? Things are going along normally. Then, out of the blue, somebody starts to croon. The next thing you know, the entire village is engaged in an elaborate dance number. I don't get it." Moreover, this response is not confined to newcomers. As Dwyer and Patel note, films of "the Hindi commercial cinema . . . are criticized" for a number of things, prominently including "their song and dance sequences" (7); indeed, "Song sequences . . . are often used to denigrate" the "Hindi film" (37).[1] This reaction is in some ways peculiar. After all, the musical is well established in the United States. Though less prominent in Hollywood, it is a staple of Broadway, and has certainly made its way into mainstream cinema. Nonetheless, the musical format—which dominates Bombay film—serves as a salient marker of difference for many non-Indian viewers. It is, in a way, a symptom of the alienness, not only of Hindi film, but of the culture it represents and expresses.[2]

Even leaving aside Broadway and Hollywood musicals, this evaluation is, I believe, deeply mistaken. Far from being a disruptive case of cultural difference, song and dance numbers in Indian cinema are—like the stories, themes, and emotions we have considered thus far—cultural specifications of universal patterns. There is nothing truly alien about them.

More exactly, in studying the song interlude, two basic issues arise in a cognitive context. The first concerns provenance. Just what principles generate the song and dance numbers in Indian films? The second issue concerns reception. What effects does or should the song interlude have on viewers? Equivalently, how can viewers come to understand and appreciate such interludes—or to criticize them for particular features in individual cases (rather than dismissing them generally)? In fact, the two issues are closely related. The universal principles that give rise to the interlude do so because they manifest universal functions. Those functions define just what it is that the song interlude should do, and thus what aspects of the interlude are most important for our understanding and response (our attentional focus, encoding, and so on) as viewers.

## Narrative Junctures: On the Sources of the Song and Dance Interlude

So, what universal principles lie behind the song interlude? Where does it come from and what effect is it supposed to have? To answer these questions, we need first to understand something about the structure of narrative. As a range of narrative theorists have noted, stories proceed in segments. The segments are joined at points where there is some significant change. Two thousand years ago, the Sanskrit narrative theorists referred to these moments of transition as junctures (see Chapter Twenty-one of Bharatamuni). About fifteen years ago, the cognitive narratologist Keith Oatley referred to them with the same term, rediscovering the idea and the metaphor.

Plots provide instances of an objective series of events that force a clear change in a character's situation and possibilities. Romeo and Juliet pursue romantic union. In the course of this pursuit, real events sharply alter their situation, as when Romeo is exiled. However, a juncture may be subjective as well as objective—as when Hamlet contemplates suicide. For example, the hero may simply lose heart or suffer doubt as he or she seems to make no progress, although there is no particular catastrophic event. In connection with this, the Sanskrit theorists referred to one very important juncture as the "pause." The pause is a moment where the hero rethinks his or her goals and actions, reflecting on his or her condition in light of preceding efforts and larger interests.

A somewhat peculiar feature of junctures is that, cross-culturally, they are often marked by distinctive non-story features. In other words, they are not solely a matter of plot. They frequently involve some discursive or related changes as well. Sometimes there is an authorial intrusion or evaluative commentary. Sometimes—as in the "pause"—there is an extended reflection by a character. Most important for our purposes, there are also more narrowly formal ways of marking junctures. For example, a wide range of traditions have used poetic verse at such points. Thus a number of Chinese novels portray characters as composing poems at crucial transitions. Japanese travel writings may highlight key moments with haiku. Sanskrit dramas insert short verses at points of separation or reunion.[3] Needless to say, the different forms of junctural marking may be combined, as in Shakespeare's soliloquies. Shakespeare may preserve iambic pentameter throughout most of a play; nonetheless, the soliloquies of Hamlet, Macbeth, and other great characters—usually delivered at moments of pause, in the Sanskrit theorists' sense—remain distinctively poetic elaborations.

More exactly, in technical terms, we have a universal structural principle by which narrative is organized into a junctured sequence of objective or subjective events. In addition, we have two universal development principles. The first is that junctures may be elaborated—for example, in authorial intrusion or extended reflection by a character. The second is that junctures may be formally distinguished. Finally, the default procedure for generating formal distinction is to increase formal patterning. The most obvious way of doing this is by shifting from prose to verse.

It is worth considering the formal development principle and its default procedure a bit further. The shift to verse entails the patterning of syllable stress or syllable length. It commonly includes the enhancement of alliteration, assonance, and other techniques of patterning the sounds of the words as well. These aspects do not exhaust the possibilities for formalization, however. Pitch, gesture, and bodily movement may also be systematically structured. While rhythm, rhyme, and so forth may be regularized in verse alone, song organizes pitch, and dance adds patterning to gesture and bodily movement.[4] Thus song and dance structure aspects of speech in just the way verse does, giving them a distinct formal organization.

Now we are in a position to give a preliminary explanation of the musical interlude in Bombay cinema. It is a particularly extensive formalization and elaboration of narrative junctures. The formalization employed in verse is extended to pitch and motion. Moreover, the nature of this formalization fosters a more extensive elaboration, as the singing and dancing are developed, repeated, and varied.

This extensive elaboration is probably one reason why the song and dance interludes may appear obtrusive. In other formalizations, the elaboration may be more limited, thus easier to ignore. But that does not seem to be the whole problem. Shakespeare's soliloquies are shorter than song and dance interludes. But they certainly seem long enough—and mimetically implausible enough—to prompt questioning. This brings us to a further, crucial characteristic of the interlude—its narratively ambiguous status. Unlike Macbeth's or Hamlet's imaginations and worries, we may not know whether we should take the interlude to be part of the story.

One of the standard distinctions in film criticism is between diegetic and nondiegetic music. Diegetic music is music that occurs in the story (e.g., when a juke box is playing in a bar). Nondiegetic music is heard by the viewer, but does not occur in the story (e.g., when an orchestra plays while the main character tries to pick his or her way across a mine field). The song interlude in a musical cannot strictly be fitted to either category. On the one hand, the characters do sing and dance. (In contrast, the soldier does not react to the music that accompanies his or her attempt to avoid the mines.) On the other hand, suppose one of the characters in a song interlude returns home after the episode ends and is asked, "What were you just doing?" He or she will not say, "Singing and dancing with everyone in the town square."

We might refer to narrative segments of this sort as "paradiegetic," for they are, so to speak, "alongside" the story without being quite part of the story. In paradiegetic sections of a work something does happen in the story, but what happens in the story is not what is directly represented in the discourse (here, on the screen). Like the junctural structure of narrative and the development principles we have considered, paradiegesis too is universal. Moreover, it is not at all confined to song and dance sequences. Probably the most common instances of paradiegesis are to be found in metaphors. For instance, when Lorca tells us that his "heart of silk/is filled with lights,/with lost bells,/with lilies and bees" (11), he is telling us something about himself as a character in his own story (in this case, a poem). But he is not telling us that a bee has gotten stuck in his artery. In this respect, the musical interludes are akin to metaphors.

The obvious question to ask at this point, however, is—just why should one follow these universal principles, creating paradiegetic episodes? Clearly, junctural formalization and elaboration are "optional," not "obligatory" development principles,[5] for there are many works that involve neither. Why, then, would a director or screenwriter combine and intensify these principles, further complicating them with paradiegesis, to produce the musical interlude? Or, rather, why would such a practice develop in the course of a tradition and even become predominant within that tradition, as occurred in India—again, not some idiosyncratic, marginal tradition, but the largest film industry in the world? Here we need to consider the function or functions of the interlude.

The most obvious place to look for such a function is in the distinctive characteristics of narrative junctures. Such junctures are not a matter of indifferent changes in condition or thought. They are moments of particularly intense emotional experience or transition—not only for the characters, but even more significantly for the reader or viewer. Given this, the elaboration and formal marking of a juncture must almost necessarily function, first of all, to modify that emotional experience or transition, most obviously by intensifying it. Indeed, emotional intensification does appear to be the basic function of the song interlude, what allows it to find a place in film initially. But to say that this is its first function is not to say it is its only function. Once a structure is generated by a combination of universal development principles operating in relation to one particular function, it may be "exapted," to use a term from evolutionary biology (see Gould 1232). Unsurprisingly, the second function of the song interlude bears on the second main purpose of literature (following the communication of emotion)—the communication of themes. Specifically, it often serves to clarify or elaborate such themes. Finally, while narrative junctures are centrally a matter of emotion, paradiegesis per se is a matter of narrative status. As such, it is bound up with the communication and status of narrative information. In keeping with this, the third important function of the song and dance interlude is the regulation of narrative information as this is made possible by the difference between story and discourse.[6] I consider each of these functions in turn, beginning with the last. In each case, I illustrate the discussion by reference to Karan Johar's mega-hit, *Kabhi Khushi Kabhie Gham . . .* Before going on, however, we need to consider the paradiegetic operation of the interlude in more detail.

## Discursive Uses of the Interlude: On Private Metaphors and Ambiguous Ellipses

The main discursive (i.e., discourse-related) function of the paradiegetic interlude derives from the general feature that makes it so obtrusive—it interrupts the ordinary flow of the narrative. The interlude is clearly marked off from the surrounding story. The music begins, the characters start their singing and dancing, and we understand that this episode is somehow different from what went before. When there is a sharp change of this sort, we commonly infer that there is a disruption in the discourse. When the main character looks off into the heavens and his or her face goes all wavy, we know that we have entered his or her mind and are now witnessing either a fantasy or a memory, which lasts until the wavy close-up is repeated.

The song interlude too signals an alteration in the discourse. It is similar to the wavy close-up in that it is distinctly marked. However, it is different in that its meaning is not precisely specified. Indeed, it permits a range of uses.

One common use of the interlude is to suspend ordinary time constraints. A song sequence allows us to experience the elaborate development of a romantic relationship in the course of a few moments. For example, lovers sing to one another in a series of verses. Perhaps they change locations for each verse. Perhaps they change clothing. In any case, the development of the song communicates the development of their relationship. Interestingly, this need not be matched by a corresponding lapse in time in the actual story. Thus an interlude may begin and end at the same moment in story time. In a sense, the passage of time in such an interlude is metaphorical, rather than literal. It suggests the common experience of lovers that even brief moments together have advanced their mutual understanding and affection vastly.

Beyond temporal ellipsis, the discursive shift in the song interlude allows the film to shift points of view. Thus it allows us access to the inner life of the characters. Moreover, it does so in a way that need not be entirely internal. The paradiegetic nature of the interlude allows the suggestion that everyone present overhears the inner thoughts being expressed in the song. But at the same time, it indicates that no such feelings really have been expressed. As a result, the song interlude may approximate actual experience in a way that realistic representations rarely do. Lovers indirectly and uncertainly communicate a great deal to one another in the course of their interactions. The song interlude easily portrays this wealth of intense and exhilarating, but indirect and ambiguous communication.

Indeed, the possible ambiguity of the interlude is important in itself. The precise status of any moment in a song interlude may be uncertain. This ambiguity is enhanced by the fact that a particular interlude may combine a range of different meanings. At one moment, we may have a clear indication that we are witnessing the inner life of one character; at another moment, we may have an equally clear indication that we are witnessing the inner life of a different character; subsequently, it may seem that we are viewing the elliptical presentation of a developing relationship. The interlude may be disambiguated, if the director decides to do so. But directors are no less likely to make use of this ambiguity. For example, we may witness a song sequence that seems to suggest that the lovers have consummated their relationship. Nonetheless, we may still not know whether this has occurred in reality, in one or both characters' fantasies, or simply in our own imaginations.

This is related to another feature of the song interlude—indirect representation. Ordinary discourse may represent the actions and thoughts of the characters directly or suggest them indirectly. The use of indirectness is unusually intense in the song interlude, particularly in the area of sexuality. This is especially important in mainstream Indian film, where the portrayal of sexual contact has been highly constrained. The song interlude allows the filmmaker to represent the sexual attraction of the couple. As I have just indicated, it even allows the director to suggest actual sexual relations. The undulating movements of the dance sequences are often clearly erotic in nature. The physical interaction of the lovers continually approaches a sort of sexual mime. The lyrics of the songs continue the use of sexual metaphors, often through the well-known imagery of the ghazal (a central genre of Persian and Urdu poetry).

These references to metaphors lead us to a final discursive use of the song interlude. The interlude is not simply akin to a metaphor in its paradiegetic quality. It is bound up with metaphors, both explicit and implicit. Indeed, the song interlude itself frequently enacts a metaphor. In a novel, the lover might be spoken of as "dancing with joy" or "singing the praises of his beloved." In the song interlude, we witness this metaphor—not its interpreted meaning, but the metaphor itself. Of course, the musical interlude need not express a single metaphor. Moreover, its metaphorical operation is not necessarily based on something so idiomatic, so commonplace as "dancing with joy." In most cases, the precise metaphorical implications of the interlude are multiple and complex, and can only be inferred through interpretive effort.

## Regulating Narrative Information: The Lovers' Discourse, and Their Story

*Kabhi Khushi Kabhie Gham . . .* (*Through Smiles through Tears . . .*) includes many exemplary interludes. "Suraj Hua Maddham" ("The Sun Dims into Twilight") provides a particularly relevant illustration of the preceding points, for it brings together a range of discursive operations and meanings.

For readers who are unfamiliar with the film, I should note that *Kabhi Khushi Kabhie Gham . . .* is "the highest grossing Indian film in the overseas market."[7] It is a prime example of contemporary Hindi commercial cinema. It is also a brilliantly crafted film. For our purposes, the main events concern Yash Raichand, a fabulously wealthy businessman; his wife, Nandini; their adopted son, Rahul; their younger, biological son, Rohan; and Anjali, the daughter of an ordinary man who owns a small sweetshop in Delhi. We learn early on that Anjali's father, called "Bauji," is ill. Rahul meets Anjali. They fall in love. But Yash refuses to accept the marriage, preferring Naina, the daughter of a wealthy friend. Initially, Rahul agrees to break off his relationship with Anjali. However, when Anjali's father dies, Rahul marries her despite his father's condemnation. This leads to a split in the Raichand family. Rahul and Anjali travel to England, where he becomes a fabulously successful businessman. He has no contact with his adoptive parents or his young brother, though he misses them terribly. When Rohan grows up, he decides that he should travel to England, find his lost brother, and reunite the family. Concealing his true goals, he convinces Yash that a stay in England is necessary for his education. Once there, he finds Rahul and, after some further complications, reunites Rahul with his parents. Along the way, he falls in love with Anjali's sister, whom he marries at the end of the film.

In the scene I wish to consider, Rahul and Anjali are at a fair in Chandni Chowk in old Delhi. They have just engaged in a discussion about what Rahul wants. The discussion includes a number of double entendres that prepare us for what follows. (Technically, they prime ideas about sexual relations, which are then more readily available for interpreting subsequent events.) Up to this point, Anjali has been oblivious to Rahul's romantic intentions, believing instead that he was plotting to take over her father's small business. Their discussion at the fair leads to a juncture where Anjali comes to understand Rahul's feelings, and to accept her own feelings for Rahul as well. The scene culminates in Rahul gently pressing Anjali's hand through a set of bangles, asking over and over if he is hurting her. The suggestion of sexual penetration seems unmistakable.

From here, the song sequence begins. This lengthy interlude, first of all, presents an elliptical account of the flowering romance between the two lovers. It accomplishes this by a number of means, including the repeated changes in costume. As often happens in such interludes, the costume changes, roughly a dozen in number, do not indicate a literal passage of time. But they do suggest developments in the relationship between the lovers. In this case, the disjunction from literal time makes particular experiential sense following the paradiegetic representation of sexual relations that preceded the interlude.

Indeed, the interlude itself involves clear implications of sexual union. It communicates these implications most obviously through the highly sexualized nature of the lovers' dance. But it does so more subtly—and more definitively—through the details of their costume changes. At the start, their clothes may seem to vary without any pattern. However, Anjali appears in red three times. This associates her with that color. Rahul, in contrast, tends to appear in white or black. About two-thirds of the way through the interlude, Anjali suddenly appears in black, with Rahul in red. Anjali sings verses that suggest there has been a sexual culmination represented by this switching of colors: "The colors of our souls have melted into one," she sings, and "I can't say which of me is you and which of you is me." The verses continue with the lines, "O beloved, it's the waves of your love that drown me before transporting me to the shore." This leads directly to a scene where both characters are in a pool, drenched by the water, with the visual consequences (clinging, semi-transparent clothes) and metaphorical implications one would expect from wetness. After this culmination, and a few intervening shots, we return to the real world where Anjali is drenched in rain.

While the episode is, in my view, quite powerfully erotic, the sexuality is never explicit. Thus, in the manner described by Richard Maltby (discussing classical Hollywood cinema), viewers are free to imagine innocent play or elliptical sexual relations, as they see fit. As will become clear below, this dual construction of the audience is a recurrent feature of the film. It is particularly evident in the interludes. This is unsurprising, as the ambiguity and metaphorical nature of the interlude facilitate such duality.

"Suraj Hua Maddham" also incorporates the inner, mental life of the characters. This is signaled by the doubled presence of the main characters at certain points in the interlude. For example, in one section, Rahul—unperceived by anyone in the scene—watches Anjali interact with his family and ultimately with a second version of himself (see Figure 4.1). This is paralleled by a subsequent sequence with Anjali, who appears twice in the frame, watching herself receive a brief kiss from Rahul—rather far in the background (see Figure 4.2).

Do these sequences suggest, then, that the entire interlude is a fantasy? I do not believe so. The sections that we know to be fantasies are clearly signaled by the presence of a fantasizing observer. Moreover, the sections without a doubled Rahul or Anjali—thus, the non-fantasy sections—are themselves marked by a palpable decline in representational realism. The fantasy sections represent Anjali's and Rahul's imaginations

*4.1. Rahul sees himself with Anjali and his family.*

*4.2. Anjali observes herself receiving a kiss from Rahul.*

of future events. Thus they are constrained, at least to some extent, by real world possibility. The non-fantasy sections, in contrast, are not constrained in this way. Rather, they are free to diverge widely from mimetic realism, in the manner of metaphors. Indeed, that divergence is, to a great extent, guided by implicit metaphors.

Consider, for example, locations. The non-fantasy sections do not take place in, say, the Raichand mansion or Chandni Chowk, but in isolated, exotic locales, such as the Egyptian Sahara. The choice of these locations for the unrealistic scenes is consequential. Here, as in other Hindi films, the various places in the interlude are not simply a matter of "visual attractions," as some writers have claimed (see, for example, Dwyer and Patel 30, 35–39). They carry significant, metaphorical implications. In this case, the lovers feel transported; they feel as if they are alone in the world; they experience their love as timeless, as ancient and eternal as the pyramids that figure prominently in two sequences of the interlude. Indeed, the ancient and eternal quality of their love is indicated directly in the lyrics, which refer to the idea that lovers rediscover each other in every incarnation. Thus Rahul sings of "our love, traveling through centuries," and Anjali replies, "Let us meet throughout lives and lives." In addition, the lovers' eventual union in the water is a form of relief from the literal and metaphorical heat, and the water is a source of new life after the barrenness of the desert. Of course, putting it this way is banal—but that is often the case with translated metaphors. The suggestive richness of the metaphor is in the image, not in a paraphrase.

Finally, when the episode ends, it is as if no time has passed at all. This yields a crucial ambiguity. Are we to imagine that the lovers go through this sort of developing relation in a period stretching out after that moment at the fair? In other words, are we to imagine that this is a paradiegetic flash forward? Alternatively, did the brief touch of the lovers communicate so much; was there such intensity of understanding that it was equivalent to a developed relationship? Or should one completely accept the sexual implications and assume that there has indeed been a consummation? Or perhaps it was, after all, entirely a fantasy, with some parts merely indeterminate as to which one of the lovers was dreaming? The ambiguity is important to our cumulative understanding of the film and to our interest in and uncertainty about what will happen next. In short, not only the possible meanings, but the very fact of their ambiguity organizes—and enhances—our engagement with the film.

## Themes and Suggestions: Is It Really All about Loving Your Parents?

Again, a second important function of the song and dance interlude is the communication of themes. *Kabhi Khushi Kabhie Gham . . .* is no less remarkable—and no less carefully ambiguous—in its thematic developments than in its manipulation of story and discourse. Specifically, Karan Johar has provided us with a moral for the film, and he has done so in his own voice. "It's all about loving your parents," he tells us—on advertisements, on the box for the DVD, even in the movie itself, immediately following the title. The explicit statement of the theme orients viewers, who are free to view the film as a son's love letter to his father and as a statement of everything that Indian parents want a movie to be.

But, at the same time, the film is open to another thematic reading. In this way, it in effect generalizes the sort of dual audience technique described by Maltby. Indeed, the film follows the standard structure and thematics of romantic tragi-comedy, which is hardly all about loving your parents. The father in Johar's film, though not entirely unsympathetic, is unequivocally the bad guy. He is trying to force his will on his son, controlling his marriage in the name of tradition. The entire development of the film indicates that Rahul is right to marry Anjali, and that it would have been cruel, and even immoral, to abandon her due to his father's wishes.

But if the film is not "all about loving your parents," what is it about? Or, more important, how do we infer what it is about? Johar is evidently not communicating his primary themes directly, through the explicit moral. But how, then, is he communicating those primary themes?

Johar directs us toward the implicit themes of the work—often themes of religious or national identity and tradition—through what the Sanskrit theorists called "dhvani," usually translated as "suggestion."[8] Dhvani is a very broad concept, encompassing all one's associative connections with a given term or image. These connections include not only meanings, but facts and even episodic memories. For example, the dhvani of Rāma encompasses such narrative events as his defeat of Rāvaṇa and his exiling of Sītā. It also includes criticisms and revisions of Rāma's character, memories of politicians invoking Rāma, images of temples devoted to Rāma. In short, it includes all mental contents activated by the idea of Rāma. Clearly, only some of these activated contents or suggestions will be broadly shared, and only some of those will be relevant in any given context. One task of a poet or filmmaker is to trigger the right associations at the right points in order to fulfill his or her thematic (or emotional, or narrative) purposes.

Since *dhvani* is such a general term, it may be useful to distinguish between suggestions that primarily concern ideas, objects, or events outside the film and suggestions that operate primarily within the film. In other words, it may be useful to distinguish between suggestions that relate the film to the real world and suggestions that relate one part of the film to another. I will refer to these as "allusion" and "patterning," respectively. Needless to say, allusion and patterning may be found in any section of a film. However, they are particularly prominent in the song and dance interludes. The freedom of the interlude—released as it is from ordinary diegetic constraints—allows for an intensified use of both techniques.

First, consider allusion. There are obviously many ways in which a song and dance may allude to matters outside the film. For purposes of illustration, I will focus on one set of these—the ways in which song and dance may tacitly suggest cultural genealogies. Music does not appear out of nowhere. It relates to traditions and histories. These relations regularly have metaphorical resonances in Indian films. One simple way in which this occurs is through cultural marking. Some music and dance are traditional Indian folk arts; others are Indian classical; others are western classical; others are western popular; others are mixed. The association of a particular character or event with a culturally marked dance or piece of music encourages us to transfer the cultural marking to that character or event. Thus a character introduced with a classical Indian composition or rāga and classical Indian vocal techniques is likely to be associated with elite Indian tradition. In contrast, suppose a character's choice of a spouse is elaborated through an interlude in a discotheque. This suggests that his or her choice in marriage reflects westernization. Obviously, such marking has particular relevance to thematic treatments of tradition—whether the connection is straight or ironic, positive or negative.

Simple cultural marking is far from the only element of the interlude that has bearing here. Dances have isolable mythic and narrative connections. Songs have individual histories—times and places where they were written or performed. Moreover, there are many components in both music and dance. For example, the words, melody, and instrumentation may interact, sometimes necessitating more complex cultural judgments, as when the instrumentation is western, but the scale is Indian. This too may have metaphorical significance. Most obviously, it may suggest that the associated characters and situations themselves combine culturally heterogeneous elements. To make things still more complicated, some interludes are segmented into strikingly different musical styles.

Of course, music has internal as well as external associations. In other words, its thematic operation is not confined to allusion. Even if one does not recognize a particular rāga or style, one may recognize the repetition of a melodic motif—or a particular dance movement, rhythmic cycle, or instrumentation. That allows music to create patterns within a film. When we hear the same motif played in connection with two characters or events, we join them metaphorically. This joining may lead us to think that the characters share personality traits, that the situations have related causes, that a sequence of events is about to be repeated or varied. In each case, the connection may foster thematic generalization—about types of people, cycles of life, the results of particular sorts of behavior. Moreover, as is usually the case, this metaphorical link may be straightforward or ironic. Thus we might just as easily find striking oppositions between the linked characters, events, and situations. The important point here is that, through their relatively unconstrained use of patterning, interludes contribute in often crucial ways to the establishment of pointed comparisons and contrasts within the work. They lead us to conjoin characters, events, and scenes, to think one through or against the other. In this way too interludes may be deeply consequential for thematic interpretation.

Johar works to communicate his implicit themes through both patterning and allusion. The task is particularly complex as his actual themes largely contradict the stated moral of the film. In part as a result of this contradiction, Johar relies heavily on the freedom of the song and dance interludes to convey his ideas. In the following sections, I will take up two exemplary instances of this. In the first case, I will focus on internal patterning, particularly examining a drum motif associated with Rahul. In the second case, I will turn to allusion, considering some of the ways in which Johar connects his film with, and implicitly comments on, current political and social conflicts in India.

## Themes and Patterns: Rahul among the Rich and Famous

Early in the film, the Raichand family is singing the title song while celebrating Dīpāvalī. The melody of the song provides a motif that will serve to remind us of familial bonds many times in the course of the film. In this case, the entire family is present at the ceremony—except for Rahul. Late in the interlude, Rahul is introduced. His entry is preceded by drumbeats, which fuse with the rhythmic propeller strokes from the Raichand helicopter that is transporting him to the event. The harshness of the strokes and the quick rhythm of the drums interrupt the fluid and sentimental song. The entire sequence may be seen as foreshadowing the separation of Rahul from his family. The musical contrast in particular has marked him as different. But the precise nature of the difference is unclear. An obvious interpretation would be that Rahul is mechanical (like the propeller blades), while his family has human feeling. But this is not at all borne out by subsequent developments. Given that Rahul is adopted, we might simply take it to suggest a different origin, a distinct heritage. But, even then, the content of that heritage is unclear.

The significance of linking Rahul with the drums becomes comprehensible only in a subsequent interlude ("Say 'Shava Shava'"). Rahul's adoptive father and Anjali's father were born on the same day, so of course their birthday celebrations fall on the same day as well. The Raichands are fabulously wealthy. Anjali's family has a modest income. Again, they are ordinary people. The Raichand party begins with a rendition of the western "Happy Birthday" song, in English. In fact, English is sprinkled throughout the speech of the Raichands. "Happy Birthday to You" is followed by a strange sequence in which the patriarch, Yash, sings a celebratory song about a desirable young woman. While singing, he is surrounded by a group of mini-skirted female dancers who also provide the chorus in the style of some American pop music.

The celebration for Anjali's father or "Bauji" is intercut with the Raichand party. The former takes place in the streets of old Delhi, while the latter takes place in the Raichand mansion. Needless to say, there is no singing of "Happy Birthday" at Bauji's celebration. Johar does have Anjali's family and friends sing a song that is recognizably the same as the second tune sung by the Raichands. However, in this case, the shared melody is arranged and choreographed in such a way as to make it into a folk tune, and the dancers are all wearing Indian clothing. Thus we have a direct parallel, with the two families celebrating a father's birthday by singing the same basic tune. However, this similarity permits a striking contrast. The Raichands and their multi-millionaire friends are highly westernized; their modes of social interaction and self-expression are imbued with globalized

American pop culture. There is also something very campy about the Raichand performance, with Yash engaging in some self-consciously awkward dance moves, and gyrating a little too erotically with a young girl at the end. In contrast, the men and women attending Bauji's celebration express an indigenous folk culture. Their song and dance manifest a joyful sense of community, rather than an apparently westernized sexual exhibitionism. Moreover, the praises for Yash seem smarmy and excessive, a matter of getting in good with a powerful man. Even when apparently sincere, they are hyperbolic to the point of absurdity. The daughterly affection of Anjali could also be seen as hyperbolic. Specifically, she sings that her father is her heaven and her earth and asks what she will do without him. However, this has a context that, in my view, makes it affecting, rather than cloying. The context for Yash's celebration is, in part, his vast wealth. The context for the eulogizing of Bauji is his illness. Anjali's praise is not flattery. It is the expression of her fear that her father will soon die.

But what does this tell us about Rahul? Are we to infer that he is simply one of the aristocratic sycophants? Rahul does praise Yash extravagantly. And he moves among the elite with ease. Yet there is a sort of disconnect between Rahul and this society as well. The point is made most strikingly when Rahul repeatedly sees Anjali at the Raichand party, although she is far away in old Delhi. In a nice touch, Johar changes Anjali's costume (and the costumes of the dancers around her) in order to mark Rahul's fantasy or illusion more clearly. The real Anjali is wearing blue—in parallel with Rahul's mother. However, Rahul's imagined Anjali wears bright red, perhaps reminiscent of a wedding sari, such as that worn by Anjali's friend when she becomes a bride a little later in the film. In any case, Rahul's imagination of Anjali and her companions connects him with that other celebration, partially removing him from his own immediate surroundings. It may even suggest that he belongs with the ordinary people dancing in the streets of Delhi, rather than the elite guests at the Raichand mansion.

Perhaps more important, the shift from the Raichand party to Bauji's celebration is marked by vigorous drumming, reminiscent of the drumming that introduces Rahul initially. This occurs at the first cut from one scene to the other. Subsequently, we witness the Raichands engaged in ballroom dancing. This sequence ends with a medium close-up of Rahul, not dancing, but looking doubtful about the whole business. When we cut away from this to Delhi, we actually see the drums in the foreground of the new shot. This emphasizes the association between the drumming and the folk culture of Anjali's family. It also re-emphasizes the tie between the drumming and Rahul. This in turn serves to link Rahul more firmly with the popular folk practices of ordinary Indian people. The connection fits with his mysterious origins. It also fits with his eventual fate. Again, when Rahul first arrives, the drumming motif interrupts the sentimental familial celebration. It is appropriate that the drumming links Rahul with ordinary folk, for it is his affinity with the common people that eventually leads to the disruption of the Raichand family, when Rahul marries Anjali against the demands of his adoptive father. Moreover, this link reinforces our sense that the union of Rahul and Anjali is right, whatever Yash might claim. Indeed, in rejecting Rahul's marriage to Anjali, Yash specifically invokes a discrepancy in "tradition" between the two families. Patterns such as the one we have been considering serve to undermine Yash's claims implicitly. The two families do have distinct traditions. But this only supports Rahul's choice.

From what I have been saying, it may seem that Johar is celebrating indigenous culture and criticizing westernization. But that is not the case. Rather, the themes of the film are much closer to the standard romantic affirmation of individual choice. Indeed, Johar seems to respect all ways of being Indian—whether one is a folk-dancing Indian or an American-pop-music-imitating Indian—as long as they are not authoritarian. This becomes clear only later in the film. But there is a suggestion in this interlude that Johar is not making a simple traditionalist movie. Specifically, toward the end of the interlude, Anjali rushes to carry sweets from Chandni Chowk, in downtown Delhi, to the Raichands' estate. This brings the two worlds together physically. The significance of this joining begins to emerge when one keeps in mind that Anjali's jog from Chandni Chowk to the mansion makes no geographical sense. The radical reduction of physical distance in the conclusion of this interlude metaphorically suggests that the cultural distance between the two groups is not as great as it might initially appear. They are both part of a single space. That one space may be understood as India, or as a global community that has room for Indian folk dance and American pop. The fusing of the two groups is made still clearer by the convergence of the two songs, as both groups culminate their celebration with the enthusiastic cries of "Shava shava."

## Themes, Allusions, and Irony: How to Have Fun with National Anthems

As the preceding discussion already suggests, the complexity of Johar's thematic concerns and his consistent development of two audiences for his film are inseparable from his cultivation of irony. We find touches of irony throughout the film, but it is particularly effective, and thematically consequential, in the interludes. Moreover, it is often bound up with allusion.

Again, in the "Say 'Shava Shava'" interlude, we see both Indian traditional and American pop culture. The end of the interlude suggests that these two apparently opposite tendencies have a great deal in common. Sharing a melody, a physical space, and parallel forms of exuberant dance, perhaps the two communities are fundamentally the same. But, if so, what does Johar intend by making this point? What does the film indicate about that continuity of seemingly disparate cultures?

One recurring concern in the film is the contrast between human relations, on the one hand, and identity categories, on the other. Identity categories are, simply, the set-defining properties that we believe are essential to our sense of self, properties that place us in groups we see as defining us in some fundamental way. All of us have countless properties. However, we feel that some of those properties are basic and necessary, that they indicate "who we are." These categories most often include race, ethnicity, religion, and class. In keeping with the usual principles of romantic tragi-comedy, Johar implicitly criticizes the invocation of identity categories in any way that inhibits the freedom of human relations.

The crux of the entire plot is the father's rejection of his son's choice in marriage. This rejection is inseparable from the assertion of identity categories. Yash objects to the marriage of Rahul and Anjali on the grounds that she cannot share their "paramparā," their tradition—a concept that, in this case, includes not only religious beliefs, but a network of ideas and practices bound up with class standing. The objection is fundamentally that Anjali is not "one of us," a member of our group.

Even without the musical interludes, any viewer of the film would recognize that Yash's objection to the marriage is wrong from the perspective of the filmmaker. However, one might take this to be a particular criticism of a single, mistaken invocation of identity categories. In fact, the film implicitly sets out a general critique of identity categorization. This critique is brought out almost entirely by the use of music. One noteworthy instance of this occurs when Anjali's nationalism inhibits her own relations with English people. Living in England, she has assumed the xenophobic nationalism that sometimes flourishes among emigrants who are nostalgic for their old home and angry at the racism they encounter in their new home. Her assertion of a limited national identity category is challenged when her son's grammar school class, full of little white children, sings the Indian national anthem. Indeed, this event is doubly relevant, for the anthem—written by India's most famous universalist, Rabindranath Tagore—celebrates the unity of diverse groups.

Perhaps the most striking instance of Johar's critique occurs in the song and dance interlude that marks Rohan's arrival in London. Before going, Rohan has to speak with his father about the trip. When his father asks why it was necessary for him to leave India for Europe, Rohan explains, simply, "Paramparā, Dad. Paramparā." The response is both suggestive and ironic in a number of ways. First, the idea that going to England is traditional seems absurd, especially in light of the ancient Hindu prohibition on crossing the sea (see, for example, the two-thousand-year-old *Laws of Manu* 3.158 [Doniger and Smith]). Nonetheless, this is, precisely, the family tradition. The point suggests, once again, that the practices of the Raichand family are far from "traditional" in any usual sense. On the other hand, we know that Rohan is traveling to England in order to reunite father and son—a truly traditional and familial act. Complicating the dhvani of the statement still further, we remember that Yash's earlier invocation of paramparā is what caused the familial separation initially. Finally, the very phrasing, which combines the English *Dad* with the Sanskrit *paramparā*, suggests the mixed and global character, not only of the language spoken by the Raichands, but of the culture they practice. Such a combined and international set of practices does not fit well with Yash's narrow assertion of categorial identity.

After the leave-taking scene, we cut to a series of aerial shots of London. These are accompanied by a toe-tapping version of "Vande Mataram." This too is both highly suggestive and highly ironic. In this case, the suggestiveness and the irony are both bound up with the external references of the interlude, which is to say, its allusiveness. The song is based on the tacitly anti-Muslim nationalist poem by Bankimchandra Chatterjee. It appeared in his novel *Anandamath* in connection with a Hindu rebellion against

Muslim rule. The song is sometimes seen as an alternative to Tagore's national anthem and, unsurprisingly, it is particularly championed by Hindu nationalists. Viewers of Satyajit Ray's *The Home and the World* will recall that the phrase—meaning "Hail Mother" or "Hail Motherland"—is chanted by the bigoted and destructive Hindu militants in that film. In short, the poem, the song, and the phrase *Vande Mataram* are bound up with an insular, even communalist nationalism, which is to say, a rigid affirmation of a narrowly defined identity category. Hearing this nationalist mantra sung over a montage of the main sights of London is, for me, laugh-out-loud funny.

But it is not only funny. It is also significant. From the start of the scene, it suggests the absurdity of insular nationalism, for it implicitly hails England as the Motherland, not India. On the other hand, this is not some colonialist paean to the civilizing effects of Europe. As the song continues, we see international shops, shows, and people. There is nothing narrowly English about the London presented in this sequence. For example, we see a group of Indian women dressed as the Indian flag, and another group performing traditional Indian dance. Rohan, in European clothing, joins in. Subsequently, we come across a group of white women, also dressed as the Indian flag, and Rohan dances with a group of European women, just as he danced with the Indians. Through parallels such as these, the interlude insists on the exchangeability of cultures. The point seems to be that the Mother/Motherland is, as Tagore would have it, not India or England, but the world, and that Indians and Europeans can equally choose European or Indian culture as they prefer. The interlude suggests a radical criticism of categorial identity, of valuing one culture over another or of tying one culture to a person as his or her essence.[9]

The irony of this interlude is so sharp that it is surprising the film has not been denounced by the Hindu right. I imagine it has been saved by common presumptions, already mentioned, regarding popular entertainments. It seems to be widely assumed that commercial Indian cinema—at least in its wholesome varieties—could not engage in blatant mockery of something we are all supposed to treat piously. Indeed, this presumption is probably even stronger when it comes to the song and dance interludes, which are commonly understood, even by Indian viewers, as a sort of crazy fun in which nothing really needs to make sense. The presumption gives the filmmaker a surprising degree of latitude in treating controversial themes.

## Feelings and Nothingness

Again, the primary function of the interlude—understood as a form of narrative juncture—is the intensification of emotion. Indeed, this is not only the primary function of the interlude generally. It is also the primary function of the interlude in *Kabhi Khushi Kabhie Gham* . . . Before considering a particular case, however, we need to develop a little further just what constitutes such intensification.

The primary way in which the enhancement of a juncture—through elaboration or formalized marking—affects the reader's or viewer's feeling is, of course, by amplifying a current emotion. Thus the song interlude may serve to deepen our sorrow over something that just happened in the story or intensify our suspense over what is about to happen. On the other hand, in the right circumstances, junctural enhancement may be used for what is apparently the opposite purpose, suspending a current emotion. There is one feature of human emotion that, at times, inhibits the effectiveness of junctural prolongation. That is our tendency to experience habituation. Repeated or continuing exposure to certain sorts of emotion triggers will eventually result in our desensitization to those triggers (see Frijda 318–321). At first, a loud shriek is frightening. However, if it is prolonged or repeated beyond a certain point, it stops being frightening and becomes merely annoying. In order to prevent habituation, an author or filmmaker may interrupt the main emotion. For example, he or she may provide comic relief in the course of a sorrowful story. As this indicates, however, both forms of junctural enhancement function ultimately to intensify our emotional experience. The difference is simply that, in one case, the intensification operates directly by continuing and increasing the predominant emotion. In the other case, the intensification operates indirectly by reducing the likelihood of habituation, with its corresponding loss of emotional force.

Of course, in either case, the song and dance must have emotional effects on the audience. To understand these effects, we need to consider the operation of emotion a bit further. As discussed in Chapter Three, emotions have two sources—innate emotion triggers and emotional memories. The emotional memories are themselves produced by pleasurable or painful experiences. These experiences are associated with particular events or objects that, in turn, come to define new (i.e., non-innate) triggers for the relevant emotions. It is easy to see how this works in the case of, say, fear. Some things (e.g., bared fangs) cause fear innately. Other things (e.g., flower shops, after a painful run-in with soccer hooligans) cause fear through emotional memories. Moreover, it is easy to see how such rasas as the romantic/erotic could be fostered in song interludes by a combination of innate triggers (e.g., Anjali's hip movements in "Suraj Hua Maddham") and emotional memories (e.g., memories of one's own romantic experiences). The same point holds for most of the bhāvas and rasas, such as disgust/the odious, anger/the furious, and so forth. Indeed, with a little thought, it seems relatively easy to account for all the bhāvas and rasas in these terms. There is, I believe, only one exception to this—sorrow.

The problem with sorrow is that it is largely a matter, not of the presence of some trigger, but of its absence. More generally, it is not clear how the preceding account of emotion can explain what might be called "emotions of nothingness," emotions that bear on some lack. It might explain one's horror at seeing a corpse. But how does it explain one's grief months after someone has died? In discussing melodrama, I referred to compassion for the panic of children who are separated from their parents. This works perfectly well in the system we have been discussing, for that compassion is related to specifiable emotion triggers (e.g., a child's sobbing) and to emotional memories (e.g., of being lost as a child). But what the account does not explain is just why the child himself or herself would feel panic in the first place. The problem is that the child's emotion is not caused by something that is happening (e.g., a dog growling and baring its teeth), but by something that is not happening (e.g., Mom coming back from wherever she went).

I cannot give a full account of such emotions of nothingness in the present context. However, I can outline some of the principles that are necessary to treat these emotions within the basic framework outlined in Chapter Three. Specifically, to explain emotions of nothingness, I need to explore two complications in that model of emotion.

First, it is important to recognize that our emotional response to any situation is not limited by immediate sensory experience, on the one hand, and memory, on the other. In fact, it is inseparable from our ongoing imagination of possible outcomes. In other words, we do not simply respond to what is occurring right now. Our response to present conditions is inseparable from our projection of what is about to happen next. The point bears on both our perception and our action, including such actions as where we turn to look, whether or not we tense our muscles (in preparation for flight or attack), and so forth. As Robert Jourdain explains, "The brain perceives by anticipation. . . . Imagery arises from the unfolding of such anticipatory schemes in the absence of actual perceived objects" (163). Moreover, "the brain makes the body move not merely by shouting commands down the corridors of the nervous system, but also by anticipating the sensations that will result from those commands. We project a flux of such anticipations before us in whatever we do, testing them against incoming sensation" (302).

Here is a simple example. Suppose I see a car one hundred yards from me. I will probably not have any emotional reaction. However, suppose I see a car two hundred yards from me, turn away briefly, then turn back and see that it is one hundred yards from me. In this case, I might have a reaction of fear. Clearly, the fear is not due to the car being one hundred yards away. Rather, it is due to my imagination. Based on the relation between the two perceptions, I imagine a third moment when the car is right on top of me. Indeed, my brain calculates the car's trajectory automatically (see van Leeuwen 272). Moreover, when I decide to move out of the way, I simultaneously imagine what will result if I run one way rather than another. For example, I imagine my relation to any cars coming in the opposite direction. My brain also automatically calculates my relation to those cars, and to other objects (e.g., lampposts).

Thus an emotional experience involves a sequence of roughly the following sort. I perceive something. Depending on the nature of the perception, this may to some degree excite innate emotion triggers. For example, an ambiguous motion seen from the corner of my eye may give some activation to triggers associated with rodents, snakes, and so on. This leads to attentional and motor effects. For example, it causes me to turn my head. Simultaneously, the (still ambiguous) information is sent to other systems, including memory. There, it may partially activate memories of similar perceptions. These memories may reinforce the innate triggers (e.g., if they are memories of having seen a snake in some similar location), or they may contradict and thus partially inhibit such triggers (e.g., if the memories involve leaves blowing in the wind). Finally, and also simultaneously, I am continually imagining future events. What I imagine is in part determined by the emotion triggers and the memories. But the causal sequence is not uni-directional. My imagination also sends information back to the innate emotion circuits and episodic memory. For example, emotion triggers and memories may lead me to imagine that the ambiguous motion is made by a snake slithering toward me. But as soon as I imagine this, information about the imagined object and its likely trajectory is sent to the emotion circuits and to memory, leading to further activation of emotion triggers and emotional memories.

To clarify the operation of this imagination, we need to distinguish two sorts of anticipation. One sort involves extended, self-conscious processes of inference. Through these processes, we determine what we believe to be the most likely outcomes of various events or situations. When asked what we believe or expect to happen in a given situation, we respond by describing this sort of anticipation. However, inferences of this kind have only a very limited impact on emotional response. Suppose Jones is afraid of flying. He may *believe* that airplanes are safer than cars. Thus he may self-consciously expect everything to go well on a particular flight. Indeed, he may reasonably be said to *imagine* that the plane will take off, fly, and land smoothly, without incident. Nonetheless, he is afraid of flying, and of this particular flight. The discrepancy between Jones's emotion and Jones's self-conscious inference may be due entirely to emotion triggers and emotional memories. However, it may also be due to a discrepancy between his extended, self-conscious processes of inference and another, unself-conscious sort of imagination.

Specifically, along with long-term, self-conscious inference—what we might call "elaborative imagination"—we continually engage in short-term, spontaneous imagination; we continually produce sensory projections of anticipated experiences and actions. These anticipations are not the result of logical or self-reflectively controlled statistical inference. Again, they do not involve time-consuming, self-conscious reasoning and do not themselves treat long-term sequences. Rather, they are generated spontaneously and swiftly. Moreover, they treat only proximate outcomes. For example, research indicates that there is an actional anticipation preceding movement by .5 to .7 seconds. This is distinct from self-conscious decision, which appears to occur about .2 seconds before the action, when the possibility of inhibition arises (see Walter 248–250). Presumably, sensory projections fall somewhere in the same range. In any case, this sort of imagination does not concern such lengthy events as a plane crash. It concerns, rather, a very temporally constrained set of immediate experiences, both relatively passive experiences and experiences of one's own action.

For example, in particular cases, one element of a fear of flying may be a form of claustrophobia. Claustrophobia is in part a matter of innate triggers. But it is also bound up with one's imagination of action—specifically, escape. When one feels claustrophobic, one feels that one cannot get out of a particular enclosure. This means that one's imagined actions all encounter some obstacle—not an obstacle in the long term, but a direct and concrete obstacle that is imagined as part of a very short sequence of events and actions in the immediate future. In cases such as this, it is short-term, spontaneous imagination—more properly, perceptual and actional projection—that has the crucial emotional effects. My contention is that this is true generally. Thus, even when long-term, self-conscious imagination appears to have emotional consequences, these consequences too are the result of perceptual and actional projections that occur as part of longer-term imaginations.

One crucial point about perceptual and actional projection is that not all components of such projection draw attentional focus. For this reason, and due to the brevity of projection, emotionally consequential images that arise in projection need not be recognized as such and incorporated into long-term memory. Indeed, it seems likely that we become self-consciously aware of only a tiny fraction of what we produce in perceptual and actional projection. As Boyer explains, "That we have precise expectations is not something we are aware of. It is made manifest only when some aspect of physical reality around us violates the principles" (98–99). Suppose I pick up a glass of orange juice and take a sip, then recoil. Someone asks, "Does it taste bad?" I respond, "No, I just didn't expect it to be hot." The implication is that I expected it to be cold. But I did not ever think, "This is orange juice, so it will be cold." Had it been cold, I would never have become aware that I had such an expectation.

Now we may turn to the second complication in our account of emotions, a complication already suggested by the example of the oncoming car and by the subsequent discussion. A given emotion, such as fear or joy, may be triggered by the properties of a current situation. But it may equally be triggered by a comparison of properties across two situations (or two moments of one situation). Moreover, the relevant situations involve not only objects, but also our own bodily states, including emotional states. In other words, emotion triggers are not simply defined by such object properties as, say, another person's bodily orientation or facial expression. They are equally—perhaps even more importantly—defined by relations across object properties (e.g., changes in someone else's bodily orientation or facial expression) and relations across bodily/emotional experience (e.g., changes in one's degree of sorrow or anxiety). In part, this is a matter of spontaneously imagined outcomes, as when we envision the trajectory of the oncoming car. But it is not only a matter of such imagined outcomes. We are very sensitive to changes in our environment and in our bodies. Certain changes appear to have emotional consequences for us, independent of the outcomes we imagine.

For example, suppose I meet Jones and he is deeply distressed. I am likely to have some empathic response to his sorrow. Now suppose I am at a party celebrating Jones's birthday. In this festive atmosphere, Jones receives a telephone call. He goes from laughing to looking deeply distressed. I am likely to feel somewhat worse for Jones in this case, even though his sadness is the same. In other words, I am likely to respond emotionally not only to Jones's emotional expressions themselves, but to the change in those expressions as well.

For our present purposes, the most important cases of this sort concern our own bodily/emotional experiences, such as our sense of being, say, more frustrated or less fearful from one moment to another. As Antonio Damasio has emphasized, our brains are continually monitoring our bodily condition, and our emotions are inseparable from this continual monitoring (see Damasio xiv). My contention here is simply that one crucial part of this monitoring concerns changes in our emotional states, and that those changes themselves are emotionally consequential. In other words, the very alteration of our feelings is itself a cause of further alterations in our feelings.

This returns us to emotions of nothingness. Emotions of nothingness are generated by the discrepancy between the emotional states derived from expectation (as produced by perceptual projection) and the emotional states derived from subsequent experience. For example, disappointment results from the arousal of positive emotion in anticipation, then the subsequent absence of positive emotion in actual experience. The discrepancy is what triggers the negative feeling. Relief, in contrast, involves the arousal of anxiety (again, through perceptual projection), then the subsequent absence of anxiety. Here, the discrepancy produces positive feeling.

But does this account for all emotions of nothingness, including such apparently complex emotions as grief? I believe it does. Indeed, I would argue that grief operates in much the same way as relief or disappointment. Grief appears to be an enduring state. However, it seems more likely that it is a ongoing series of relatively short grief episodes. This is in keeping with Greg Smith's persuasive account of emotion as much more punctual than we commonly imagine (see *Film,* 37). These relatively short episodes of grief, like the experience of disappointment, are produced by the shift in emotion caused by expectation, itself produced by perceptual and actional projection. The point may be illustrated by a brief anecdote. Many years ago, not long after my grandmother died, I came upon my mother weeping piteously. She explained that she had read something that she wanted to tell my grandmother, had gone to the telephone and dialed half the number before she realized that there would be no one there to answer at the other end. Her grief episode was precipitated in an obvious way by the discrepancy between her expectation and her subsequent experience—in this case, an experience produced by the activation of a memory (that her mother had died). Her extended mourning was, by this account, a matter of the repeated occurrence of such episodes, along with such factors as the priming of sorrowful memories and other forms of mood-congruent processing (which tend to produce a more mildly, but more continuously, sorrowful state).

This anecdote also suggests the importance of a particular variable in the triggering of certain emotions, especially emotions of nothingness—the gradient of emotional change. In general, the intensity of an emotion is increased as the gradient of change from one bodily/emotional state to another is increased (on the intensification of emotion by contrast and by a steep gradient of change, see Ochsner and Schacter 177 and 180). The point is a simple one. If my imagination of a particularly dreadful outcome is slowly diminished, I will feel less relief than if it is suddenly and swiftly diminished.

Before returning to *Kabhi Khushi Kabhie Gham . . .*, I would like to remark on two implications of this account for our understanding of human emotional response to art. First, there is a surprising aspect of our response to literature and film that, as far as I am aware, has not been well explained by previous accounts of emotion. Specifically, surprise or the violation of expectations is part of our enjoyment of a narrative. That is why it is considered so important not to learn the endings of certain films (e.g., *The Crying Game*) before we see them. In itself, this does not seem strange. Novelty engages and stimulates us (see LeDoux, *Emotional,* 289 on the neurobiological basis for this). Surprise intensifies emotional response. On the other hand, we may enjoy seeing the same film or reading the same book many times. This too is not inexplicable. We experience many sorts of enjoyment in literature and film. Eliminating surprise may end one type of enjoyment, not all of them. However, what does seem difficult to explain is the fact that we continue to experience tension and excitement when watching films or reading novels, even when we know perfectly well what the outcome will be. There is most often some reduction in that tension and excitement, but the feelings do not disappear, and in many cases their reduction is minimal. The intellectual difficulty here is that our emotional experience of expectation is only partially affected by knowing the outcome of a series of events. One might have thought that the emotional effects of expectation would be entirely undermined by the first reading of a book or the first viewing of a film.

The preceding analysis allows us to explain this apparent anomaly. First, it accounts for the easy part—the reduction of our tension and excitement on a second viewing or reading. However, it does this in a complex way that does not imply a complete elimination of tension. Specifically, according to this analysis, our surprise at the ultimate outcome of a film is in part a matter of our long-term inference or elaborative imagination. That elaborative imagination has emotional consequences *insofar as it involves perceptual projection.* In, for example, *The Crying Game,* most of us simply do not have the actual outcome as an imaginative option the first time we see the film. Thus it is not part of our elaborative imagination of the full trajectory of the plot. Thus it cannot affect our ongoing, perceptual projection of proximate outcomes. When we see the film a second time, however, the ending becomes a salient part of elaborative imagination. Indeed, it is likely to have a fairly constant prominence in that imagination. As such, it is likely to be incorporated into our perceptual projection at various relevant points in the film. Because of this, the emotional effect of the culminating surprise is almost certain to be diminished as the gradient of change from one state (ongoing expectation) to another (actual experience) is almost certain to decrease.

More important, the preceding analysis also accounts for the difficult part. It gives us a way of understanding the continuation of tension and excitement on re-readings or re-viewings. As we are watching a film, the operation of our perceptual projection results primarily from our moment-to-moment experience of the film. That experience is guided only partially by elaborative imagination. In other words, only a small number of our memories from an earlier viewing affect our short-term projections at any time. As a result, a great deal of our ongoing, short-term expectations remain the same or nearly the same when viewing a film a second time. Thus the emotional effects of those expectations will not be undermined by a first viewing. In watching a mystery or a thriller, perhaps I know that the hero will escape a particular attack. Nonetheless, my spontaneous generation of imagined proximate events may be almost entirely isolated from that knowledge. That is important because my experience of narrative tension comes from those spontaneously imagined proximate events. Indeed, given that seeing a film twice changes our encoding of the film, usually increasing our acquisition of information, there will even be cases where the emotional effects are stronger on re-viewing. For example, we may notice dangers to the hero that we missed on the first viewing. Those dangers may make our perceptual projection generate even more fearful proximate outcomes, thus producing greater tension and, ultimately, greater relief, despite the fact that we know the outcome beforehand. In any event, the important point here is that, in each case, perceptual projection is the crucial factor governing our experience of narrative tension and related emotions (such as relief). Such projection is only partially determined by our more encompassing knowledge, including knowledge about actual outcomes.

This account also suggests a way of further clarifying sentimental emotion, in the sense of Tan and Frijda, which is to say, "emotion characterized by an urge to cry or a state of being moved with a strength in excess to the importance we attach to its reason" (49). It seems likely that sentimental responses often derive from a very steep gradient of change from an expected outcome to an actual outcome. The sentimental emotion (e.g., tearful joy) may seem inappropriate to a particular outcome state (e.g., finding out that someone is not injured), since it is triggered, not by the outcome state itself, but by the gradient of change from expectation. This account may also explain the feeling of helplessness that Tan and Frijda argue is crucial to sentiment. Our sense of control over our environment is complex. But certainly one important factor is our feeling that we can predict outcomes of independent events and of our own actions. The steeper the gradient of change between an expected and actual outcome, the greater our sense that we have miscalculated in important ways. The greater our sense that we have miscalculated in important ways, the greater our sense that we are not in control of our environment. Note that this is true even in cases where the actual outcome is significantly better than our projected outcome. Thus, at least in certain contexts, a sharp gradient of change from spontaneous expectation to experience should give rise to the excessive emotion and the sense of helplessness identified by Tan and Frijda.

## Emotion and Anticipation, or Why I Cry Every Time Rahul Marries Anjali

Many of the interludes from *Kabhi Khushi Kabhie Gham . . .* would provide good illustrations of the emotional principles just discussed. I would like to consider one episode that is not precisely a song and dance interlude. However, it is similarly structured and functions in the same way—the marriage of Rahul and Anjali.

Up to this point in the story, the senior Raichand has shown a fondness for Naina, in some ways an excessive fondness. In keeping with his own preferences, he has arranged the marriage of Naina and Rahul. In the scene immediately preceding Rahul's marriage, Rahul discusses his love for Anjali with his father. Yash insists that Rahul cannot marry Anjali due to their family's "ethics" and "tradition." With no discernible logic, he concludes that Rahul has disappointed him and hurt him deeply. A flash to white is followed by a black and white shot of a tearful young boy. We recognize the scene from earlier in the film. It is Rahul, just after he learned that he was adopted. We remember that, immediately after this, Yash embraced the boy and announced that his adoption would never be mentioned again. Henceforth, he would simply be Yash's son. Recalling this episode, Rahul weeps and promises to do whatever his father asks.

The following scene takes place in Chandni Chowk. Since Rahul has just promised his father that he will break off his relations with Anjali, the viewer at this point cannot help but expect the worst. Moreover, since the sound track for the film is typically released before the film, many first-time viewers are aware that one part of the sound track involves Vedic chanting for a wedding ceremony. (Vedic chanting is chanting of Sanskrit verses from the ancient religious texts, the Vedas.) This, of course, suggests that a highly traditional wedding will take place in the film. One cannot help but assume that it will be a marriage approved by the family patriarch as a fulfillment of paramparā, tradition.

As the scene begins, it is raining. This recalls the conclusion of the "Suraj Hua Maddham" scene discussed above. That scene ended with Anjali playfully interacting with Bauji and stealing his umbrella. We are reminded of that moment particularly as Rahul wends his way through a crowd of black umbrellas. When he emerges at the other side, he finds Anjali all in white, the color of mourning. The illness we learned of earlier has now caused Bauji's death. Anjali is predictably devastated. She looks at

Rahul with her swollen, tear-filled eyes. For the viewer, the effect may be enhanced by the contrast with the earlier, playful scene. In a voice-over, we hear Yash speaking of their family's "ethics" and "tradition." The most obvious inference is that, recalling his father's words, Rahul is steeling himself for the difficult task of rejecting Anjali. This outcome, initially operating in both perceptual projection and long-term inference or elaborative imagination, is only enhanced by the mythic and other resonances of the film. For example, Rahul is in some ways paralleled with Rāma. Again, in one of the most notorious passages of the *Rāmāyaṇa,* Rāma rejected his beloved Sītā because his duty to society demanded it. We cannot help but expect the same thing from Rahul. Thus everything points to an intensely melodramatic ending of their relationship as Rahul approaches the grief-stricken girl.

But when he begins to raise his hand, we hear the beginning of a Vedic marriage chant. There is a flash to white, recalling Rahul's memory of learning that he was adopted. But this time, the white screen becomes a wedding ceremony, the marriage of Rahul and Anjali. As long as the chant continues, we flash between the funeral and the wedding.

Personally, I find this scene deeply moving. The suddenness of the change, the dizzying steepness of the gradient from anticipated sorrow to joy at the lovers' union, brings tears to my eyes. It is precisely one of those moments of helpless sentiment discussed by Tan and Frijda. Most important, this happens to me every time I see the film. Admittedly, there has been some decline in the force of this response after repeated viewings. But it has not at all disappeared. This response results, I believe, from my perceptual projection of the scene. Despite my knowledge of the outcome, I continue to imagine the tragic result automatically and implicitly. Specifically, I see Rahul's determined, harsh expression as he approaches Anjali. I also see Anjali's expression. As she looks at Rahul, apprehension mingles with the grief on her face. This is a standard scenario of aggression and fear. The aggression is suggested by Rahul's facial expression and movement. The fear is suggested by Anjali's facial expression and immobility. This is the sort of scenario to which we are highly emotionally sensitive for both innate and experiential reasons. Presented with such a scenario, our minds almost inevitably project from aggression to violence on one side and from fear to pain on the other. When Rahul begins to lift his arm, I spontaneously project the beginning of his aggressive act. More important, I project Anjali's devastated expression, a strong trigger of empathic emotion. But Rahul has barely moved his hand when the Vedic chanting begins. To make a somewhat crude analogy, it is like watching a wild animal move with intense determination toward a frightened, wounded child, only to see the animal lick the child's wound. I am, of course, aware that the chanting will begin. However, that is an awareness removed from the progress of the scene. For the obvious causal reasons, it is not a likely projection from Rahul's approach and lifting of his arm. Moreover, until I wrote this analysis, I was uncertain of the precise point at which the chanting began. Indeed, I consistently misremembered the chant as beginning when Rahul places his hand on Anjali's head. In other words, when I reconstructed the memory of the scene, I, not surprisingly, placed the start of the chanting at the end of Rahul's gesture, rather than in the middle of that gesture. This has undoubtedly affected my response to the scene, for each time I see the film, the chanting begins earlier than I expect. In any event, whatever the precise mechanism, it appears to be the case that my perceptual projection is largely unmodified by the recollection of information from prior viewings. The resulting discrepancy between my perceptual projection and the actual outcome causes my tearful delight when the Vedic chant begins and we see that the lovers are to be united.

But, of course, this does not fully explain my response. My feeling has a particular character. It is a specific sort of joy—the sort that, in Sanskrit aesthetic theory, defines the precise rasa of the scene. It is important to consider the rasa in this case because it is, I believe, somewhat unexpected. Moreover, in its unexpectedness, it suggests a connection between sentimental emotions and emotions bearing on childhood. Indeed, it may indicate that the sense of helplessness isolated by Tan and Frijda is particularly connected with a steep gradient of emotional change that bears on our empathic relation to children.[10]

Specifically, the emotional power of the scene derives, I believe, from the way it mobilizes, not eros, but parent/child affection, vātsalya. However beautiful Anjali may be, our primary relation to her in this scene is the relation to someone who is suffering. Insofar as we are responding to the events of this scene (rather than, say, the physical appearance of the actress), our primary concern at this moment is, in effect, parental. It is the hope that this girl who has been orphaned will not suffer the loss of her lover on the same day. Any viewer with normal human sympathies is likely to feel this way in viewing the scene. One does not need to have studied Sanskrit aesthetics to be moved here. But our experience of the rasa is enhanced, I believe, by a sensitivity to vātsalya. Indeed, the force of the vātsalya is increased by the contrast between this and other scenes. First, we have come to think of the relation between Rahul and Anjali in terms of sexual love, the erotic or romantic rasa (śringāra) that was expressed so strikingly in the "Suraj Hua Maddham" interlude. When Rahul touches Anjali in the funeral scene, this recalls the sexual touch when he slipped the bangles on her arm. But there is nothing sexual in this contact. It is a gesture of comfort and protection. The same point holds when, during a brief glimpse of the wedding, we see Rahul slip a ring on Anjali's finger—an act both very similar to and very different from the slipping on of the bangles. Second, we cannot help but keep in mind the directly preceding scene, for it apparently explains Rahul's current visit to Anjali. In that scene, we witnessed Rahul's vātsalya for his father. But from Yash, we saw nothing but bigotry and selfishness. The flash to white just before the wedding ceremony recalls the flash to white when Rahul remembers learning about his adoption. They are both moments when an orphan has been accepted into a new home, thus moments of comfort in a child's sorrow and abandonment, comfort allowed by a feeling of vātsalya.

Here Johar suggests that Rahul would have been betraying his own familial tradition or paramparā rather than following it had he rejected Anjali. Moreover, the Vedic chant tells us that Rahul's defiance of his father is far more a matter of following broader ethical or dharmic traditions than any filial obedience would have been. Rahul has ethical obligations to this woman, whether we assume that they have consummated their relationship or not. To follow his father's whim would have been unethical in this context—and, Johar suggests, a violation of something fundamental in the traditions that Yash claims to preserve.

The fact that Rahul is accepting an orphan into a new home, thus following both ancient ethical tradition and familial paramparā, is emphasized by the fact that, in the wedding ceremony as we see it, Anjali continues to wear white, the color of mourning. Indeed, this suggests that what we see is not the actual wedding ceremony at all. Rahul and Anjali are, indeed, married. But what we are shown is, like the more standard song and dance interludes, paradiegetic. The white sari is not what Anjali would have worn at her wedding. Nor would a traditional Hindu ceremony be likely to take place so soon after the death of the bride's father. But, by presenting the marriage in this paradiegetic way, Johar has not only communicated important story information through a shift in the discourse. He has also communicated crucial thematic ideas. Perhaps most important, he has intensified the emotional impact of this major narrative juncture—an emotional impact that is, in turn, crucial for the effect of the film's social and ethical themes as well.

CHAPTER FIVE

# Seeing Indian Style

## The Brain and Its Visual Culture

### *Umrao Jaan* and *Fire*

There has been a great deal of cognitive research on vision, much of which is directly consequential for the study of film. I will consider some of the most relevant material in two broad categories. The first concerns figures. The second concerns light, both color and brightness. More exactly, the first section takes up some of the main implications of research concerning figural vision, particularly as this bears on expectation and emotion. This relates most directly to editing, especially those aspects stressed in the continuity editing system. In keeping with this, the second section treats continuity editing in Muzaffar Ali's *Umrao Jaan.* In the third section, I turn more briefly to the research on perception and light, focusing in particular on brightness and boundaries. The chapter concludes with an examination of light intensity, boundary definition, and color in Deepa Mehta's *Fire.*

### Looking Well: Figural Vision in the Cinema

In his important book, *Visual Intelligence: How We Create What We See,* Donald Hoffman abstracts a series of rules that, he argues, govern our cognitive construction of the visual world. Empirical research has demonstrated that there are many rather surprising patterns in the way humans take ambiguous visual information and turn it into the relatively unambiguous visual world we experience. Through careful examination of the relations between objective facts about the visual world and subjective visual experience, Hoffman is able to abstract a set of principles that predict what we will see, given certain visual data. Many of these principles seem banal. For example, his fourth rule is "Interpret elements nearby in an image as nearby in 3D" (32). But they are not banal. There is nothing actually projected onto our retinas that requires this interpretation. Indeed, that is part of the value of such cognitive work as Hoffman's. It takes processes that we might otherwise find too obvious to consider and makes them explicit.

On the other hand, there is something to the view that Hoffman's rules are commonsensical. This is not at all an objection to Hoffman's isolation of these rules. However, it does suggest something that the rules have in common. Hoffman's rules, insofar as they accurately represent the mechanisms of our visual system, are the result of evolutionary developments. As such, they should approximate some function. The function is, obviously, to get the world right. Since visual data are ambiguous, it will not be possible to develop mechanical principles that get the world right all the time, at least not on the first try. This is particularly significant given a second functional constraint. The mechanical rules should get the world right with enough speed that we can act in a way that ensures our survival. To put it differently, there is an evolutionary trade-off between speed and accuracy. We need mechanisms that give us as accurate and complete a representation of the world as possible. And we need mechanisms that do this as quickly as possible. If I can get perfectly accurate and complete information about a predator, but it takes a long time to process, I will be eaten before I can make use of the information. On the other hand, inaccurate or very partial information will not help much even if I get it very swiftly. Finally, since these are mechanisms, not functions, they may err. For this reason, their results should not be rigidly fixed. Rather, they should be open to correction.

Thus we should expect evolution to produce mechanical principles that operate very quickly and that, in most situations—and particularly in reproductively crucial situations—provide extensive and accurate information. At the same time, we should expect these mechanical principles to be flexible enough that they allow for adjustments when we get something wrong. This is, of course, just what happens. Our visual system is very quick, and usually gets things right. On the other hand, sometimes my visual system miscalculates. Sometimes I make a mistake (e.g., I try to thread the needle, but fail). In such cases, I can seek more visual information (e.g. by looking at the needle more closely). Sometimes I might actually change my visual experience. If I first see someone and think he is Smith, then look again and realize he is Jones, I subsequently see him as Jones. My subjective experience of his face changes. In other cases, as with objects in the rear-view mirror (which are always closer than they appear), my visual world continues to be inaccurate no matter what I do, so I have to compensate for the inaccuracy through another cognitive system.

The various mechanisms that allow this combination of accuracy, speed, and flexibility will largely conform to some broader meta-principles. This is because mechanisms cannot be accurate if they do not generally cohere with principles of valid empirical inference. As mechanisms, they are not identical with those principles. However, they must generally operate as if they are instances of those principles. In fact, it turns out that the mechanisms approximate the general principles very closely. This is where we return to the intuition that some of Hoffman's rules are obvious, for one of these meta-principles is the ordinary scientific principle of simplicity. Consider, for example, our construal of rigid motion. If we are shown a number of points moving together rigidly, we will see these as points on a solid object. This is because, given the general operation of the real world, the world in which our visual system developed, the simplest way of accounting for rigidly coordinated movement is by reference to a shared, solid body. If we see several white spots moving rigidly on the other side of some foliage, that may result from the remarkably coordinated movement of several animals, each with one white spot. However, it is much simpler to explain it by reference to a single animal with several white spots. Of course, the visual system does not "know" that a particular construal is simplest. Rather, the visual system developed particular mechanical properties in evolution because they approximate the functions served by simplicity, producing the same inferences in most cases, and doing so more swiftly.

But simplicity alone does not account for Hoffman's rules. This is, again, true for functional reasons. Even perceptual accuracy is not an end in itself. Rather, it is valuable precisely insofar as it facilitates reproduction, first of all through facilitating survival. In this way, I did not put the evolutionary imperative accurately. It is not really crucial that perception should be accurate and complete. As to completeness, it is only crucial that perception give us the information needed for increasing the likelihood of reproduction (e.g., for increasing the likelihood of survival). As to accuracy, the information may be inaccurate, so long as any inaccuracy increases (or at least does not decrease) the likelihood of reproduction. Thus the rules isolated by Hoffman should show a further characteristic. In cases where simplicity is not likely to enhance reproductive success, we may expect a bias toward greater complexity, thus toward a higher likelihood of inaccuracy. For example, in a given case, the simplest construal of a particular visual array may identify it as a stick. However, a slightly less simple construal may identify the array as a snake. If the object really is a stick, it probably does not matter to our survival if we mistakenly see it first as a snake, then correct our initial error. However, if it is a snake, then it obviously does matter to our survival whether we first see it as a snake or as a stick. Thus we expect our visual system—and, indeed, our other sensory systems—to be biased toward complexity in such cases. In other words, we can expect there to be certain systematic deviations from simplicity that are not merely a matter of evolutionary inefficiency, but are, rather, a matter of enhancing reproductive success (e.g., by enhancing the likelihood of survival).

Specifically, in addition to construing the visual array so as to approximate simplicity, our visual system construes the visual array so as to make certain sorts of opportunities and threats particularly salient. Thus we might isolate two meta-principles: 1. Assume the simplest explanation of the data. 2. Highlight possible opportunities for and threats to reproduction (prominently including opportunities for and threats to survival). Though he does not discuss the data in these terms, Hoffman presents research that is very striking with respect to the second meta-principle. For example, blackbird nestlings respond to "two adjacent disks, one having a diameter about a third that of the other" as if they constituted the mother blackbird. However, "if the ratio of their diameters deviates much from one third," then the nestlings do not respond in this way (8). It seems that the nestlings follow one set of principles—presumably principles congruent with simplicity—when responding to most disks. However, they forego simplicity when faced with a visual array that may suggest an opportunity for feeding. Research on chickens and ducks shows that they have little response to "a cross moving in the direction of its long end," but respond with fear to "a cross moving in the direction of its short end," presumably because of its similarity to a hawk (9). For chickens and ducks, then, the possibility of a threat trumps all other interpretations, no matter how simple. (Of course, I am speaking loosely here. The blackbirds, chickens, and ducks are acting out mechanisms. The point is that these mechanisms approximate distinct, functional meta-principles.)

The mention of fear obviously returns us to emotion. This is just what we would expect, for the opportunities and threats to which our visual system is sensitive are identified by precisely the visual features that constitute our emotion triggers. In connection with this, I should like to isolate one particularly important complex of such features, a complex that is crucial for vision and emotion bearing on interpersonal interactions. I am referring to features that express emotions. These include bodily orientations and postures, hand gestures, and other things. Perhaps most consequentially, they include the human face. The face provides us with crucial information about a person's identity, attention, and attitude. Facial information is often critical for assessing another person's likely status as a threat (e.g., an enemy in conflict) or opportunity (e.g., an ally in conflict). For this reason, our visual system is biased against simplicity in the case of data that bear on faces, particularly as those faces express emotions. Indeed, it is biased against simplicity in construing visual information as a face—a fact that is obvious from ordinary experience, where we are likely to see faces in almost anything that has even the vaguest face-like features (e.g., the moon). This sensitivity to faces has a range of consequences. For example, we not only construe and recognize faces with great ease, we also experience congruent or complementary emotions when we see someone's face. Thus we may feel sorrow on seeing someone weep, and fear on seeing someone angry. (The former is a congruent emotion; the latter is a complementary emotion.)

Our various perceptual sensitivities resulting from opportunity/threat bias clearly have significant implications for the study of film. This is true most obviously in shots of emotionally expressive faces. However, these sensitivities may be taken up in more complex and unexpected ways as well.

Mechanisms relating to the other meta-principle of simplicity have important implications for the study of film as well, and particularly for our understanding of emotional response to film. To spell these out, we need to return to the notion of perceptual projection. Again, perceptual projection involves the ongoing, implicit representation of likely proximate sensory outcomes. Our various forms of visual imagination follow the same general principles as visual perception, using the same brain areas. As Gerald Edelman puts it, "mental images arise in a primary-conscious scene largely by the same neural processes by which direct perceptual images arise" (105; see also Kosslyn 295, 301, 325, and Rubin 57 and citations). The mechanisms instantiated in imagination, then, presumably approximate the meta-principles of simplicity and opportunity/threat bias as well. Why is this significant? Among other things, it indicates that, in keeping with simplicity, our perceptual projection is likely to assume a certain sort of perceptual constancy. Specifically, our perceptual projection in effect presumes that things stay the same. If something is moving at a particular velocity, we expect—and concretely imagine—that it will continue to do so. More exactly, we expect continuity relative to our own bodily movements, head movements, and so forth. Discontinuities beyond those entailed by our movement (e.g., our blinking) draw our attentional focus, partially activating relevant emotion systems and, in connection with this, they lead us to look for causes.

Finally, there is a broad division in sensory processing between the recognition of objects and the identification of spatial location. These bear on distinct systems in the brain such that sensory information is processed through two distinct circuits, commonly referred to as the "what pathway" and the "where pathway" (see Ramachandran and Blakeslee 77). Unsurprisingly, we are acutely sensitive to spatial relations. These are important, not only for instrumental action, but for emotion as well. Our emotional responses to people and events are inseparable from our sense of their proximity or distance and changes in that proximity or distance. Here too perceptual projection is crucial. We judge approach or withdrawal to be unexpected when it violates our concrete imagination of where someone will be at a certain point. Since change in proximity is an important variable in our emotional response, it seems clear that a sharp gradient of change from expected to actual proximity will also have strong emotional effects. The point holds no less in film than in real life. Indeed, as Persson has noted, there is even a cinematic equivalent to the distinction between my movement toward (or away from) a person and that person's movement toward (or away from) me. This difference too is consequential for emotional response and thematic inference.

To a certain extent, the principles of continuity editing, as developed in Hollywood, are an attempt to minimize our experience of attention-triggering deviations from our perceptual projection. Before going on, I should explain what I am not saying here. First, I am not saying that anyone in Hollywood, or anywhere else, formulated the purposes of continuity editing in this way. Obviously, they did not. Rather, they recognized that certain film practices have certain effects. They wished to enhance some of these effects and diminish others. My comments about perceptual projection and simplicity, if correct, explain their intuitions. Second, I am not saying that all aspects of continuity editing have this function. I am only saying that many features of continuity editing do. Finally, I am not saying that continuity editing provides the only way of avoiding certain disruptions of perceptual projection. In some cases, I suspect that the continuity editing system does hit on the sole solution to this problem. In other cases, however, continuity editing presents only one possible solution. The crucial point here is that—as authors such as David Bordwell and Noël Carroll have argued—continuity editing is not merely conventional (see Bordwell, "Convention"). Bordwell and Carroll have focused on aspects of standard editing practices that direct attention in a way that is relevant to the purposes of the filmmakers (see Bordwell's *On the History* and Chapter Two of Carroll's *Engaging*). I am emphasizing the other side of this, the function of continuity editing in *not* drawing attention in irrelevant ways, specifically, not drawing attention to discontinuities, thus not triggering a search for explanations of those discontinuities. Given this goal, continuity editing adopts a solution that relies on the nature of our visual system and, related to this, our perceptual projection.

Of course, there is no reason one should adopt the particular purpose of avoiding experiences of discontinuity. Indeed, many filmmakers have self-consciously chosen to defy principles of continuity editing. Muzaffar Ali presents us with one case of that sort. On the other hand, even in Ali's film, the violation of continuity principles is necessarily local. Ali disrupts our ongoing visual expectations at particular points, affecting our emotional response and prodding us to search for reasons for the disruption. But the bulk of the film necessarily conforms to our perceptual projection. Indeed, it is this conformity that allows the particular cases of discontinuity to stand out and have consequences.

In sum, our visual experience of a film is highly complex, but also structured in specifiable ways. That structure includes a propensity to construe current experiences and anticipate proximate outcomes in keeping with simplicity, but simplicity qualified by an emotion-laden sensitivity to opportunities and threats. Any disruptions of anticipation—including those caused by violations of continuity editing—are likely to have emotional effects and to spur attention to causes. Attention to causes is, in turn, likely to foster thematic inference and the reconstrual of story elements. We can see these principles at work, quite strikingly, in Muzaffar Ali's violations of continuity editing in *Umrao Jaan.*

## Continuity Editing and Its Discontents: Expectation in Muzaffar Ali's *Umrao Jaan*

*Umrao Jaan* is one of many Indian films that treat courtesans and their patrons. It also explores aspects of Muslim aristocratic culture in the nineteenth century—another recurring concern in Indian cinema. In connection with this, it develops a story that is not only moving, but that also takes up complex and subtle metaphysical issues from Islamic mysticism. Most important for our purposes, its emotional impact and its thematic development lean very heavily on its distinctive visual style. This style includes great visual beauty, through its attention to color, set design, costuming, and so forth. It also involves editing practices that are, at points, obtrusively unorthodox. Ali not only deviates from the standard practices of continuity editing. He actually flouts those practices, violating them—and thus our ongoing expectations—in salient and sometimes startling ways.

The story begins about 1840 and continues past the 1857 uprising. It concerns a young girl, Umrao, who is kidnapped shortly after her engagement ceremony and sold to the cultivated madam of a prosperous brothel in Lucknow. The education of a courtesan at this time included training in classical music and dance. Umrao becomes not only proficient but renowned in both arts. She also becomes a great poet. There is a Maulvi or learned Muslim teacher who lives in the brothel. He tutors her in poetry and philosophy. Specifically, he helps her to become a master of the ghazal, drawing on the motifs and imagery of the Persian and Urdu literary traditions, their standard, if often implicit narratives of love, and their recondite mystical themes, taken over from Ṣūfism.

Umrao's poetry attracts the young Nawab Sultan to the brothel. On hearing Umrao sing her ghazals and seeing her dance, he is overcome by love. He pursues Umrao and soon becomes the love of her life. The couple encounters a number of obstacles, as one expects in a romantic plot. There is a brief conflict with Nawab Sultan's father, and, less predictably, a murder which prevents him from returning to the brothel. It appears that they are to be united at last when the Nawab explains that he cannot marry her because his mother will not accept her as his bride. There are shorter sequences in which Umrao is united with lost friends, then separated from them as well. There is also a second lover, who tries to take Umrao away from the brothel, but is killed. The film culminates when Umrao is briefly reunited with her mother. She has been driven from Lucknow by the 1857 uprising and is giving a performance in the town where she was born. She senses that her mother is nearby and leaves to meet her. After a brief reunion, Umrao and her mother are separated again, for Umrao's brother enters and drives her out of the home as a disgrace to the family. The film ends as Umrao returns to a house she purchased some time before. She enters a room that has, it seems, not been used in many years. She walks to a mirror at one side of the room. She reaches out and wipes the dust from its glass. We see her face in the clear surface of the mirror. The film ends with a freeze frame of this shot.

Emotionally, the film fosters our identification with Umrao, our desire that she escape her confining life, that she be united with her lover and her mother. Thus we experience her repeated isolation from loved ones—lovers, friends, family—as deeply tragic. At the same time, our response is qualified by Umrao's sense of resignation, communicated by Rekha's fine, understated acting and Ali's use of tight close-ups of her face. Our response to her resignation is twofold. It lessens the tragedy of particular miseries. But, at the same time, it enhances our sense that her entire life is tragic. Her resignation is inseparable from her complete lack of human comfort and trust, her sense of utter isolation. This is related to the thematic concerns of the film as well. Fundamentally, the film treats the cross-cultural theme of false happiness, a theme that points to the ultimate inadequacy of all forms of happiness and our general inability to know just what (if anything) will make us happy. Umrao's disappointments are unusually intense. But they are, in a way, inevitable. She could not be united with her lover, her friends, or her mother "happily ever after." These bonds always end. Like so many literary works, the film suggests something undeniable, that ephemeral things lead only to temporary happiness. But, of course, the film does not treat this theme in a merely general way. It specifies the point, in this case through Ṣūfism.

Ṣūfism is a mystical version of Islam that stresses the longing for union with Allāh. At the same time, Ṣūfism has clear affinities with Vedāntism. Indeed, Ṣūfism was influenced by Vedāntic thought from the outset (see Chaitanya 113–114), and the influence only deepened in India (see Waines

149). More exactly, Ṣūfīs begin with the view that distance from God is pain and falsity. The only truth and the only happiness are to be found in union with God. In developing this idea, some Ṣūfīs advocate a form of monism. Specifically, they take up the fundamental precept of Islam—the unity, singularity, and absoluteness of God. However, they do not interpret this merely as a criticism of polytheism, trinitarianism, and related doctrines. Rather, they extend the idea of this unity, singularity, and absoluteness to the entire universe. In this view, the essence of one's own individual soul is God. Everything else is falsity. As Chaitanya puts it, "Not only is there no god but God, but there is no being but God" (111). True spiritual realization, and thus true bliss, are attained only when one fully realizes one's absolute unity with God. In Chaitanya's words, "The man, whom self-knowledge has enlightened . . . ceases to know himself as a separate individual and sinks into his divine element, like a wave into the sea" (122).

However, unlike Vedāntism, which holds a place of high esteem in Hinduism, Ṣūfism has commonly been seen as unorthodox within Islam. In many cases, it has been stigmatized as heretical and Ṣūfī mystics have been executed for blasphemy (see, for example, Levy 94–95 and Davis 10–13). In this context, it is perhaps unsurprising that Ṣūfism has been closely tied to romantic tragi-comedy. On the other hand, in a cross-cultural context, such a connection is unsurprising anyway. Specifically, there is a cross-cultural pattern in religious devotion whereby the universal narrative prototypes serve as models for a devotee's relation to God.[1] Mysticism often draws on the romantic plot. In the case of Ṣūfism, the connection is most obviously developed in the ghazal tradition. As Russell explains, much ghazal poetry concerns two lovers who are separated by some representative of social authority. Allegorically, the lovers are the Ṣūfī aspirant and God; the representative of social authority is the religious dogmatist who represses Ṣūfism (see Russell 38). But the use of this model is hardly confined to ghazals. Indeed, it is not even confined to literature, for it is found in philosophy and theology as well.

Perhaps most important, Ṣūfism defines a "path" to achieve unity with God, and this path reflects the broad structure of romantic tragi-comedy. As Lichtenstadter explains, for Ṣūfīs, "Love" refers to the "means" for achieving union with God, who is, in turn, characterized as the "Beloved" (83). The romantic emplotment of the Ṣūfī path begins with a recognition that one's only true happiness lies in union with God. This recognition must involve not only an intellectual acknowledgment, but a deep passion for union as well. This passion requires trust in Allāh, what is sometimes called "abandoning every refuge except God" (Abū ʿAbdillāh al-Qurashi al-Junayd, quoted in al-Kalābādhī 92; on the place of this in the Ṣūfī path, see 141–142). Just as the lovers pass through a period of separation in exile and near death (in the prototypical romantic plot), the Ṣūfī mystic passes through a period where everything seems hopeless. At this point, the aspirant is aware of the "abyss" between himself or herself and Allāh and of his or her own "insufficiency" (Waines 142). He or she can emerge from this only through death—not literal death, but death to the self.[2] That is what allows the ultimate, complete extinction of one's personality in God and the culminating bliss of union—a bliss that really does allow one to live "happily ever after."

The romantic emplotment of devotion also leads to recurrent motifs and imagery—particularly "erotic imagery" (Chaitanya 109)—by which Ṣūfīs express this union. As Levy explains, "The Sufi poet . . . was compelled to use his experience of passionate emotions" in representing spiritual devotion. As a result, "Sufi symbolism turns about the pivotal points of Love, Wine, and Beauty," giving a "hint of union with the Divine." Specifically, "Love is the intoxication of the Wine of Unity and is an intimation of the Divine" (96). Moreover, as Davis points out, this love is commonly "love that flies in the face of either social or sexual or religious convention" (19). Thus it incorporates the conflict with social norms that is a standard feature of the romantic plot. Again, in this case, that conflict is bound up with the orthodox evaluation of Ṣūfism as heretical. Finally, one of the most prominent Ṣūfī images is that of seeing the face of God, the Beloved. There is considerable emphasis on the face in Ṣūfī writing, a point with obvious relevance for film. One implication of monistic Ṣūfism is that the face one sees is ultimately one's own, for, as al-Kalābādhī puts it, "The seeker is in reality the sought, and the Sought the Seeker" (al-Kalābādhī 141). Unsurprisingly, this leads to the use of mirror imagery in connection with ultimate spiritual realization.

Though Ṣūfism focuses on romantic separation and reunion, it draws models from friendship and parent/child relations as well. These aspects of devotion are more fully elaborated within the Hindu tradition of "bhakti" or devotion. But in India, the two traditions developed together and influenced each other. Bhaktas (or devotees) took up emotional commitment to a deity—not worship per se, but love—as the primary means of achieving spiritual realization. This love was understood in terms of Indian theories of emotion or bhāva. In keeping with the principles of rasa theory, writers on bhakti treated romantic love and vātsalya as important models for bhakti. They added to this sakhyabhāva or the emotion of friendship, which had only an ancillary place in rasa theory. *Umrao Jaan* is primarily a Muslim, and specifically Ṣūfī, work. At the same time, like Indian Ṣūfism generally, it is not insulated from the bhakti tradition. Thus it includes not only the romantic model for divine love, but the models of vātsalya and friendship as well.

As the preceding discussion suggests, there are two ways in which Ṣūfism commonly enters into literature, prominently including the ghazal tradition. These are also the ways it enters into Ali's film. First, as already indicated, a romantic plot often serves as an allegory for the Ṣūfī path. A story about the separation and reunion of lovers suggests a parallel story about the soul's separation from and reunion with God. As just noted, this allegory may be extended to the separation of friends or family members also, as we find in *Umrao Jaan*. The second way in which Ṣūfism commonly enters literature is through the false happiness theme. Tragic plots in particular indicate that the separation of lovers or family members is inevitable, and thus even the most intimate and fulfilling human bonds can never be a source of true happiness. Frequently, the two methods of incorporation are combined. The romance of the lovers suggests the longing of the soul for union with God. Indeed, it is part of that longing for ultimate union. The desire of the lovers is, in a sense, a limited form of the desire for union with all souls in God. However, while the longing of the lovers is a partial realization of the true longing of the soul for God, it is a partially false longing as well, longing based on error—thus longing that leads inevitably to loss, even despair. Still, not everything is bleak in this version. A sense of desolation is, after all, a necessary stage in the Ṣūfī path. In consequence, the error of the lovers is not, ultimately, a bad thing. It is an error that may in fact be necessary for insight.

*Umrao Jaan* develops these thematic ideas implicitly, but clearly. The presence of the Maulvi and the unmistakable allusions to Ṣūfī thought in Umrao's poems provide a context for interpreting the events of the story in relation to spiritual aspirations. Specifically, Umrao moves through a series of separations, partial reunions, then final separations that recall the Ṣūfī path allegorically, but that are also inadequate to that path and leave her, in the end, in desolation and nothingness. Perhaps most obviously, there is the story of her love for Nawab Sultan, a standard romantic tragedy that leads to separation. There are also the initial separations from her two friends, her reunions with them, and her final separations from them. The more important of these is intertwined with the romantic plot. It concerns a girl with whom Umrao was kidnapped. When they meet again, Umrao learns that this girl is now married to Nawab Sultan. Clearly, there is no future for their friendship, just as there is no future for Umrao's relation with Sultan. Finally, there is the encompassing love of her entire life, the love of the mother from whom she was stolen as a young girl. The hope for reunion with this woman has driven Umrao from the time when she was first kidnapped and sold into prostitution. In a way, her strivings to be united with her friends or even her lover are only variations on this unresolved attachment to her mother. In a Ṣūfī context, that unresolved attachment to her mother is itself only an unwitting manifestation of the universal and encompassing passion for union with the true Beloved, God. This divine connection ennobles all Umrao's mundane loves. But at the same time, it entails that they are inadequate to the ultimate, encompassing passion. To put it differently, earthly loves are a part of divine love, but a part that has been misunderstood, and thus a part that will lead inexorably to the suffering of isolation, rather than the bliss of union. The film ends when Umrao's foundational, mundane passion—the love of her mother—is rendered hopeless and she is left with nothing, except her own image in the mirror from which she has wiped away the dust.

For our purposes, what is most important about the film is the way that Ali uses visual style, primarily editing, to enhance the emotional impact of the film and to develop its themes. This is largely a matter of Ali's violations of continuity editing principles. In order to analyze these violations, we need to begin by distinguishing different aspects of continuity editing.

The first aspect we need to consider in effect reduces to simplicity considerations. As discussed in the preceding section, our perceptual systems tend to follow rules that approximate simplicity evaluations. Other cognitive systems are similar. One aspect of this is that we assume continuity of most states unless we have reason to believe otherwise. If I look over at the corner of the room, turn briefly, then look back, I assume that the corner will be much the same both times I look at it. If there is no one standing in the corner the first time, I expect no one to be standing in the corner the second time—unless I hear footsteps moving in that direction or otherwise have a positive reason to expect a change. Obviously some cases of perceptual projection are still more strict than this, more difficult to alter. For example, suppose I look at Smith, then blink. When I first see him, he has gray hair. I expect him to have the same color hair when I open my eyes after blinking. Many aspects of continuity editing merely accord with these sorts of perceptual projections or spontaneous simplicity expectations.

Consider, for example, the jump cut, in which there is a very limited discontinuity that we experience as a jump from one point to another. Suppose we have a medium close-up of a man putting on a hat. He lifts the hat up and places it on his head. We have a jump cut if we delete some portion of the man's action or if we slightly shift the position of the camera. For example, if we cut from the man lifting the hat just above his waist to putting the hat on his head, we have a jump cut. We may refer to this as a jump cut on action. Similarly, we have a jump cut if we cut from one camera position to, say, a camera position a foot or so to one side. We may refer to this as a jump cut on perspective. What is peculiar about the jump cut is that the movement that is deleted (e.g., dollying the camera to the left) has to be very limited for us to feel that there is a jump. If the first shot is a man lifting his hat and the second is the man going outside (with the hat on), we do not perceive this as a jump, even though the discontinuity is much greater.

This seems at first to be a mere matter of training. We are accustomed to the cut from a man lifting his hat to the same man going out the door. We are not accustomed to the cut from a man lifting a hat to the same man placing the hat on his head. However, I do not believe that this is a matter of training. Rather, it is a matter of how our perceptual and related cognitive systems construe events. When I see a man begin to lift a hat toward his head, I spontaneously imagine his arm moving through space up to his head. When part of this is cut, there is a direct contradiction between my expectation and my experience. The contradiction is a result of my identifying the experienced event and the perceptually projected event as following the same proximate sequence—as being, in other words, the same event. In other words, I change my attention all the time. I am listening to a piece of music when the telephone rings. I do not hear the telephone as a bizarre musical development. I hear it as a distinct event, unrelated to the music. My ongoing expectations about the music are suddenly interrupted. However, they are not violated in the way they would be if the music took an unexpected turn (e.g., if it shifted in style or genre). Similarly, with big enough differences between shots, we do not see the change as part of the same proximate event. In encoding, we do not segment and structure the entire sequence as one event. Thus we do not apply our ongoing expectations. The disconcerting effect of jump cuts appears to result from the fact that we encode what precedes and what follows a jump cut as parts of a single structure. The difference between the two shots is too slight to alter this encoding and thus make us discard our ongoing projection of outcomes. However, it is large enough that it is salient.[3]

Another set of principles in continuity editing—the ones that are most often discussed by film theorists—serve in effect to create expectations, or perhaps more accurately to narrow expectations. These principles are usually not entirely arbitrary. However, they do not result directly from our perceptual capacities and ordinary perceptual projections. Indeed, to some degree, they operate to retrain our perceptual projection through repetition across films. Take the standard shot/reverse shot sequence. Jones and Smith are speaking. When Jones speaks, we have a three-quarters face shot of Jones, taken from over Smith's shoulder. When Smith speaks, we shift to the parallel shot of Smith from over Jones's shoulder. David Bordwell has argued cogently that there are important perceptual and cognitive reasons for this configuration. For example, as Bordwell explains, there is "some experimental evidence that for human faces in pictures, the three-quarter view may be more easily recognized than other orientations" ("Convention," 98). In addition, we almost certainly expect to see the person who is speaking. We almost certainly project our own action of turning toward the speaker. However, Bordwell has also pointed out that shot/reverse shot is not simply naturalistic in that it does not mimic what an observer would see if he or she were watching the conversation. (An observer would probably stand to the side and between the speakers, swiveling his or her head back and forth as they speak.) We may infer from this that our ongoing imagination of dialogue shots has to be trained by watching films. Note that this is different from saying that we have to be trained to infer what is going on. We probably have no difficulty understanding the dialogue situation the first time we see shot/reverse shot. But it seems unlikely that we expect it initially. In other words, it seems unlikely that we spontaneously imagine it in perceptual projection. This changes as we see more films and come to expect dialogues in the canonical shot/reverse shot mode.[4]

Since continuity editing often mimics our naturally spontaneous expectations or trains our expectations through repeated exposure, violations of continuity editing will often violate our expectations as well. These violations may be of various sorts. I would like to isolate two—violations that do not create a sense of some anomaly in the story world, and violations that do create such a sense.

The first, more common, sort of violation primarily affects trained expectations as well as untrained expectations bearing on our own movement (e.g., turning our head or shifting our visual focus). One might equally say that these bear on formal expectations, expectations having to do with editing itself, rather than with the story. Violations of this sort serve primarily to intensify our emotional response, though they may also have narrative or thematic consequences. We find numerous cases of this sort in *Umrao Jaan,* particularly in connection with shot/reverse shot. Thus we find that Ali will sometimes shoot Nawab Sultan in the canonical three-quarters face shot over Umrao's shoulder, but then cut to a tight close-up of Umrao facing directly into the camera. The effect is generally one of fostering intensified empathy with Umrao. This is particularly striking when Umrao's expression betrays great sorrow. In this case, the result is due not only to the violation of expectation, but to the precise nature of that violation. First, it involves a human face, which is almost always an emotion trigger (see, for example, Adolphs and Damasio 196). Second, relative to our expectation, it involves greater proximity to the object of our feeling (here, Umrao as the object of our compassion), which is almost always an intensifier of emotion. Finally, Umrao's relative immobility during these shots fosters the sense that we are entering her space unexpectedly, rather than the reverse (to use Persson's useful distinction). This imitates the standard actional outcome of "approach" emotions, such as sexual desire, affection, and compassion. A peculiar thing about emotion is that the activation of any distinctive part of an emotion circuit tends to activate other parts as well. For example, smiling is, first of all, an expressive outcome of happiness. But, if we smile even without any reason, it tends to make us somewhat happier (see, for example, Damasio, *Descartes',* 148–149 and Plantinga, "Scene," 242–243 and citations). In this case, the feeling that we have approached Umrao helps to activate approach emotions, thus intensifying those that are already activated by other aspects of the film.

Violations of the second sort (i.e., violations that create a sense of anomaly in the story world) operate primarily on our untrained expectations regarding object identities and event trajectories. Specifically, there are certain sorts of deviation from expectations that lead us to question just what is going on in the story world. In other words, they violate not only our perceptual expectations, but our understanding of the way the world operates. They produce a sense of contradiction in our ongoing construction of the world. As usual, this leads us to seek an explanation for the contradiction. The most obvious cases of this sort involve the supernatural. A man suddenly turns into a wolf. Our initial expectation (that he will keep being a man) leads us to posit a causal explanation (that he is a werewolf) and to re-imagine the story world accordingly. Ali also uses techniques of this sort, but not in a supernatural way. In other words, his use of these techniques gives rise to anomalies that are not easy to accommodate in a revised imagination of the story world (e.g., through the addition of werewolves). For example, in one sequence, he cuts from a shot of Umrao dancing and weeping to a shot of her continuing the dance, but with a dry face (see Figures 5.1 and 5.2). The continuation of both the song and the precise motion of the dance suggest that no time has passed between the first shot and the second. Nonetheless, Umrao's face is wet with tears in the first shot and dry in the second. This creates a sense of anomaly, a sense that something is not right in our understanding of the story world. However, there is no obvious way of adjusting our understanding of the story world in order reconcile this contradiction.

Such narrative anomalies certainly have emotional consequences. However, their main function tends to be thematic. Unable to accommodate the anomaly in a coherent narrative structure, we try to understand it in relation to the extra-narrative purposes of the work. In the case of *Umrao Jaan,* the relevant theme is a variation on the Ṣūfī view that everything that is separate from Allāh is false. The anomalies of the story world—especially the anomalies that bear on happiness and sorrow—cannot be real. They are the stuff of dreams. But at the same time, they are part of the material world. In consequence, that world too must be the stuff of dreams.

Jump cuts are somewhere between these two sorts of violation. In one way, they are a formal matter. However, we find them obtrusive because they bear on the way we perceive and understand object identity. Thus they do not face us with an anomaly in the story world. But they are also not simply a violation of trained expectations or a constraint on our projected movement. Rather, they often give us a sense of uncertainty about our own observation of the scene. They are in a sense anomalous with respect to our place as observers.

*5.1. Umrao with tear-filled eyes and tracks of a tear from each eye to the sides of her chin . . .*

*5.2. . . . then Umrao with dry eyes and a dry face, though the scene is apparently continuous.*

Ali uses jump cuts with some frequency as well. For example, in one scene, he begins with a centered, middle distance shot of Khanum, Umrao, and other women in the brothel. He cuts from this to a shot of the same group, continuing the same actions with only the small difference that the camera has now moved slightly off center and slightly closer. Jump cuts may be taken up for narrative or emotional ends—perhaps including the widely discussed emotional effect of creating distance or alienation from the feelings of the characters or the scene. However, in Ali's case, their primary function appears to be thematic. Ali uses jump cuts in the way just discussed—to create some degree of uncertainty in the viewer regarding his or her own position in relation to the story world. However, Ali's use of this technique is not merely general. It is culturally embedded. Specifically, his jump cuts—particularly his jump cuts on perspective—have precisely the function of a Ṣūfī lesson. One crucial aspect of Ṣūfī teaching is that the aspirant should never become settled into a particular doctrine or a set of certainties. The Ṣūfī teacher must continually challenge the aspirant's beliefs and attitudes. Indeed, Ṣūfī writing routinely involves sequences of mutually contradictory ideas or representations. For example, referring to Attar's great Ṣūfī poem, *Conference of the Birds,* Davis writes that "logic is often deliberately flouted so that we are, as it were, teased or goaded—rather than logically led—into understanding" (17). Specifically, "just as the reader has worked out" what means what in the poem, "he will find that he has to change his mind or suspend judgement" (18). This is not sloppiness. It is a self-conscious effort to continually disrupt settled convictions that will prevent spiritual realization. In other words, the Ṣūfī teacher must repeatedly shift the aspirant's perspective, so that he or she does not get stuck at a preliminary stage on the way to realization. Jump cuts in Ali—particularly those involving a literal change in perspective—often have the same function.

The film begins with the engagement ceremony of the young Umrao, intercut with the titles. Here, Ali already introduces some violations of standard cinematic practices. For example, one of the women in the ceremony stares directly into the camera (Figure 5.3), which can make the viewer self-conscious about the unreality of this apparently real scene—an idea that, in a Ṣūfī context, may be carried over to the world outside the

*5.3. An observer at the wedding—centered in the frame and in sharp focus—looks directly at the camera.*

*5.4. Umrao is facing forward . . .*

*5.5. . . . but a jump cut on action shows her facing left immediately after.*

film as well. More important for our purposes, there is a jump cut on action which has a similar effect. Umrao is facing forward, then there is a cut to her facing left (Figures 5.4, 5.5), but the camera position is the same and the song is continuous, suggesting that there has not been any passage of time.

Subsequently, Umrao is kidnapped from her home in Faizabad and taken to Lucknow to be sold into a brothel. Her mother weeps and cries out to Allāh. Just after we hear her mother crying "Allāh," Ali cuts to Lucknow, where the muezzin is calling out "Allāh." While Ali often goes out of his way to create discontinuity within scenes, he also employs techniques such as this to create continuity across scenes. Together, these discontinuities and continuities have the effect of working against our expectations of

*5.6. Young Umrao, Khanum, and others from one perspective . . .*

*5.7. . . . then the perspective shifts, though the scene is otherwise continuous.*

both sameness and difference. This is just what one would expect from a film that takes up the teachings of Ṣūfism, according to which all the world is simultaneously false diversity and ultimate, unified truth. In this case, the connection is particularly apt as the one reality is Allāh, and "Allāh" is precisely what is repeated across the two scenes, drawing together Umrao's home and her place of exile.

In the first scene at the brothel there is a very disconcerting jump cut on perspective. This is the scene I described earlier. Khanum (the madam), Umrao, and the others are all seated together. Khanum is speaking. In the middle of Khanum's sentence, there is a cut and the camera position shifts slightly but noticeably to the left and slightly closer to the group (see Figures 5.6 and 5.7). It is as if the viewer has changed position without moving through the intervening space. In the context of the film as a whole, this shift suggests the instability and even unreality of our perspective on the world.

Soon after this, Umrao begins her singing lessons. The first lesson starts by invoking Allāh, but the first song is a Hindu devotional piece, suggesting the Ṣūfī synthesis of Hindu and Muslim traditions. Moreover, this song particularly stresses the importance of romantic love in bhakti or devotion. It culminates in the sexual play of the devotee with the god, Kṛṣṇa. Ali particularly stresses Kṛṣṇa's flute playing in this context—a point that has important resonances later in the film.

As the song proceeds, there is a series of cuts. In the middle of the sequence, one cut moves us from the child Umrao to the adult Umrao. The continuity of the song is most obviously interpreted as suggesting the repetition of practice over many years. However, in relation to the Ṣūfī themes and Ali's play with continuity and discontinuity elsewhere in the film, it also suggests the unreality of the passage of time. A peculiar aspect of the shot with the adult Umrao is that the teacher is not visibly older. He is not wearing his hat, and this reveals some gray hair on top. But the hair on the sides of his head appears to be less gray than it was in the preceding shots.

There is a remarkable shot later in the sequence that confirms this play with the viewer's sense of time and reality. The adult Umrao is dancing in the foreground. In the background to our left we see the singing teacher. The center and right background are simply a wall (Figure 5.8). We cut in to a shot of Umrao in the right foreground and the teacher in the left background (Figure 5.9). Our attention is drawn primarily to Umrao, who continues to make the facial and hand gestures of the dance. However, Umrao is out of focus, and there is a sharp focus on the teacher. This effect is disorienting for, as with so much else in the film, it works against our expectations—in this case regarding our own action of visual focus—and our related spontaneous interests. Indeed, it works against the interests created by the shot itself, which encourages us to focus on Umrao, even while keeping her out of focus. At the same time, there is a way in which the slight blurriness of Umrao's image fosters a sense of intimacy, a feeling that she is too close to focus on. As Umrao continues the dance, the camera pans right and moves back to reveal Khanum, seated against the wall, with bolsters, and so forth (Figure 5.10). There is no suggestion that she has just entered hurriedly. It is as if she has been there the entire time.

*5.8. Umrao dances with no audience . . .*

*5.9. . . . as the dance continues, the visual focus of the scene violates the viewer's focal concern with Umrao . . .*

*5.10. . . . and finally the camera reveals an audience that had not been there previously.*

Alternatively, it is as if there has been a change in time and this is a subsequent performance. But neither interpretation is entirely consistent with what we have just seen and heard. The space was empty when the camera dollied in initially, and, though there has been a cut, the costumes, action, and music have been perfectly continuous.

If it was not clear before, Ali's play with our sense of what is real and what is not becomes unmistakable in this scene. Of course, at this point, watching the film for the first time, we do not know just what the significance of that play may be. There is some conflict in the presentation of time, of possibility and reality, of subjective experience and the objective world, but for all we know Ali could be leading us to postmodernism. The next scene clarifies just how we are to think about these disruptions thematically. Right after the dance, Ali cuts to Umrao receiving her first lesson in poetry and Ṣūfism from the Maulvi. He explains that the ultimate goal of Ṣūfism is a "mindless" state of absolute union, a state in which there is no distinction between self and other. This scene also prepares us to interpret the subsequent romantic narrative in Ṣūfī terms, as the Maulvi stresses the importance of love for both motivating and achieving this union.

The second scene with the Maulvi, not long after this, includes one of the most affecting sequences of shot/reverse shot editing in the film. In this sequence, Ali continually disrupts our expectations. First, he sets up a dissymmetry between the shots of the Maulvi and those of Umrao. The former are canonical three-quarter face shots from a position next to Umrao. But when Ali cuts to Umrao, it is a tight close-up, what might be called an "intimate reaction shot" (see Figures 5.11 and 5.12). The effect is to make us share Umrao's feelings in the scene all the more intensely. A second type of disruption occurs when Ali does not consistently pair visuals with dialogue, so that sometimes we see Umrao's face when the Maulvi is speaking. This too fosters our empathy with Umrao, as our focus of attention is as much on her reaction as it is on the Maulvi's words. Finally, just as we are coming to expect an alternation between canonical shots of the Maulvi and intimate reaction shots of Umrao, Ali changes things yet again, giving us a two shot of Umrao and a third character, Gohar Mirza, who is seated behind her (Figure 5.13). Moreover, the focus is on Gohar Mirza, with Umrao, out of focus, in the foreground—recalling the earlier shot with the singing teacher.

The subsequent dance sequence employs jump cuts on action as Ali cuts from one hand gesture to the next, deleting the intervening motion (see

*5.11. A canonical shot of the Maulvi leads the viewer to expect a canonical reverse shot . . .*

*5.12. . . . however, we are given an intimate reaction shot, which changes our expectations . . .*

*5.13. . . . which are in turn violated when a two shot with unexpected focus replaces the expected intimate reaction shot.*

Figures 5.14–5.18). Since song and dance sequences sometimes do violate continuity editing, this would be unremarkable on its own. However, in context, it furthers the Ṣūfī themes suggested earlier in the film. It also intensifies our emotional response as the hand gestures are partial emotion triggers (due to their relation to innate features of emotional expression and, for some viewers, due to emotional memories of their use in dance and elsewhere).

One might wonder at this point if Ali's visual style will produce its own habituation. That is, in fact, a danger. It could easily happen that we come to expect, say, dissymmetrical shot/reverse shot sequences, so that they lose their emotional impact and their force in inspiring thematic reflection. However, Ali does routinely return to the practices of continuity editing. For example, Nawab Saheb is introduced and has a conversation with Khanum. This is done entirely in canonical shot/reverse shot form. Moreover, Ali's disruptions of our expectations are not always the same.

Umrao's first meeting with Nawab Sultan is particularly remarkable in this regard. Just before the meeting, we have a brilliant sequence presenting Umrao before her dressing table. The sequence begins with two shots of Umrao's face in mirrors. In the first, we see the frame of the mirror (Figure 5.19). But, in the second, we must infer that it is a mirror image, noting that her jewelry is not reversed with respect to the first mirror image (Figure 5.20). In keeping with the Ṣūfī themes, the self simultaneously faces us everywhere and is difficult to recognize in its true form. As Nawab Sultan is about to enter, we see Umrao's face in the two mirrors simultaneously (Figure 5.21). The effect is not only beautiful in its symmetry and visual patterning; it is also thematically suggestive. In meeting Sultan, one might infer, Umrao is in some sense doubling herself. This makes thematic sense insofar as we understand their romance as an allegorical depiction of the spiritual aspirant's relation with God, or as a partially misunderstood instance of that relation. Their initial dialogue is shot in more or less canonical shot/reverse shot format—except that there is almost no coordination between who is speaking and who is photographed.

The visuals become still more complex as the scene continues. At one point, we learn that Sultan is from Faizabad. This serves to link Sultan with Umrao's lost family and facilitates our assimilation of her longing for Sultan to her longing for her family. This assimilation fits with the Ṣūfī themes of the film as Ṣūfism ultimately brings together all forms of longing for union by linking them to longing for union with Allāh. What

*5.14. Gestures . . .*

*5.15. . . . in Umrao's dance . . .*

*5.16. . . . are shown only . . .*

*5.17. . . . in their culminating forms . . .*

*5.18. . . . with the transitions deleted.*

is stylistically noteworthy here is that, as soon as we learn that Sultan is from Faizabad, the camera cuts in much closer to both Sultan and Umrao. Ali continues with the shot/reverse shot sequence, but he now alternates close-ups of the two speakers. The effect is obviously to enhance our sense of intimacy with the lovers. But this enhanced intimacy does not bear on our relation to the two lovers equally. It is based on, and itself extends, our identification with Umrao, not Sultan. Umrao never tells Sultan that she is from Faizabad. Thus the information about Sultan's origins can only affect their intimacy from Umrao's point of view, not from Sultan's. In coming closer to the couple, our increased emotion repeats that of Umrao.

From this point, a remarkable sequence begins. My suspicion is that many viewers will take the sequence to be continuous, even though there is some suggestion that a great deal of time passes. Specifically, we have a number of shots of the lovers that are easy to view as continuations of the

*5.19. Umrao in the first mirror, with a visible frame.*

*5.20. Umrao in the second mirror, with no visible frame.*

*5.21. Umrao in both mirrors.*

*5.22. Umrao and Sultan . . .*

*5.23. . . . then again, moments later, or days, or weeks.*

same initial meeting. The editing does nothing to signal a change in time. Indeed, the scene is edited in such a way as to give a sense of continuity. However, dialogue and changes in clothing suggest that time has passed. At one point, the lovers embrace, then move down below the frame. After a cut to two figurines in a niche in the wall, the camera reveals the lovers again. It seems that this must be the same scene. They descended to the bed, then we followed. It can only be a moment later. Moreover, Umrao's clothes are evidently the same. But Sultan's clothes are different (see Figures 5.22 and 5.23). This may, then, be another day, another meeting, even another place. Once again, Ali has used editing to give us a false sense of spatial and temporal continuity, only to reveal discontinuity—or, in this case, uncertainty—in temporal and spatial relations. The disruptions of our ongoing expectations are clear, as is the thematic relevance of these disruptions.

*5.24. Umrao and Sultan before the screen . . .*

*5.25. . . . then beyond the screen.*

Subsequently, Sultan shoots an abusive patron at the brothel. This murder leads to the separation of the lovers. When they are reunited, Ali positions them before a screen, Umrao on the left and Sultan on the right, both brightly lit (Figure 5.24). He cuts immediately to the other side of the screen (Figure 5.25). Now both are silhouettes—Sultan on the left and Umrao on the right. From here, Ali moves to a sequence of extreme close-ups of their hands, eyes, and lips. At the end of the sequence, we find that the positions of the lovers are reversed. They are now before a wall, brightly lit, but Sultan is on the left and Umrao on the right. In the context of the film's Ṣūfism, the reversal suggests the ultimate identity of the lovers. There are also hints of Ṣūfī themes in the pairing of fully visible figures with shadows and the play between what is before us and what is beyond a veil that obscures and darkens what we are able to see. In a later reunion, Umrao and Sultan walk toward the camera. As the lovers pass on the left, the camera pans slightly right to a field of flowers. It begins to move slowly in through the flowers, in the opposite direction from the path of the lovers. There is a cut, but after the cut the camera is still moving through the flowers at the same pace. Our unreflective assumption is that it is moving in the same direction, thus away from the lovers. Now, however, there is something just beyond the flowers. The camera racks focus to reveal Umrao and Sultan seated in a clearing. Once again, editing that leads us to imagine continuity is disrupted by discontinuity. In this case, it is ambiguous whether the discontinuity is in the physical events of the story or in our perspective. Either way, it suggests a lack of sureness and fixity—in reality itself or in our knowledge of reality.

There are three subsequent meetings between Umrao and Sultan. In the first, they discuss Sultan's marriage. Umrao says that he should marry his cousin, to whom he has been betrothed since they were children. She explains that, for his sake, she is even willing to accept a co-wife.[5] Obviously, Umrao takes it as unquestionable that she and Sultan will be married. Shortly after this, Sultan explains that his mother will not approve of his marrying Umrao. Here, again, Ali uses a dissymmetrical shot/reverse shot, substituting an intimate reaction shot of Umrao just as she learns that she will not be married to Sultan (see Figures 5.26 and 5.27). The effect of Umrao's disheartened expression (exquisitely portrayed by Rekha), as it follows the sudden overthrowing of her certainty about union with Sultan, is very moving. It is clearly enhanced, not only by the tight close-up itself, but by our expectation of a more distant shot, in keeping with the canonical shot/reverse shot pattern.

Their next meeting occurs when Sultan comes to announce his wedding. As he enters, we—and presumably Umrao also—see him in her mirror (Figure 5.28). Again, in context, this seems to suggest their identity, for it is, first of all, Umrao's image that should be (and usually is) visible in her mirror, not Sultan's.

Their final meeting occurs when Umrao is briefly reunited with her friend Ramdei. As children, she and Ramdei had both been abducted from their families and were kept together before being sold. One day, Umrao is asked to sing at a celebration. As she speaks with the woman of the house, she realizes that it must be Ramdei. Their reunion is deeply emotional and suggests the possibility of a lasting bond, the positive resolution of at least some worldly longing. But this suggestion is quickly undermined. Ramdei explains that her husband is out of town and will return the next day.

*5.26. Canonical shot of Sultan leads the viewer to expect a canonical reverse shot of Umrao . . .*

*5.27. . . . but this expectation is violated by an intimate reaction shot.*

Umrao begins to sing, "What a favor the passage of time has done me." In the course of the song, the husband returns. No one remarks that he is early. It appears that he has, indeed, arrived the next day. Once again, the film establishes, then challenges our construction of temporal sequence. As it turns out, Ramdei's husband is Sultan. This not only reminds us of Umrao's loss of Sultan; it also entails her loss of Ramdei. Sultan convinces Umrao to stay and sing another song. What she sings could stand as a statement of the main themes of the film. She begins, "I did not find what I looked for," and continues, "Life, I think I only saw you in a dream." This dreamlike quality of life is, again, the quality communicated by the film's visual style.

This ends the story arc treating Umrao's romantic longing for Sultan.

It also concludes the film's treatment of lost friendship.[6] At this point, then, two of the three models for spiritual love have been treated. Again, both have partially allegorized that spiritual love, and partially pointed beyond worldly bonds toward divine love as providing the only possibility for lasting happiness. All that remains now is vātsalya, the love of parents and children. The crucial scene comes when the women of the brothel are forced to flee Lucknow during the aftermath of the 1857 uprising. They stop for the night outside Faizabad and Umrao escapes.

Umrao's return to Faizabad is accompanied by a song that comes close to making the Ṣūfī themes explicit. Umrao sings, "That which has no face, that which has no name, / Why do I long for such a thing?" The verses suggest, first, that Umrao cannot envision what it is she truly desires. This itself has two meanings. It means that she cannot recall her mother's face, and it means that she does not really know what she desires. The verses also suggest that what she truly desires is precisely what has no face and no name, thus God. Ṣūfī mystics accept the orthodox view that Allāh is without any representable attributes (thus that he "could not be 'seen' . . . , but was only visible . . . through his 'signs' (*ayat*) in nature" [Waines 14]). But at the same time, they maintain that there is a sense in which Allāh does have such attributes—including, crucially, a face (see, for example, al-Kalābādhī 16). That face is the face of the true beloved, a face that always remains hidden until one achieves realization and recognizes the face—which, again, in monistic Ṣūfism is one's own face.

In the next scene, Umrao performs in a courtyard just across from her

*5.28. Sultan enters the scene by an image in Umrao's mirror.*

*5.29. Umrao dances before a light background . . .*

*5.30. . . . but, while the dance and music are continuous, the background is suddenly dark.*

childhood home. Singing, she asks, "What place is this?" She dances before a red backdrop, but suddenly there is a cut. The song is continuous. Umrao's movements are continuous. But the background is black (see Figures 5.29 and 5.30). Again, our expectations, and related sense of reality, are disrupted. It is as if she has been transported out of any space. Then we have the first cut away to Umrao's mother. Umrao describes the place, "Where I have no control over sorrow or joy," thus marking it as the material world of pain and falsity, not the world of divine and eternal bliss. We return to the red background. But then in another cut, a cut that preserves the camera position across shots, the background goes black again. There are further cuts to Umrao's mother. Umrao weeps in a close-up. Tears roll down her cheeks. Ali cuts to a tighter close-up, from the same camera angle, as Umrao's singing continues without interruption. But now her face is dry (see Figures 5.1 and 5.2). The enlargement of Umrao's face on the screen emphasizes the sudden absence of the tears. Again, our spontaneous perceptual expectations are undermined. Again, our sense of the reality of the story world is disturbed—though in this case the disturbance implies the fleetingness and falsity of worldly sorrow, rather than the fleetingness and falsity of worldly happiness.

Umrao sings "Beyond the blinds who beckons me?" and we cut to her mother beyond the blinds in her childhood home, visible through the doorway and across the courtyard from where Umrao is performing. The line certainly refers to Umrao's mother. But it refers equally, or more, to Allāh. It is, ultimately, God who is calling to her—through Sultan, through Ramdei, through her mother. In Ṣūfī thought there is only one true call. The blinds, in that sense, stand for everything that conceals reality from us, the entire material world where we mistakenly place our hopes for happiness. Following this, Umrao wanders off the stage and out, through the gateway, and into her family courtyard. The song continues, but her lips do not move. It is impossible to say just what is happening. Is she imagining this departure from the performance? Or is she only imagining the continuation of the song? Or has the song suddenly become mere cinematic accompaniment, with no status in the story world—perhaps a reminder to us of what should have happened? It is all like a dream, and once again we cannot retain a sense that the material world has fixity, that time and space are real.

When Umrao meets her mother, the dialogue is a tentative discussion between two people who suspect that they are mother and daughter. But much of it is also a sort of Ṣūfī allegory. When the mother asks about her identity, she responds, "How can I say who I am?" Her history makes her identity uncertain. But at the same time, if someone realizes that his or her true nature is Allāh, he or she cannot define himself or herself as having a distinct identity. When the mother asks about Umrao's "real home," she responds that it is the place "where I am standing now." This is literally her childhood home. But the response is also fitting for someone who has achieved realization of the ubiquity of Allāh, and thus experiences wherever she stands as home. The first part of the dialogue is in standard shot/reverse shot mode. But after Umrao's mother begins to ask questions that have both literal and spiritual resonance, the camera lingers over the mother's shoulder so that we focus entirely on Umrao's reactions (Figure 5.31). When Ali returns to canonical shot/reverse shot format, we are suddenly in the past (Figure 5.32). The result is that our expectations are disrupted, once again, toward the usual thematic ends.

Finally, mother and daughter recognize one another. There is a reunion. Seeing the film for the first time, we do not know if perhaps now it will end; perhaps the implication is that Umrao has indeed found her real home.

But then Umrao's brother enters. She goes to greet him, but he repudiates her, saying, "You should have drowned yourself." Ali shoots the interaction dissymmetrically. The brother is presented in medium shots (Figure 5.33). But, rather than parallel presentations of Umrao, we are given intimate reaction shots (Figure 5.34). Rekha, who rightly won the National Film Award for Best Actress for this role, communicates the utter despair that this denunciation brings. Throughout her entire life after the kidnap-

*5.31. Extended shot of Umrao, without a reverse shot when her mother speaks . . .*

*5.32. . . . then, when there is a reverse shot, we are suddenly back in Umrao's childhood.*

*5.33. Umrao's brother in a medium shot suggests that Umrao will be shot in the same way . . .*

*5.34. . . . however, Umrao appears in an intimate reaction shot.*

ping, Umrao held onto the hope of reuniting with her mother. Now, just at the moment when it seemed to be fulfilled, that hope is shattered. As she runs weeping from the home, we know that she has reached the lowest point. In Ṣūfī terms, she has no support other than Allāh; she has been thrown into the desolation, nothingness. Returning to the dialogue with her mother, we may say that she has not found her "real home." Indeed, she no longer has any idea where that real home may be—because she has not yet recognized who she is.

The next scene is the final one of the film. Umrao walks through her house in Kanpur. No one lives there. The furniture has been thrown about. There is debris everywhere. She enters a second room through glass paneled doors. As a sarangi plays on the soundtrack, she moves toward the light

*5.35. The final freeze frame of the film; Umrao wipes clean the mirror, revealing her face in the polished arc.*

streaming in from a window. A large mirror comes into view. As Umrao's face appears in the mirror, a flute begins to play, recalling Umrao's first song and the devotee's romantic union with the flute-playing god, Kṛṣṇa. It may be too much to call the flute joyful, but it contrasts strikingly with the unmistakably mournful quality of the sarangi. The mirror is dusty. Umrao reaches out and wipes clean a swath. Just as her face reappears in the newly cleared patch of the surface, Ali freezes the frame (Figure 5.35). That is the end—Umrao seeing her face in a clean mirror. On the one hand, her face remains sorrowful, her eyes brimming with unshed tears. That is part of what makes this conclusion so moving. But at the same time, this ending may suggest the possibility of true happiness. Having reached the moment of despair, Umrao should, by Ṣūfī teaching, be closer to the moment of bliss, the moment of recognizing her true self and her true Beloved—a moment aptly suggested by her appearance in the mirror. This freeze-frame is a final disruption of our expectations[7] and particularly of our sense of time. Perhaps it adumbrates the timelessness of such a culminating recognition.

## Orange Crush: Colors, Boundaries, and Brightness in Deepa Mehta's *Fire*

The use of color in film is, for the most part, straightforward. We have the ability to match colors, and we do this regularly and self-consciously in ordinary life. Indeed, we routinely isolate patterns, not only by shape, but by color as well. This universal sensitivity in life allows us to be sensitive to color motifs in movies. Moreover, cultural particularity is, in this case, straightforward as well. Colors take on meanings, and these meanings vary from place to place and time to time. Of course, these meanings are not entirely arbitrary. For example, given the color of fire, it seems unlikely that any culture would associate heat with green. However, many associations of color are a result of historical accident.

Light is somewhat more complicated, as it involves a number of elements to which we respond emotionally, but unself-consciously, in ordinary life. One of the most important aspects of lighting—in life and in films—is direction. Hoffman points out that our perceptual apparatus assumes overhead lighting and construes the visual array in those terms unless there is specific reason to assume another directional source of lighting (117). (In evolutionary terms, this derives from the fact that our usual source of light, the sun, is overhead.) This default assumption contributes to the effects of unusual lighting sources, such as lighting from beneath in horror films. Direction of lighting is a standard topic in discussions of visual style in films.

The manipulation of lighting direction is related to another parameter of lighting that is not so widely discussed in film studies—the difference between brightness and boundary. Hoffman explains that "you can construct changes in brightness without also constructing borders. . . . But typically you construct both together" (50). Through the use of light diffusion, photography may separate our experience of brightness from our experience of boundaries. Torben Grodal suggests that any form of nonnormal lighting has emotional consequences ("Film"). Grodal is referring specifically to deviations from overhead lighting. But, if correct, the same point should apply to brightness separated from boundaries in diffusion. Indeed, our preceding discussion suggests that the point should apply to any lighting that deviates from our short-term, perceptual expectations. This includes expectations that are produced by film practices (such as the standard practice of adding a fill light to soften shadows and increase visibility beyond what it would be in natural conditions). Moreover, such deviations commonly have thematic consequences as well.

Unlike some viewers, I am not convinced that *Fire* is entirely successful as a literal story.[8] However, it is, I believe, remarkable for its use of color and for its subtle use of lighting in relation to figure boundaries. One might have expected some concern with light and color, given the film's title. Moreover, seeing is a recurrent motif in the film, from the opening vignette in which a little girl (young Radha) attempts to see the ocean with her eyes closed. But neither point suggests the profound importance of visual style to the emotional effect and, even more, to the thematic exposition of the film. Indeed, I would argue that the main themes of the film are not fully recognizable without careful attention to visual style, particularly color.

Consider, for example, what is probably the most illuminating and scholarly treatment of the film to date—the sixth chapter of Jigna Desai's *Beyond Bollywood*. Desai analyzes *Fire* valuably in terms of heteronormativity and globalization. She also discusses the apparently contradictory comments by Mehta, who seems to say that the film both is and is not about lesbianism. My contention is that *Fire* treats many issues, including globalization and lesbianism. However, it organizes these issues in relation to an overarching theme that one will simply miss if one focuses on plot and dialogue, while ignoring the film's visual patterning. Specifically, the film is a critique of male, Hindu nationalism[9] and an implicit statement that the only positive possibilities for the future of India lie with its women and with such syncretistic religious movements as Ṣūfism. There are certainly non-visual suggestions of this, as when Mehta repeats music from the film *Bombay*, which treats Hindu/Muslim intolerance and violence. Specifically, Mehta begins and ends the film with music from the beginning and ending of *Bombay*. Thus, at the start, she may be seen as suggesting that Hindu/Muslim conflicts provide an important context for the film. At the end, we might infer that the culminating union of Sita and Radha in a Ṣūfī shrine is in some way parallel to the unification of Hindus and Muslims that ends *Bombay*. But these are only very brief hints. The visuals are crucial for working out these themes.

The basic plot concerns an Indian family that runs a video rental store and restaurant. The widowed mother, Biji, suffered a stroke that left her mute. She has two sons—Ashok, the elder, and Jatin, the younger. Ashok is married to Radha. Since Radha cannot have children, Ashok has taken a vow of celibacy. He has become the devotee of a swami and has set himself the spiritual goal of eliminating all desire. To test himself, he sometimes asks Radha to lie beside him. His aspiration is to experience no sexual arousal in these circumstances. Jatin is in love with Julie, a Chinese woman, with whom he is having an affair. However, Julie refuses to marry him. Due to family pressure, Jatin has agreed to marry Sita. However, even after the marriage, he spends all his time with Julie. Abandoned by their husbands,

Sita and Radha begin a sexual affair themselves. Once discovered, they reject their husbands and set off to start a new life together.

Looking solely at the story, it is reasonable to assume that the film is, first of all, about lesbianism. However, one might equally argue that the literal treatment of lesbianism is rather a weak point in the film. For example, Shabana Azmi (Radha), one of the most renowned actresses of Indian cinema, is far from convincing in her love scenes with Nandita Das (Sita). More important, the film never makes clear just how the lesbian relationship develops. Radha apparently desires sexual relations with her husband. It seems unlikely that, deprived of sex with her husband, she would simply turn to the one available woman for sex. Moreover, the film includes some mocking comments on Ashok's relation with his swami as semi-sexual. If the film were made primarily in support of homosexuality, such mockery would seem misplaced. All this suggests that perhaps the film is not, first of all, about lesbianism. Rather, its thematic focus is on something else, of which the relation between Radha and Sita is an instance. This is where the film's visual style becomes critical. It turns our attention to the particular historical problems of India at the time and suggests that, in Mehta's view, those problems are the result of patriarchal, sexually repressive, and communalist Hinduism.

Consider, for example, a particularly striking use of color. Ashok has just discovered Radha and Sita in flagrante delicto. One might have expected him to respond with feelings of anger and abandonment. However, he is struggling against sexual arousal. We already know that this struggle manifests a pathological repression and that his subordination of Radha has been inseparable from this repression. He sits on the curb outside his home, tortured by the idea that he is having an erection. Looming above him is a soda machine, bright orange in color, emblazoned with the beverage advertisement: "Crush." (See Figure 5.36.) The significance of "crush" is obvious, for Ashok is trying to crush his sexual impulses, and those of his wife. The orange color, the fact that this is an orange soda, is perhaps less self-explanatory, at least for western viewers. The color here alludes to the traditional saffron of Hinduism, the color worn by Hindu activists. The conjunction suggests that Ashok's perfidious sexual repression comes from Hindu fundamentalism.[10] Moreover, the conjunction implies that this fundamentalism involves a sort of phobic rejection of women and femininity. Finally, by using the western soda, Orange Crush, to communicate this,

*5.36. Ashok suffers from Orange Crush.*

the scene also suggests that Hindu nationalism itself is inseparable from colonialism, and globalization. Indeed, this is just the argument that has been made by post-colonial theorists such as Ashis Nandy (see Chapter Three of Nandy et al.; see also Nandy, *Intimate,* especially 22–26).

Of course, one cannot draw these conclusions based on this scene in isolation. Crucially, the use of color in this scene is part of a broader, allusive pattern that pervades the work. Specifically, the film is visually organized around three colors—orange, white, and green, the national colors of India. Orange, again, represents Hinduism. Green represents Islam. In the Indian flag, white symbolizes the peaceful unification of the two religions in the nation. Mehta's use of the color, however, is somewhat more complex. We encounter these colors in the first scene of the film when the child Radha sits with her mother and father. Radha wears orange; her mother wears green; her father wears white.

This opening scene also introduces the important theme of envisioning possibilities that go beyond anything in one's current experience. Radha's mother refers to a legendary "old woman" who spoke of imagining the ocean that one had never seen. Radha says that she does not understand. At the end of the film, just before Radha leaves her home to join Sita in a new life, we have a flashback to the child Radha. Standing in a field, with the ocean nowhere in sight, the child Radha says that she can, indeed, see the ocean. In other words, she has imagined possibilities outside what is actually given in her experience. This is, of course, just what the adult Radha does when she leaves the traditional family structure for a new life with Sita. Again, this new life is a life of lesbian union. But the crucial point, I take it, is that it is a thorough rejection of the tradition that went before. Lesbianism is only one form of such a rejection.

For our purposes, three further points are crucial about this opening story. First, the imagination of unexperienced possibilities is passed down from a legendary old woman, through Radha's mother, to Radha. This indicates that new possibilities are to be found in a specifically female heritage. In connection with this, it may be significant that the father does not sit between the mother and daughter, but beside them. Thus the color white does not come between the orange and the green, as it does in the Indian flag. As we shall see, this is consistent with the use of diffused white light in the course of the film. Rather than being associated with the peaceful unity of Hindu and Muslim, it is linked with the patriarchal tradition that separates them. In this way, Mehta may be drawing on the standard Indian association of white with death and mourning. That is certainly the most common cultural suggestion of the color outside the context of the national flag. Finally, it is no accident that the source of the new imagination comes from the mother who is dressed in green. Mehta repeatedly hints that Islam is the source of national renewal, and that Hinduism is the stifling tradition that needs to be overcome.[11]

The last point is suggested partially in the following scene. We are now in the present. Jatin and Sita are on their honeymoon at the Taj Mahal. The tour guide explains how the Taj is a monument to love. The rest of the film takes pains to show us that Hinduism, at least in the form of Rāma worship, undermines romantic love between husband and wife. The Taj seems to stand as a vast testament to the importance of love in Islam. The scene is not without criticism of this testament. The tour guide explains that the emperor who built this monument to his beloved wife also cut off the hands of the architect. Nonetheless, it is difficult not to see the contrast between Shah Jahan's devotion to his wife and Jatin's extreme indifference to Sita.

When Jatin and Sita return from the honeymoon, the three women of the household sit together. Biji is in white; Sita is in orange; Radha is in green. Here too we must recall the national flag. Sita and Radha repeat Radha and her mother from the opening. Biji is ambiguously linked with the "old woman" of Radha's mother's story (because she is a very old woman) and with Radha's father (due to her white clothing). The second association is enhanced by the fact that Jatin too is in white, and the clothes of Ashok and the male servant, Mundu, are largely white as well. This is in keeping with Biji's status and function in the film. On the one hand, she is part of the female heritage that the film seeks to explore and extend. But at the same time she is perhaps the most vehement guardian of patriarchal tradition. Indeed, her white clothing is the traditional clothing of a widow, a woman perpetually in mourning for the death of her husband.

The following scene takes us into Jatin's room, where the association between masculinity and violence is stressed by the film posters that decorate the walls. Repeatedly, we see muscle-bound, gun-toting film stars. Here too Mehta makes her point not through dialogue, but through the visual presentation of the film. This scene also furthers the association of Biji with tradition and patriarchy. Sita discards her sari, puts on pants, pretends to smoke, and dances to pop music. As this is going on, Biji soils herself. The literal, narrative connection is simply that Sita fails to come when Biji needs attention. But the conjunction obviously has metaphorical implications as well. Moreover, when Sita appears in pants, Biji objects vehemently.

The following scenes begin the explicit treatment of Hinduism and the association of Hinduism with repression, both sexual and patriarchal, as well as communal intolerance. First, we hear Ashok's swami lecturing an all-male audience about desire, and we hear Ashok's summary, "Desire is the root of all evil." Thus we are introduced to Hinduism as a sexually repressive, masculinist religion, represented by the swami and Ashok. Admittedly, the swami may not at first appear to be overly masculine. But, subsequently, we learn that he suffers from a painful ailment that Mehta surely intends to be symbolic—enlargement of the testicles, a literal excess of masculinity.

After the swami's lecture, Mehta presents us with the figures that many Hindus consider the ideals of masculinity and femininity, Rāma and Sītā, through the televised version of the *Rāmāyaṇa*. Specifically, we see the notorious scene when Rāma and Sītā are reunited and Rāma demands that Sītā pass through the fire to prove her purity. Later, we see the scene again, in a folk theater production, which also includes Rāma's subsequent exiling of Sītā. The patriarchal elements of the scenes are obvious. But the political significance of the scenes is not confined to these elements. As Indian viewers of the film would be well aware, Hindu nationalism—with its prominent strain of anti-Muslim communalism—has developed over the last two decades in part through a cult of Rāma worship. As Mishra puts it, "the discourse of fundamentalism congealed around the heroic figure of the Hindu God Rama" (204). The television *Rāmāyaṇa* contributed to that cult, and to the related, reactionary political movements.

Some subsequent scenes point to the intolerance and communalism of some contemporary Hindu politics as well. The most direct treatment of this occurs when Jatin is having dinner with Julie and her family. One of them remarks that there is "no place for minorities here." Though the literal reference is to Chinese immigrants, the comment applies most obviously to Muslims.

All this prepares for what is, in my view, the most powerful use of color in the film. This occurs when Radha and Sita are together in bed for the first time. It is the moment when they make the first decision to break with tradition and to affirm desire and love over social convention. Radha is wearing orange. Sita is wearing green. The white sheets are between them. The configuration vividly recalls an Indian flag. More important, it suggests a genuine, loving union of the two largest and most antagonistic groups in South Asia—Muslims and Hindus. The scene hints that the only peaceful future for India lies in the union of its women, their rejection of a patriarchal tradition that is bound up with political and economic oppression, sexual repression, violence, and communalism. This rejection involves a loosening of sexual constraints, and thus a rejection of heteronormativity. In this way, the film is indeed about lesbianism. But it is not solely or even primarily about lesbianism. Rather, its treatment of lesbianism is the consequence of a larger thematic concern—again, the rejection of oppressive, repressive, intolerant, violent, and communalist patriarchy.

On the other hand, to say that the scene is anti-communalist is not to say that it treats all communities equally. As we have already seen, in Mehta's film, the destructive patriarchy is allied with the religious majority. It is linked with Hindu nationalism and the fundamentalist Hindu imagination of an ideal society, which is modeled on the "rule of Rāma." Mehta uses the *Rāmāyaṇa* story of Sītā's fire ordeal as a synecdoche for the ideology of Hindu nationalism. Rāma's rejection of Sītā symbolizes what Mehta evidently sees as a broader, Hindu repudiation of femininity—a repudiation that makes the solidarity of women all the more urgent.

Indeed, Mehta draws the title of her film and its culminating events from this episode of the *Rāmāyaṇa.* Just before Radha leaves for her new life with Sita, she has an argument with Ashok, who demands that she touch his feet in worship. When she refuses, Ashok pushes her away. The edge of her sari falls onto one of the gas burners of the stove and catches fire. Ashok watches as the flames rise up around her and she struggles to put them out. Eventually, he decides to carry Biji out of the room, apparently leaving his wife to die. The scene is suggestive in many ways. First, it harshly criticizes Rāma's treatment of Sītā in demanding the fire ordeal, for Rāma looked on as Sītā passed through the flames, just as Ashok looks on here. It also recalls the actual situation of some women in India today, most obviously the reports of "bride burning," in which "husbands engineer an 'accident' (frequently the bursting of a kitchen stove) when they feel the obligatory marriage dower (gifts from in-laws) is not enough" (as explained by UNICEF). Only a "tiny percentage" of the murderers "are brought to justice."[12] In addition, we can read Ashok's action—taking up Biji—allegorically. He, like the Hindu nationalists, chooses to preserve tradition rather than save the life of a real, suffering woman. Finally, it is important to recall that Radha does, indeed, survive her fire ordeal. The implication is that Radha is like the mythic Sītā in being pure. After they spend their first night together, Sita asks Radha if they have done anything wrong. Radha responds firmly, "No." This fire ordeal seems to confirm that judgment.

In sum, the film suggests that the choices of women, working together to overcome masculinist, Hindu traditions, are morally right and are necessary to bring the nation out of patriarchal oppression and communalist violence into peaceful unity. But there is an obvious objection here. How can Hinduism, masculinity, and violence be viewed as inseparable, and as a danger to the nation, when the greatest nationalist of India, Mahatma Gandhi, was a Hindu and a man, but also the world's greatest advocate of nonviolence? Moreover, Gandhi was assassinated for his supposedly excessive sympathy toward Muslims (for discussion, see Ganguli). How can this possibly be reconciled with the implicit judgments on Hinduism in the film?

In fact, Mehta anticipates this objection. The film responds by implicating Gandhi himself in the same masculinist violence that is represented so overtly in Jatin's film posters. The difference is that, in Gandhi's case, the violence is concealed. Mehta's response here has two parts. First, she suggests that invocations of nonviolence are often hypocritical. When Sita calls Jatin a "fool," Jatin slaps her. He then explains why he does not beat her more severely—"You're lucky I don't believe in violence." Not only has he already slapped her, it is clear that his general behavior constitutes "hiṃsā" (violence) in the traditional sense, for he continually acts in such a way as to cause her suffering. Moreover, despite his yogic aspirations, Ashok's behavior too is marked by hiṃsā, most obviously in the scene where he pushes Radha into the fire, then fails to rescue her.

But, of course, none of this implicates Gandhi himself. The second part of Mehta's response is more damning. Ashok simultaneously subordinates his wife and repudiates any connection with anything feminine. He does this, most directly, through his vow of chastity and his use of Radha to test himself. This strange practice, in which Radha is reduced to a sort of antisexual sex object or counter-phobic phobic object, refers directly to what is perhaps Gandhi's most notorious practice. For a period in his late 70s, he engaged in what he called "brahmacarya" or chastity "experiments." In these experiments, he would lie naked with young women. His goal was to be certain that, even in these circumstances, he would not become sexually aroused (see Brown 377–378). As I have already noted, the fire ordeal—repeated by Ashok and Radha—is a synecdoche for the cruelty of Rāma and the Hindu fundamentalists who invoke him. In a similar way, Gandhi's brahmacarya experiments—also repeated by Ashok and Radha—are a synecdoche for the more concealed patriarchy of Gandhi and the politicians who (most often, hypocritically) invoke him. Moreover, the allusion to Gandhi's experiments contributes to the tacit anti-communal themes of the film, indirectly suggesting the inadequacy of any anti-communal initiatives undertaken in a patriarchal and Hindu framework. Specifically, Gandhi claimed that his self-sacrifice in the brahmacarya experiments would help to end Hindu/Muslim divisions (see Wolpert, *Gandhi's,* 228).

These harsh criticisms of Hinduism contrast directly with the representation of Islam in the film. Indeed, Mehta clearly indicates that, in her view, it is Islam (combined, of course, with women's solidarity) that holds the possibility for inter-communal harmony, as well as other sorts of liberation (e.g., sexual liberation) in India today.[13]

I have already noted the contrast, early in the film, between the Hindu repudiation of desire and the Muslim celebration of love in the Taj Mahal. The point is developed more strongly when Sita and Radha go to the shrine of Nizamuddin, a Ṣūfī mystic renowned for his acceptance of people from all religious backgrounds and for his emphasis on the spiritual importance of love. The shrine is, in part, painted green. After presenting her offering at the shrine, Sita expresses the wish that she and Radha will be able to leave the extended family and live together. The scene implies that she has appealed for the saint's aid in achieving this union. The end of the film suggests that Sita's prayers have been answered—hinting at both the supernatural efficacy of Islamic devotion and Allāh's acceptance of lesbianism.

More significantly, when Radha and Sita decide to leave and to begin a life together, they meet at this same shrine. There could hardly be a sharper

*5.37. Sita and Radha appear as tiny figures in the Ṣūfī shrine.*

contrast than that between the two final scenes of the story (interrupted briefly by a flashback to Radha's childhood). In the first scene, Radha is trapped by patriarchal Hindu tradition into re-enacting the fire ordeal of Sītā. In the next, she is in the free space of the Islamic shrine, cooled by life-giving rain, and beginning a new, anti-patriarchal life with her beloved. Indeed, the final union of the lovers is shot from a distance so that Sita and Radha are simply small figures in the encompassing Muslim structure (Figure 5.37). The shot emphasizes the religious context more than the lovers' embrace. Of course, it is crucial that this is not just any Islamic structure, but a specifically Ṣūfī shrine. As I have already noted, Ṣūfism, though a form of Islam, is the product of Hindu/Muslim synthesis (see, for example, Waines 149 and Chaitanya 111–113). As such, it is sometimes seen as a religious alternative for a non-communalist India. For example, Khizer maintains that "if the national integration is to be achieved, we need to revive the spirit of Ṣūfism" (123).

In this way, Mehta's film is not simply anti-Hindu and pro-Muslim. The importance of synthesizing the two religions is suggested visually at the end of the film as Sita, dressed in orange, waits for Radha in the shrine, parts of which have taken on an orange hue from the ambient light. Here, the colors moderate the apparent harshness of the religious opposition. Indeed, the fact that Mehta continually joins the women in orange and green, rather than dressing them both in green, suggests that she is not urging some sort of general conversion to Islam. Rather, it suggests a combination of the two traditions. Moreover, Mehta hints that there are elements in Hindu tradition, elements specifically associated with women's heritage, that lend themselves to anti-patriarchal uses. For example, there is a suggestion of this in the characters' names. The character of Radha clearly represents the epic Sītā, most obviously in her fire ordeal. This would lead one to expect that Sita would represent the legendary Rādhā. Certainly, Rādhā showed the sexual independence of Mehta's Sita, leaving her husband's bed in the middle of the night to meet her lover, singing of her sexual desire, and so forth. Indeed, during a scene in which Radha and Sita are dancing together, we see a painting on the wall of the room. It depicts Kṛṣṇa with the gopīs, a relation most fully represented in their spiritual and erotic dance. In this way, Mehta seems to be using the sexuality of the Rādhā/Kṛṣṇa stories to oppose the martial Rāma/Sītā epic and its political uses much in the way that Sivan uses those stories to oppose the martial Kannaki/Kôvalan epic and its political uses.

Mehta's use of lighting fits with these concerns as well. For most of the film, Mehta follows standard lighting practices, much as Ali usually follows the practices of continuity editing in *Umrao Jaan*. Specifically, Mehta commonly uses a key light or main lighting source that corresponds to whatever source of light a viewer would expect in a given scene. For example, if it is night and a character is seated beside a lamp, then the key light will come from the direction of the lamp. Moreover, the key light approximates the brightness and hue of the putative source (e.g., the lamp). In addition, she almost always uses a fill light, a second light that unobtrusively illuminates important areas (e.g., parts of a character's face) that would otherwise be in darkness. Thus, if a character is seated with a lamp to his or her right, the key light will be to the character's right, but there will also be a softer, fill light coming from the character's left, so that we are able to see both sides of his or her face.

There are two repeated exceptions to this practice. In some cases, Mehta takes away the fill light. The most important instances of this occur with the two lovers. In their most intimate moments, they are often back lit and appear in profile, in silhouette, with rim lighting (in which the face is generally dark, but brightly lit along the profile edge). The other way in which Mehta deviates from standard lighting is almost the precise opposite. Indeed, this second deviation provides what is probably the most visually striking feature of the film—its almost tangible cascades of light. Brilliant white sunlight pours in from the windows and doors, diffusing in misty clouds around faces, hands, objects—and, most of all, around the white cloths that we see throughout the film.

Thematically, the dispersed sunlight might seem to suggest a beneficial fusion across boundaries—particularly in contrast with the rim lighting

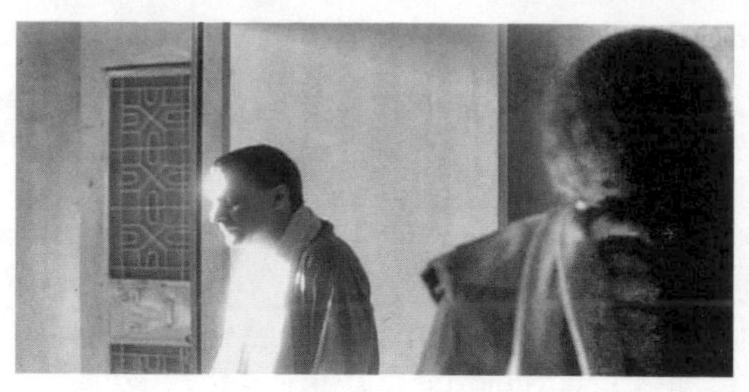

*5.38. Radiant Mundu.*

that stresses those boundaries. But that is not how Mehta uses it. Light that spills over boundaries is associated with fire in this film, and fire itself is linked, not with passion and love, but with a tradition of patriarchal control. Moreover, the wondrous luminosity of particular scenes is often in direct contrast with their content. For example, there is a very striking scene in which Mundu is threatening Radha. He says that he will reveal what he knows about her relations with Sita. As he communicates his threat, the sunlight streaming in the door spreads a cloud of white about his face (Figure 5.38). The radiance recalls the miraculous events that the Sanskrit theorists connected with wonder. But Mundu's action and intent here are sinister, closer to demonic plot than to divine revelation.

The character most often associated with this diffuse brightness is Biji. The first scene with a strong use of such light occurs when Biji is introduced. Radha is powdering and dressing her. The light coming in the window billows into the air with the puffs of powder and spreads across the room, reflecting from Biji's white hair, white sheets, and white blouse. The scene culminates when Radha pulls Biji's white, diaphanous scarf over Biji's head. It catches the brilliant light and glows like a halo (see Figure 5.39). Biji is, again, the mute matriarch of the family, the guardian of family morals. She can communicate only by ringing a bell, reminiscent perhaps of the bells rung as part of worship in Hindu temples. Her white hair is obviously a sign of her age. Her white sari is a symbol of her widowhood. The powder applied by Radha is a reminder that she is disabled and cannot care for herself.

In these and other cases, the diffuse light suggests a sort of spiritual reverence, a reverence for morality (as in Mundu's disapproval of Radha and Sita), a reverence for ancient tradition, of which Biji is almost a personification. But, in each case, there is something deeply wrong. Mundu has just masturbated in front of Biji in a display that is likely to fill many viewers with disgust, both physical and moral. Biji herself does not suggest a living and vibrant tradition (such as that of the old woman spoken of by Radha's mother). Rather, everything about her suggests disability and death.

In direct contrast, the dim lighting of the furtive lovers communicates intimacy (the opposite of disgust) and an affirmation of life. Mehta uses this technique perhaps most effectively when Sita first kisses Radha. The women are seated in bed, facing one another. We see the right side of Radha's face and the left side of Sita's face. One might expect that the faces would be lit in the same way. However, they are not. Both are back lit. There is a fill light on Radha's face, in keeping with standard lighting practices. However, Sita's face, only a few inches away, is not illuminated by a fill light. Rather, most of her face is dark, with a strong rim light on the profile (Figure 5.40). This has a number of functions. In terms of narrative, this suggests that Radha and Sita are not yet thinking about their relationship in the same way. With respect to theme, it indicates that darkness will be associated with love and forbidden sexuality, just as light is linked with reverence for tradition, and death.

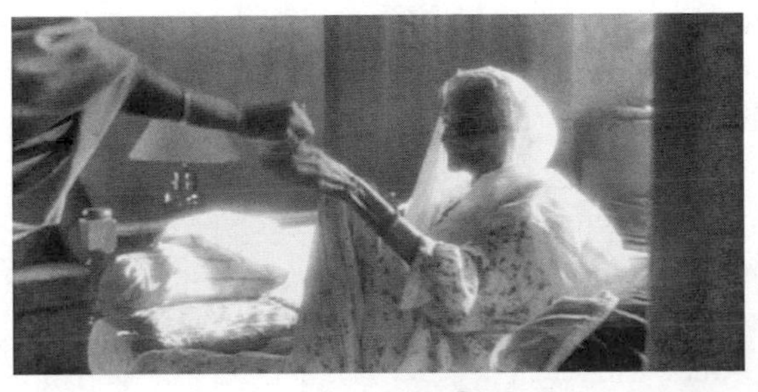

*5.39. Luminous Biji.*

*5.40. The first kiss (fill light on Radha; rim light on Sita).*

Most important, the lighting of Sita in this scene is, at least in my experience, emotionally powerful. Most obviously, it serves to make Sita more strongly erotic. The reasons for this are fairly straightforward. Darkness is associated with intimacy for most of us. Thus emotional memories play an important role in our response to this scene. On the other hand, darkness is also associated with fear. Fear is not simply a matter of darkness, however. It is inseparable from our limited ability to locate and identify moving objects. Related to this, backlighting tends to be associated with a sense of danger, especially with respect to human figures. In part, this too is a matter of identifying the object. In some ways more important, however, is that it results from our inability to see the person's face distinctly and thus to discern his or her emotional attitude. Rim lighting serves to make the contours of Sita's face very salient. It provides us with enough facial clues to recognize, thus to some extent mirror and share, her feelings. In this way, rim lighting allows us to experience the intimacy of darkness without the generation of anxiety, for it allows us to identify—and thus identify with—the character's emotional expressions.

After their first night together, Sita and Radha meet on the roof. Here, again, Mehta uses backlighting for both the women. But she drops the fill light entirely (Figure 5.41). Now they have come to the same realization, and their profound darkness contrasts strikingly with the excessive luminescence of Biji and Mundu. It is only after this scene that Radha asserts herself to Ashok—first, by not coming when he calls; second, by refusing to lie next to him in his brahmacarya experiments.

Here as elsewhere, the consequences of the lighting are not confined to narrative and theme. Emotionally this dark interaction of the lovers is very powerful as well. When their faces come close in silhouette, with the slim line of light along Sita's profile, the effect is one of shared separation from

*5.41. A later meeting (no fill light).*

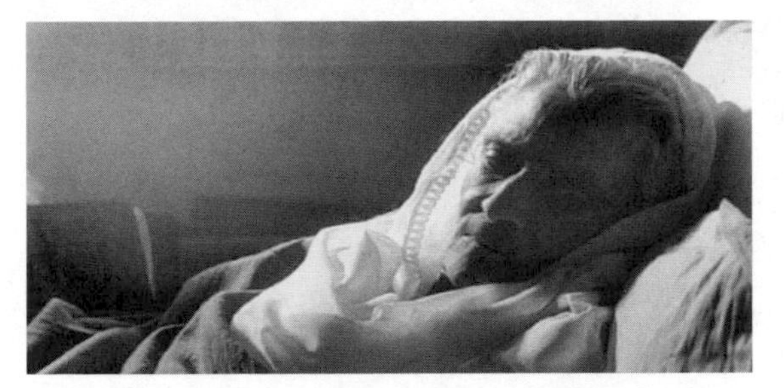

*5.42. Biji, bathed in light, watches Sita and Radha dance in a darkened area of the room (off screen in this shot).*

the rest of the world. Again, in many films, backlighting creates a feeling of threat. But here too the fear triggers are effectively disabled. In part through its association with emotional memories of intimacy, the lighting fosters our alignment with the lovers (as Murray Smith would put it), our sense of sharing their experiences and feelings. As a result, it helps make the scene not only more erotic, but more affectionate, in the rasa senses of these terms. These dark faces and bodies are brought close to us, just as the figures bathed in unbounded brightness are distanced from us.

There is one scene in which the two techniques are partially brought together. Sita is in male drag. She is dancing with Radha in the foreground. In the background, Biji lies in her white sari before a window. Bands of light fall through the window and flood the area around Biji (see Figure 5.42). Sita and Radha are in the foreground, just outside the area of streaming light. As a result, they are backlit and partially silhouetted. Though the lovers are not so dark as in the scenes just discussed, the contrast with Biji's cloud of light is unmistakable. The spaces form, in effect, two planes of light—or, rather, one plane of brilliant light, and one of partial darkness. Narratively, the scene recalls and inverts an earlier episode, the street performance of the *Rāmāyaṇa,* attended by the swami, where an actor in female drag danced the part of Sītā undergoing the fire ordeal. In their similarities and differences, the two performances suggest yet again that what is associated with luminous wonder and enlightened reverence—as well as fire—is, in fact, inseparable from sickness (Biji's stroke; the testicular enlargement of the swami), the stifling of women's self-expression (Biji is mute; a man plays the part of Sītā), and death. They also suggest that a genuine and healthy affirmation of love and life comes only from what is considered dark and impious.

*5.43. The dark, and therefore hopeful horizon of the future.*

*5.44. The bright horizon, visible only when Radha's imagination is constrained—then replaced by the dark horizon (of figure 5.43) when she can finally envision unseen possibilities.*

Clearly, in her use of these visual techniques, Mehta (working with her cinematographer, Giles Nuttgens) discards the cross-culturally standard association of good with light and evil with darkness. In reversing those associations, however, she does not rely on mere idiosyncrasies. Rather, she draws on other universal patterns and their cultural specifications. For example, she takes up the common association of mourning and death with colorless clothing. In this case, she relies on the usual Indian specification of this clothing as white (rather than the usual western specification, which is black). In a more subtle way, she connects brightness with the danger of fire—the life-threatening flames that nearly consume Radha at the end of the film, as well as the various epical and historical fires this episode suggests, from Sītā's fire ordeal to bride burning. At the same time, Mehta links darkness—prominently including shadows sculpted into facial features by a rim of light—with intimacy. The point is explicit in a lecture by the swami in which he rejects "desire night." But it is more effectively developed in the lighting itself. Mehta also connects darkness with the life-giving water that douses fire. This water appears at the beginning and the end of the film. At the beginning, it is the water of the ocean that the child Radha tries to see with her eyes closed, thus the water she tries to see in darkness. At the end, she finally does see the ocean, after closing her eyes, then opening them again and looking beyond a clearly demarcated area of light into a newly darkened horizon (Figure 5.43). That (dark) ocean is, again, Mehta's symbol for the imagined possibilities that go beyond the constraints of one's present life. Just a moment before, when Radha could not see the ocean, the horizon was bright (Figure 5.44). The child Radha's vision occurs in the penultimate scene of the film, just before the adult Radha joins her beloved Sita. In the final scene, the life-giving water appears again, now in the form of rain. In both cases—the ocean and the rain—the suggestions go beyond the personal condition of these two characters to India as a nation, to its sexual, ethnic, and religious minorities, to its women, to all groups that suffer from a tradition of patriarchal violence and repression, thus to all groups that might find hope in a dark and boundless imagination of unimagined possibilities.

# Afterword

## On Watching Indian Movies

Why do we watch Indian movies? Or, more generally, why do we watch movies at all? Recently, Lisa Zunshine devoted a book to a cognitive exploration of why we read fiction. The question about movies is directly parallel. Zunshine's answer has to do with our "Theory of Mind," our ability to infer other people's intentions and beliefs. Perhaps, she suggests, we enjoy the experience of our smoothly functioning Theory of Mind capacities (20). This is undoubtedly a motive in certain cases. But the basic reason why we watch movies is much more general. It was isolated by Ed Tan when he emphasized the production of interest. We watch movies because they engage our interest, focusing our attention. Of course, this merely pushes the question back, for it leads us to ask just what engages our interest. But this is less of a problem. Cognitive research shows that a number of things excite interest. For example, novelty combined with comprehensibility appears to draw and sustain a pleasurable attentional focus (see Anderson 117–118). The point has, in a way, been obvious to literary critics all along—thus the commonplace that the most enjoyable plot is one we cannot predict (at least not with confidence), but that makes sense retrospectively. Cognitive research adds precision to this, and a requirement that we not lose our way in the middle as well.

Of course, a mere spontaneous delight in novelty is not the whole story.

As just noted, interest engages our capacities for understanding. We feel the need to make sense out of novelty. Our effort to infer characters' motives is one case of this sort. So is our effort to infer the thematic concerns of a work, and to make sense of the work as a whole—including the characters' motivations—by reference to those thematic concerns.

Indeed, even our sense of novelty is not simple and unmediated, some sort of pure experience of the work itself. A sense of novelty involves considerable cognitive processing. For example, there are perceptual conditions for the experience of novelty, and for inference-based understanding. We may find a work banal or derivative if we do not encode those features that are distinctive and creative. We may find a work muddled or incoherent if we do not encode those features that define its organization. There are also cognitive structures that orient our ongoing, anticipatory imagination and thus our response to a work. If we do not implicitly expect certain outcomes in a story, we will not find a shift away from those outcomes to be surprising and engaging.

Perhaps most important, interest is a sort of preliminary or basic form of emotion. Indeed, it is very difficult to sustain interest in novelty if the novelty does not have further emotional consequences. Suppose Jones starts talking about beekeeping. I know nothing about beekeeping. In a sense, everything he says is novel. Moreover, his discussion is so lucid that I have no difficulty following. But I feel no emotional engagement with beekeeping. Thus his talk quickly becomes tedious; my interest flags; my mind wanders. Conversely, there are cases where interest does not require novelty or unexpectedness. The inevitable march toward an emotionally affecting outcome can very strongly provoke interest, despite its predictability.

Thus our engagement with films is bound up with a series of complex cognitive operations. Interest is inseparable from thematic inference, encoding, the structural organization of encoded information with the associated generation of expectations, and more full-blown emotional response. We might consider each in turn.

Thematic inference, by its nature, involves judging just what issues are of general importance in a society, what concerns are candidates for elaborate, particularized examination in a hugely expensive collaborative work of narrative art, such as a movie. At a general level, this is simple. An American film is unlikely to take up untouchability as a theme. An Indian film is unlikely to address anti-African racism. But it is, of course, considerably more difficult to isolate the precise issues at stake and to explore their detailed elaboration in a given case (e.g., going beyond a banal recognition that untouchability is bad to examine just what a particular film is saying about untouchability, point by point, as the story develops).

Encoding is inseparable from our perceptual habits and our knowledge of just what differences make a difference in a particular context. This is, in a sense, complicated right from the start, since we do not self-consciously choose what we encode. Americans readily encode verbal cues for race. At least at certain times and places, Hindus readily encode visual cues for caste. On the other hand, we can make self-conscious efforts to redirect our spontaneous attentional inclinations.

Our imaginative expectations are bound up with prototypes and schemas which are themselves often connected with cultural practices and narrative paradigms. When the film's hero sits down to dinner with twelve followers, westerners may begin to have particular expectations about the one follower who is different and whose loyalty is questionable. When our hero takes up a flute in a dark night and we cut to a shot of the heroine in bed, Indians may begin to have particular expectations about subsequent romantic events. Here, too, our expectations are spontaneous. Moreover, it is difficult to correct for misdirected expectations through self-conscious re-orientation. On the other hand, it is relatively easy to acquire the sorts of information that might bear on such expectations. Increased familiarity with relevant works and increased accessibility of relevant information, combined with redirected attentional focus and associated encoding, will eventually lead to the production of relevant expectations.

Finally, emotional responses are bound up with emotional memories, as well as circuits of association that link new experiences with those memories. These too are spontaneous and difficult, perhaps impossible, to produce simply by self-conscious effort. For example, there is a scene in Guru Dutt's *Pyaasa,* where Gulabo has begun to color the part in her hair when she hears that her beloved Vijay has died. I find the scene very moving. Western viewers will, of course, recognize and empathize with Gulabo's loss. But they are unlikely to recognize the sharpness of the contrast here and thus the deep pathos of the scene. First of all, they are unlikely to encode Gulabo's actions in such a way as to recognize that she is coloring the part in her hair, a sign of marriage. In keeping with this, they are unlikely to recognize the implications for Gulabo's future—that she is giving up prostitution—with its associated expectations. Finally, even if they know all this, they are unlikely to have a rich set of emotional associations with this action, associations that make this scene poignant. On the other hand, the development of such associations is not at all impossible. It is not somehow confined to people with a particular background. For everyone—Indian and non-Indian alike—the development of such associations occurs through experience, both the experience of real events and the experience of narratives, including such works as *Pyaasa*.

All this indicates that our full emotional response to a work of art—a novel, a musical composition, a movie—relies not only on extensive cultural knowledge, but on an "internalization" of that knowledge. Ultimately, it requires the incorporation of that knowledge into ordinary cognitive processes, so that we spontaneously encode the crucial aspects of a scene, so that we readily come to have the expectations tacitly anticipated by the author, composer, or director, so that we implicitly link the events with a complex of emotionally consequential memories.

The question that arises here is, of course—how can we ever achieve this? One's first impulse may be to think that, when faced with a foreign culture, we must always be like a stereotypical autistic person. According to the standard view, someone suffering from autism has an impaired "Theory of Mind module."[1] Thus he or she cannot readily understand other people, automatically imputing aims and beliefs to them. Rather, an autistic person might have to go through a laborious process of complicated inferential reasoning to arrive at even very simple conclusions about motives, feelings, desires (see Zunshine 8–9). It may seem that this is just what non-Indians have to do when faced with Indian culture, non-Americans must do when faced with American culture, and so on. Indeed, the problem repeats itself within those cultures. Won't north Indians be "autistic" with respect to south Indians, Hindus with respect to Muslims, upper castes with respect to lower castes? Fortunately, no. In fact, even the most basic familiarity with another culture allows us to experience empathic sorrow and joy, disgust and fear. It turns out that we internalize "alien" principles quite readily and come to encode or anticipate emotionally and intellectually crucial features of the social world—including those in films—with perhaps surprising ease.

Here we see, from another angle, the two sides of analysis that I have been stressing from the outset. On the one hand, there is particularity—not merely the particularity of national cultures, but the particularity of regions, religions, castes, classes, philosophies, ages, and so forth, all the way down to individuals. On the other hand, there is the common genetic heritage of the human brain, the common principles of childhood development (beyond genetics), the recurring practices that arise from group dynamics—a whole series of universal principles that we all share. (I have focused on the manifestation of these universal patterns in cognitive structures and processes, though patterns in political economy, face-to-face interaction, and other areas provide crucial cross-cultural patterns as well.) Whether we are European, Chinese, African, or Indian, Christian, Jewish, Hindu, or Muslim, it is these universals that make it possible for us to understand Indian movies and to appreciate them, rather than merely drawing abstract inferences about them, as if they were part of some inscrutable puzzle.

In keeping with this, the preceding chapters outlined a series of universal principles and patterns that are particularly important for our response to Indian movies. The opening chapter considered the general structure of the three cross-culturally predominant narrative prototypes. The second chapter turned to the cross-culturally recurring ethical attitudes associated thematically with one of those prototypes. The third chapter took up our shared set of human emotions, considering how those emotions operate in cognitive architecture; it went on to address some aspects of the evolution of emotion that are consequential for literary response. The fourth chapter examined the ways in which song is connected with universal features of narrative discourse, and how these bear on narrative information, thematic exposition, and the enhancement of emotion. Finally, the fifth chapter turned to human vision and addressed the sorts of perception-based expectation, pattern isolation, and emotional response that are shared by people generally, whatever their culture.

These universals are the underlying, relatively abstract forms that are particularized socially and historically in films and other cultural practices and artifacts. As I have repeatedly emphasized, cultural specificity is not something entirely different from one place and time to another. Someone else's culture is not an alien mystery. It is a way of thought and experience that one can internalize through its connection with the narrative, emotional, perceptual, and other principles that we all share and that themselves provide the basis for cultural development in the first place. But, of course, to experience any degree of such internalization, we need to link the other culture with the universal principles, and we need to do this by way of cultural specificity, not making the error of assuming that universal principles are particularized in the same way from one society to another.

In connection with the latter, I have sought to isolate some of the most important, recurring cultural concerns in Indian movies. Thus I have discussed ancient Indic philosophy, the main Hindu deities, the main plot lines of important epics, central tenets of Ṣūfī Islam, and so forth. These particulars of Indian culture recur continually in Indian cinema, well beyond the films considered in the preceding pages. For example, the unity of all souls in brahman is a subtle, but important element in Bimal Roy's moving criticism of untouchability in *Sujata*. The intertwining of desire and māyā or illusion is a central concern of Mira Nair's *Kama Sutra*. The lovers' tryst in Deepa Mehta's *Water* would have far less emotional—and moral—force without its iconic links to Kṛṣṇa and Rādhā. It would be almost impossible to understand some of the events in Chandra Prakash Dwivedi's *Pinjar* without a knowledge of the *Rāmāyaṇa*. M. F. Hussain's *Meenaxi* would seem a mere chaotic muddle if one did not recognize its use of Ṣūfī motifs. One could continue this list almost indefinitely.

And yet, this is hardly everything there is to Indian movies. To put it differently, the cultural topics I have outlined are not anything like a final word on Indian society—how could they be? They are something more in the way of an invitation to explore Indian cinema and culture—and human universality—further, using these ideas as a point of departure. In connection with this, it is important to make several concluding points.

First, it probably goes without saying that no cultural paradigm provides a "key" to any film, at least not any film that is complex enough to sustain one's interest for more than a single viewing. Indeed, even when we have isolated a crucial cultural connection, the precise relation between cultural principles and particular films is not always clear. Some readers seem to take any linking of a character with an epic hero or a goddess as a sort of allegory. I, rather, take it to be first of all a matter of suggestion or dhvani. In some cases, a suggestion may point toward allegory. But it may indicate something much simpler and less definite—that we should in some way evaluate or respond to the character in the context of the earlier cultural paradigm. Consider a western example, such as one alluded to earlier. Suppose the protagonist of a film is having dinner with twelve followers and one of them leaves to turn him in to the police. Does this mean that the hero allegorizes Jesus? Probably not. It does mean that we should think about and respond to the betrayal in relation to Judas's betrayal of Jesus. That relation could be one of enhancing our condemnation of the betrayal in the film, or it could be contrastive, or ironic. It could even involve a comment, not on the current narrative, but on the biblical story or on the cultural significance of that story. In other words, cultural connections are crucial for understanding films, but they are not self-explanatory.

Second, it should also go without saying that there is a great deal to Indian film that is not at all foreign to the west. Given centuries of interaction, aspects of each culture have become part of the other culture. In connection with this, it is important not to exoticize Indian movies, looking only for esoteric references to Sanskrit, seeking out Ṣūfī paradoxes, and so on. In any given case, the primary paradigms for a film could be drawn from the Christian New Testament, American popular culture, or Shakespeare. Vishal Bharadwaj's versions of *Othello* and *Macbeth* (*Omkara* and *Maqbool,* respectively) certainly involve Indian elements. But they are, first of all, reworkings and rethinkings of Shakespeare. Similarly, Guru Dutt's *Pyaasa* draws on Kṛṣṇa and Rādhā prototypes, but it is perhaps equally immersed in Christian ideas and images—as is Amit Mitra and Sombhu Mitra's *Jagte Raho.*

Third, Indian culture is obviously vast. I have introduced what I take to be particularly crucial cultural elements. But this introduction is necessarily limited. The most obvious constraints come in the areas of political and social concerns. These tend to alter much more rapidly than philosophical, religious, ethical, and related traditions. I have stressed particular, paradigmatic historical moments, such as the 1857 uprising (which continues to inspire cinematic treatment, as the 2005 *Mangal Pandey* attests). I have also introduced particular political topics that are of long-lasting importance in Indian film. For example, the issue of political violence and ahiṃsā is an enduring concern, due to the Gandhian legacy of the independence movement. Colonialism is a topic of broad and continuing interest as well. But even these topics are not always developed in the same way and with reference to precisely the same political and social policies, events, or persons. Moreover, as just noted, political topics change. For instance, in recent years, Kashmir has become enormously important for obvious reasons. In keeping with this, a spate of films have taken up the topic of Kashmir—some explicitly, some implicitly. The implicit cases are in many ways the most interesting. For example, to understand a film such as *1942: A Love Story,* it is certainly important to understand Indian nationalism, British colonialism, and the debate over violence and nonviolence, as well as universal narrative prototypes. But it is no less important to understand the situation in Kashmir, to which the film covertly refers.

Given the fact that political issues change, sometimes very rapidly, it is easy to recognize that a book such as this is necessarily limited in its coverage of political paradigms. It is necessarily limited in its coverage of more enduring cultural paradigms as well. Again, I have chosen narrative, thematic, philosophical, and other cultural particulars that are very widespread in Indian cinema, and in Indian culture more generally. However, some films draw on practices and ideas that are more confined to a region, religious sect, or other subgroup. Moreover, there is common cultural material that I have had to leave out in order to keep the book to a manageable length. To take perhaps the most obvious case, I have repeatedly stressed the *Rāmāyaṇa,* but have barely touched on the *Mahābhārata,* the other great pan-Indian epic.

In this way, the preceding chapters cannot possibly lead to a complete understanding of Indian movies—any more than they can lead to a complete understanding of the human mind. However, the fundamental cultural background they provide should allow viewers to appreciate the intellectual and emotional force of Indian films, to recognize the importance of watching those films with care, and to envision the rewards of exploring Indian culture more deeply and thoroughly—all in the context of a shared humanity that allows us (Indian and non-Indian, Hindu and Muslim, Brahmin and Dalit) to experience those movies and that culture in personally meaningful ways.

# Notes

## Introduction

1. Over the past half-century, research in linguistics has shown us that there is basically one human language—a point made cogently by Noam Chomsky (see, for example, 7). Though they prevent direct inter-linguistic comprehension, the differences among "languages" are in fact very slight, limited variations on shared basic principles. Over the past decade, a number of writers have been arguing that the same point holds for literature and related arts, such as cinema (see, for example, the special "Literary Universals" issue [6.2, August 2005] of *Consciousness, Literature, and the Arts,* available at http://www.aber.ac.uk/~drawww/journal; there is also some information available at the site of the University of Palermo's Literary Universals Project, http://litup.unipa.it).

2. See Hogan and Pandit.

3. See Chapter Four of Hogan, *The Mind.*

## Chapter One

1. On some of the evidence for this, see Holland et al. 182–183 and citations.

2. The cross-cultural narrative evidence for the prototypes is quite extensive. There is also some experimental evidence, though it is more limited. For a discussion and analysis of both the narrative and experimental evidence, see Hogan, *The Mind;* see also the entries on "Literary Universals" and "Narrative Universals" in the forthcoming *Cambridge Encyclopedia of the Language Sciences.*

3. Biographical criticism adds a third concern—the author's personal experience.

4. Some examples may be found in Hogan, "Shakespeare."

5. The indirectness of the criticism also serves to suggest the vagueness of the idea of untouchability (cf. Galanter 242 and 254 on problems with the legal definition of the concept).

6. There are hints of this connection elsewhere in the film. For example, in the morning just after her marriage to Prakash, Chhaya comes upon Bablu making a garland and singing about Sītā and Rāma.

7. I am grateful to Lalita Pandit for help with the translation here.

8. The use of the name "Durgā" varies. But it is connected with the Goddess as protector from early on (see, for example, Coburn 23–24).

9. For example, Rangoonwalla cites the song as one of the many silly, formulaic aspects of the film (76).

10. I am grateful to Lalita Pandit for pointing out this connection.

11. Some examples may be found in Hogan, "Narrative Universals, National Sacrifice" and "Narrative Universals, Nationalism."

12. After Rajiv Gandhi was replaced as prime minister, the Indian troops were withdrawn. However, only a year later, Gandhi was campaigning to be returned to office. Moreover, he stated publicly that "the India-Sri Lanka pact of 1987, under which the Indian army was sent to Sri Lanka, was not defunct" and that "he had no regrets over the Indian military deployment in the island nation" (Swamy 221). This obviously worried anyone who feared the reintroduction of Indian troops. The assassination of Rajiv Gandhi was in part a response to this situation. However, Sivan does not follow this time line. In the film, the plan to assassinate the VIP (as he is called in the film) develops while Indian troops are still in Sri Lanka. Thus, unsurprisingly, the film alters historical events by bringing them closer to the sacrificial and heroic narrative prototypes, where the devastation/foreign domination continues until the sacrifice/heroic defense of the nation.

13. Of course, there is a heroic emplotment here as well. In explicitly political versions of the sacrificial plot, the sacrificial prototype is commonly interwoven with the heroic prototype.

14. In the case of the former, it is also related to the use of undyed, white cloth for mourning dress in India.

## Chapter Two

1. Here, too, there is considerable cross-cultural narrative evidence and, in this case, significant experimental support—though, of course, the precise interpretation of the experimental findings is not uncontroversial (e.g., not everyone would explain it in terms of precisely these ethical options). For example, narrative attestations range from Homer to the Persian *Shâhnâme,* the Japanese *Tale of the Heike,* the Nyanga epic of Mwindo, and of course Indian works, such as the *Rāmāyaṇa* and the *Mahābhārata.* For an overview and analysis of some of this evidence, see Chapter Four of Hogan, *The Mind.*

2. For an informative overview of the parallel cinema, see Datta 18–43.

3. I am grateful to Lalita Pandit for pointing this out to me.

4. The film's advocacy of violence has been remarked on by a number of critics, though in a rather different context. For example, Dissanayake and Sahai maintain that the film "has the effect of glamorizing" violence (*Sholay* 61).

5. Derné reports that "G. P. Sippy . . . producer of the tremendously successful *Sholay* . . . says that Ram and Ravan, the hero and villain of the *Rāmāyaṇa,* 'are somehow brought [into every film], and the story is woven around those characters'" (Derné 51). Certainly, Sippy was not excluding *Sholay* from this judgment.

## Chapter Three

1. For a discussion of some nuances and complications of this research, see Martin; Bless; Klaus Fiedler; and particularly Forgas, "Affect and Information."

2. See Oatley, *Best,* 201, Bower 389; and Forgas, "Affect in Social Judgments," 244; on some complications of the relation between mood and memory, see Forgas, "Affect and Information," and Eich and Macaulay.

3. The practice is not entirely theory-dependent. See, for example, Tan 171 on empathic emotions and 221 on "the *dominance* of certain characteristic emotions" in particular genres.

4. Indeed, many aspects of rasa theory dovetail very nicely with recent work in cognitive science (see Chapter Two of Hogan, *The Mind,* and Oatley, "Emotions" and "Writingandreading").

5. For a lucid introduction to the theory of adaptation, see Pinker 36–44, 155–174.

6. For a fuller discussion of this idea, see Hogan, "Laughing."

7. For further discussion of the difference between tragedy and works of pathetic rasa, see Gerow. Some critics have touched on the relation of Indian melodrama to Indian literary tradition (see, for example, Dissanayake, "Introduction," 5).

8. Of course, some Indian viewers will find them contemptible also—as suggested by Shekhar Kapur's treatment of Kṛṣṇa's mischief, which we will consider in the next section.

9. We will consider dhvani further in Chapter Four.

10. For a valuable discussion of Kapoor's relation to Chaplin, see Chapter Six of Dissanayake and Sahai's *Raj.* One claim in their analysis is particularly germane to the present study: Kapoor "capitalized on the universalistic elements in Chaplin's films while Indianizing the culture-specific ones" (101).

11. I am combining slightly different versions of the manifesto for purposes of clarity, as the differences have no substantive effect on the present argument. For an examination of these different versions, see Coppola.

## Chapter Four

1. For other discussions of the interlude, see Sardar 57 and Cooper's *In Black.*

2. Gopinath points out that western critics sometimes contrast western musicals with "the illogic and unintelligibility of the Bollywood song and dance sequence" (118). The contrast is difficult to understand. How is it logical for villagers to start singing and dancing in a western musical but not in an Indian musical?

3. On these and other cases—from Persian, Sanskrit, and other traditions—see Hogan, *The Mind,* 156–160 and citations.

4. The connection with speech is particularly clear in Indian dance, which greatly emphasizes facial expressions and manual gestures.

5. For further discussion of these concepts, see Hogan, *Empire,* 203–205 and 250.

6. The story is the events as they "actually" occurred, with their precise sequence, duration, and so forth. The discourse is the presentation of the story—roughly, the way it is told.

For example, in a detective story, a fight may precede a murder, which in turn precedes the discovery of the corpse. However, in the discourse, the way the story is told, we may begin with the discovery of the corpse, turning to the fight and murder only later.

7. This quote is from the brochure that accompanies the Collectors edition DVD set from Yash Raj Films.

8. Dhvani is the central semantic concept of Sanskrit aesthetic theory. The classical discussion is to be found in Anandavardhana. See also Amaladass.

9. The interlude ends with Anjali and Rahul living in what looks like a temple. They have made their home into a sort of shrine to everything they left behind in India. Suddenly, the lovable Anjali is a (still lovable, but distressing) xenophobe. The treatment of Anjali's identity-based prejudice follows, extending the point of the "Vande Mataram" interlude.

10. Tan and Frijda give three categories of sentimental themes. Each suggests a link with childhood concerns. The first is separation and reunion, and includes "Being accepted as a son . . . by a father" (57). The second concerns justice and includes melodramas of self-sacrifice. As we have seen, these commonly focus on parent/child relations. The third treats awe, including "Being in an environment in which one feels tiny and insignificant" (62).

## Chapter Five

1. For a range of examples, see Hogan, *The Mind,* 169–171.

2. One of the best depictions of the Ṣūfī path is presented in Farid ud-Din Attar's *The Conference of the Birds.* As Levy explains, this poem depicts "the difficulties [one] must undergo on the Sufi Path," allegorically represented as a journey "through the Seven Valleys of Seeking, Love, Gnosis, Self-reliance, Acknowledgment of One-ness, Uncertainty, and lastly, Destitution and Death to Self" (99).

3. Our experience of jump cuts is probably bound up with a particular form of projection—anticipatory visual focus, which originates in the brain stem (see Matthews 223).

4. Given our cognitive/perceptual preparation for shot/reverse shot, it may be that we come to expect shot/reverse shot after only one film, or even after only one exposure. The point is simply that some training is required for us to have the expectation.

5. I am grateful to Lalita Pandit for clarifying the Urdu in this dialogue.

6. The film includes another lost friendship (in addition to Ramdei) and another lost romantic love. I am leaving these aside as they do not add significantly to the preceding analysis.

7. The point is in keeping with Grodal's claim that a "freeze-frame is often used and experienced . . . as a shift in reality-status" (*Moving Pictures,* 152).

8. In fact, I find the film often awkward in dialogue, flat in characterization, and misleading about family dynamics in India today.

9. Gopinath points out that the film is concerned with male, Hindu nationalism, and rightly stresses the ways in which nationalism is bound up with sexual ideology ("the production of normative and deviant sexualities" [134], as she puts it). However, she does not develop the thematic points of the film itself much beyond noting this general connection. This results, I believe, from the fact that she too does not pay attention to the visual properties of the film.

10. In keeping with this, when Ashok bursts in on Radha and Sita, they try to cover themselves quickly, presumably from a spontaneous sense of shame. To do this, they use a piece of orange cloth. In contrast, when they decide to leave together, thus affirming their love and setting aside shame, they agree to meet at a Muslim shrine.

11. I hope it is clear from my treatment of Hindu tradition in the rest of the book that I am not at all endorsing this idea. I am merely inferring its thematic presence in the film.

12. See www.unicef.org/newsline/00pr17.htm (accessed 16 November 2006).

13. It is perhaps worth noting that Islamic states do not appear to be unusually sexually liberatory. See, for example, Ireland on "Iran's Anti-Gay Pogrom."

## Afterword

1. I say "stereotypical" and "according to the standard view" because my very limited experience of individuals diagnosed as autistic does not seem to fit this account.

# Bibliography

Abhinavagupta. *The Aesthetic Experience according to Abhinavagupta.* Ed. and trans. Raniero Gnoli. 2nd ed. Varanasi: Chokhamba Sanskrit Series, 1968.

———. *Locana.* In Ingalls.

Adolphs, Ralph, and Antonio R. Damasio. "Neurobiology of Emotion at a Systems Level." In *The Neuropsychology of Emotion.* Ed. Joan C. Borod. New York: Oxford UP, 2000, 194–213.

Ahmed, Syed Z. *Twilight of an Empire.* Lahore, Pakistan: Ferozsons, 1996.

Ali, Maulana Muhammad, ed. and trans. *The Holy Qur'ān: Arabic Text, English Translation and Commentary.* 2nd, revised ed. Columbus, Ohio: Ahmidiyyah Anjuman Isha'at Islam Lahore, 1995.

Ali, Muzaffar, dir. *Umrao Jaan.* Screenplay by Shama Zaidi, Javed Siddiqi, and Muzaffar Ali, adapted from the novel by Mirza Ruswa. Edited by B. Prasad. Photography by Pravin Bhatt. Lyrics by Shahryar. Music by Khayyam. Art direction by Bansi Chandra Gupta, Muzaffar Ali, and Manzoor. Produced by Muzaffar Ali. 1981.

Al-Kalābādhī, Abū Bakr. *The Doctrine of the Sūfīs.* Trans. A. J. Arberry. Cambridge: Cambridge UP, 1977.

Amaladass, Anand. *Philosophical Implications of Dhvani: Experience of Symbol Language in Indian Aesthetics.* Vienna: De Nobili Research Library, 1984.

Anandavardhana. *Dhvanyaloka.* In Ingalls.

Anderson, Joseph D. *The Reality of Illusion: An Ecological Approach to Cognitive Film Theory.* Carbondale, IL: Southern Illinois UP, 1996.

Appiah, Kwame Anthony. *In My Father's House: Africa in the Philosophy of Culture.* New York: Oxford UP, 1992.

Avalon, Arthur, ed. and trans. *The Great Liberation (Mahanirvana Tantra).* Madras: Ganesh, 1963.

Bahadur, Satish. “Esthétique du film indien: Le kitsch par excellence.” In *CinémAction: Les cinémas indiens.* Ed. Aruna Vasudev and Philippe Lenglet. Paris: Editions du Cerf, 1984, 188–193.

Bakshi, Rajni. “Raj Kapoor: From *Jis Desh Mein Ganga Behti Hai* to *Ram Teri Ganga Maili.*” In *The Secret Politics of Our Desires: Innocence, Culpability and Indian Popular Cinema.* Ed. Ashis Nandy. New Delhi, India: Oxford UP, 1998, 92–133.

Beeman, Mark. “Coarse Semantic Coding and Discourse Comprehension.” In *Right Hemisphere Language Comprehension: Perspectives from Cognitive Neuroscience.* Ed. Mark Beeman and Christine Chiarello. Mahwah, NJ: Lawrence Erlbaum, 1998, 255–284.

Benegal, Shyam, dir. *Nishānt* (*Night's End*). Screenplay by Vijay Tendulkar. Dialogues by Pt. Satyadev Dubey. Edited by Bhanudas. Photography by Govind Nihalani. Blaze Entertainment, 1975.

Bhabha, Homi. “DissemiNation: Time, Narrative, and the Margins of the Modern Narrative.” In *Nation and Narration.* Ed. Bhabha. New York: Routledge, 1990.

Bharatamuni. *The Nāṭya Śāstra.* Delhi, India: Sri Satguru Publications, n.d.

Bless, Herbert. “The Interplay of Affect and Cognition: The Mediating Role of General Knowledge Structures.” In *Feeling and Thinking: The Role of Affect in Social Cognition.* Ed. Joseph P. Forgas. Cambridge: Cambridge UP and Paris: Editions de la Maison des Sciences de l'Homme, 2000, 201–222.

Bordwell, David. “Convention, Construction, and Cinematic Vision.” In *Post-Theory: Reconstructing Film Studies.* Ed. Bordwell and Noël Carroll. Madison, WI: U of Wisconsin P, 1996, 87–107.

———. *On the History of Film Style.* Cambridge, MA: Harvard UP, 1997.

———. *Ozu and the Poetics of Cinema.* Princeton, NJ: Princeton UP, 1988.

———. *Planet Hong Kong: Popular Cinema and the Art of Entertainment.* Cambridge, MA: Harvard UP, 2000.

Bower, G. H. “Affect and Cognition.” *Philosophical Transactions of the Royal Society of London, Series B* 302 (1983): 387–402.

Boyer, Pascal. *Religion Explained: The Evolutionary Origins of Religious Thought.* New York: Basic Books, 2001.

Brothers, Leslie. *Friday's Footprint: How Society Shapes the Human Mind.* New York: Oxford UP, 1997.

Brown, Judith M. *Gandhi: Prisoner of Hope.* New Haven, CT: Yale UP, 1989.

Brownell, Hiram, and Gail Martino. "Deficits in Inference and Social Cognition: The Effects of Right Hemisphere Brain Damage on Discourse." In *Right Hemisphere Language Comprehension: Perspectives from Cognitive Neuroscience.* Ed. Mark Beeman and Christine Chiarello. Mahwah, NJ: Lawrence Erlbaum, 1998, 309–328.

Carroll, Noël. "Art, Narrative, and Emotion." In *Emotion and the Arts.* Ed. Mette Hjort and Sue Laver. New York: Oxford UP, 1997, 190–211.

———. *Engaging the Moving Image.* New Haven, CT: Yale UP, 2003.

———. "Film, Emotion, and Genre." In *Passionate Views: Film, Cognition, and Emotion.* Ed. Carl Plantinga and Greg M. Smith. Baltimore, MD: Johns Hopkins UP, 1999, 21–47.

———. "The Paradox of Suspense." In *Suspense: Conceptualizations, Theoretical Analyses and Empirical Explorations.* Ed. Peter Vorderer, Hans Wulf, and Mike Friedrichsen. Hillsdale, NJ: Lawrence Erlbaum, 1996, 71–91.

Chaitanya, Krishna. *A History of Arabic Literature.* New Delhi: Manohar, 1983.

Chakrabarty, Ajit, dir. *Ardhangini.* Story by Chandrakant. Screenplay by Vishwamitter Adil and Shashi Bhushan. Dialogues by Vishwamitter Adil. Edited by C. Ramrao. Photography by R. M. Sabnis. Lyrics by Majrooh Sultanpuri. Music by Vasant Desai. Produced by Ajit Chakrabarty. Mars and Movies, 1959.

Chakravarty, Sumita S. *National Identity in Indian Popular Cinema, 1947–1987.* Austin, TX: U of Texas P, 1993.

Chandrasekhar, S. "Foreword—Personal Perspectives on Untouchability." In *The Untouchables in Contemporary India.* Ed. J. Michael Mahar. Tucson, AZ: U of Arizona P, 1972, xi–xxviii.

Chatterjee, Gayatri. *Mother India.* New Delhi, India: Penguin, 2002.

Chiarello, Christine. "On Codes of Meaning and the Meaning of Codes: Semantic Access and Retrieval within and between Hemispheres." In *Right Hemisphere Language Comprehension: Perspectives from Cognitive Neuroscience.* Ed. Mark Beeman and Christine Chiarello. Mahwah, NJ: Lawrence Erlbaum, 1998, 141–160.

Chomsky, Noam. *New Horizons in the Study of Language and Mind.* Cambridge: Cambridge UP, 2000.

Clark, Andy. "Embodied, Situated, and Distributed Cognition." In

*A Companion to Cognitive Science*. Ed. William Bechtel and George Graham. Oxford: Blackwell, 1998, 506–517.

Clore, Gerald L., and Andrew Ortony. “Cognition in Emotion: Always, Sometimes, or Never?” In *Cognitive Neuroscience of Emotion*. Ed. Richard D. Land and Lynn Nadel with Geoffrey L. Ahern, John J. B. Allen, Alfred W. Kaszniak, Steven Z. Rapcsak, and Gary E. Schwartz. Oxford: Oxford UP, 2000.

Coburn, Thomas B. *Encountering the Goddess: A Translation of the Devī-Māhātmya and a Study of Its Interpretation*. Albany, NY: State U of New York P, 1991.

Cooper, Darius. *Between Tradition and Modernity: The Cinema of Satyajit Ray*. Cambridge: Cambridge UP, 2000.

———. *In Black and White: Hollywood and the Melodrama of Guru Dutt*. Calcutta, India: Seagull, 2005.

Coppola, Carlo. “The All-India Progressive Writers’ Association: The Early Phases.” In *Marxist Influences and South Asian Literature*. Vol. 1. East Lansing, MI: Asian Studies Center of Michigan State U, 1974.

Currie, Gregory. *Image and Mind: Film, Philosophy, and Cognitive Science*. Cambridge: Cambridge UP, 1995.

Damasio, Antonio R. *Descartes’ Error: Emotion, Reason, and the Human Brain*. New York: Avon Books, 1994.

Daniélou, Alain. *The Myths and Gods of India*. Rochester, VT: Inner Traditions International, 1991.

Danvers, Frederick Charles. *The Portuguese in India: Being a History of the Rise and Decline of Their Eastern Empire*. 2 vols. London: Frank Cass, 1966.

Datta, Sangeeta. *Shyam Benegal*. London: British Film Institute, 2002.

Davis, Dick. “Introduction.” In *The Conference of the Birds*. By Farid ud-Din Attar. Trans. Afkham Darbandi and Davis. New York: Penguin, 1984.

Dawood, N. J., trans. *The Koran*. New York: Penguin, 1956.

Derné, Steve. *Movies, Masculinity, and Modernity: An Ethnography of Men’s Filmgoing in India*. Westport, CT: Greenwood P, 2000.

Desai, Jigna. *Beyond Bollywood: The Cultural Politics of South Asian Diasporic Film*. New York: Routledge, 2004.

Dhanaṃjaya. *The Daśarūpa: A Treatise on Hindu Dramaturgy*. Trans. George C. O. Haas. New York: AMS, 1965.

Dickinson, Kay. "General Introduction." In *Movie Music, the Film Reader.* Ed. Dickinson. New York: Routledge, 2003, 1–11.

Dissanayake, Wimal. "Introduction." In *Melodrama and Asian Cinema.* Ed. Dissanayake. Cambridge: Cambridge UP, 1993, 1–8.

Dissanayake, Wimal, and Malti Sahai. *Raj Kapoor's Films: Harmony of Discourses.* New Delhi, India: Vikas, 1988.

———. *Sholay: A Cultural Reading.* New Delhi, India: Wiley Eastern, 1992.

Doniger, Wendy, and Brian K. Smith, eds. and trans. *The Laws of Manu.* New York: Penguin, 1991.

Dowson, John. *A Classical Dictionary of Hindu Mythology and Religion, Geography, History, and Literature.* 12th ed. London: Routledge and Kegan Paul, 1972.

Dreyer, Carl, dir. *The Passion of Joan of Arc.* Screenplay by Carl Dreyer and Joseph Delteil. Edited by Marguerite Beaugé and Carl Dreyer. Photography by Rudolf Maté. Art direction by Hermann Warm. Société générale de Films, 1928.

Dutt, Guru, dir. *Baaz* (*The Falcon*). Story and screenplay by Guru Dutt. Dialogues by L. C. Bismil and Sarshar Sailani. Edited by Y. G. Chawhan. Photography by V. K. Murthy. Lyrics by Majrooh Sultanpuri. Music by O. P. Nayyar. Produced by Miss Haridarshan. HG Films, 1953.

Dwyer, Rachel, and Divia Patel. *Cinema India: The Visual Culture of Hindi Film.* New Brunswick, NJ: Rutgers UP, 2002.

Edelman, Gerald M. *Wider Than the Sky: The Phenomenal Gift of Consciousness.* New Haven, CT: Yale UP, 2004.

Eich, Eric, and Dawn Macaulay. "Fundamental Factors in Mood-Dependent Memory." In *Feeling and Thinking: The Role of Affect in Social Cognition.* Ed. Joseph P. Forgas. Cambridge: Cambridge UP and Paris: Editions de la Maison des Sciences de l'Homme, 2000, 109–130.

Eitzen, Dirk. "The Emotional Basis of Film Comedy." In *Passionate Views: Film, Cognition, and Emotion.* Ed. Carl Plantinga and Greg M. Smith. Baltimore, MD: Johns Hopkins UP, 1999, 84–99.

Ekman, Paul. "Cross-Cultural Studies in Facial Expression." In *Darwin and Facial Expression: A Century of Research in Review.* Ed. Ekman. New York: Academic P, 1973.

Erasmus, Desiderius. *The Praise of Folly.* Trans. Clarence H. Miller. New Haven, CT: Yale UP, 1979.

Faust, Miriam. "Obtaining Evidence of Language Comprehension from Sentence Priming." In *Right Hemisphere Language Comprehension: Perspectives from Cognitive Neuroscience.* Ed. Mark Beeman and Christine Chiarello. Mahwah, NJ: Lawrence Erlbaum, 1998, 161–186.

Fiedler, Klaus. "Toward an Integrative Account of Affect and Cognition Phenomena Using the BIAS Computer Algorithm." In *Feeling and Thinking: The Role of Affect in Social Cognition.* Ed. Joseph P. Forgas. Cambridge: Cambridge UP and Paris: Editions de la Maison des Sciences de l'Homme, 2000, 223–252.

Fiedler, Leslie. *What Was Literature? Class Culture and Mass Society.* New York: Touchstone, 1982.

Forgas, Joseph P. "Affect and Information Processing Strategies: An Interactive Relationship." In *Feeling and Thinking: The Role of Affect in Social Cognition.* Ed. Joseph P. Forgas. Cambridge: Cambridge UP and Paris: Editions de la Maison des Sciences de l'Homme, 2000, 253–280.

———. "Affect in Social Judgments and Decisions: A Multiprocess Model." In *Advances in Experimental Social Psychology.* Vol. 25. Ed. Mark P. Zanna. San Diego, CA: Academic P, 1972.

Freud, Sigmund. *Jokes and Their Relation to the Unconscious.* Trans. and ed. James Strachey. New York: W. W. Norton, 1960.

Frijda, Nico. *The Emotions.* Cambridge: Cambridge UP and Paris: Editions de la Maison des Sciences de l'Homme, 1986.

Frye, Northrop. *Anatomy of Criticism: Four Essays.* Princeton, NJ: Princeton UP, 1957.

Gainotti, Guido. "Neuropsychological Theories of Emotion." In *The Neuropsychology of Emotion.* Ed. Joan C. Borod. Oxford: Oxford UP, 2000, 214–236.

Galanter, Marc. "The Abolition of Disabilities—Untouchability and the Law." In *The Untouchables in Contemporary India.* Ed. J. Michael Mahar. Tucson, AZ: U of Arizona P, 1972, 227–314.

Gandhi, Mohandas. *The Gandhi Reader: A Source Book of His Life and Writings.* Ed. Homer A. Jack. Madras, India: Samanta Books, 1983.

Ganguli, Amulya. "Muting History." *Hindustan Times* (28 April 2003), http://www.countercurrents.org/comm-ganguly28403.htm.

Gardner, Howard. *Art, Mind, and Brain: A Cognitive Approach to Creativity.* New York: Basic Books, 1982.

Garraty, John, and Peter Gay, eds. *The Columbia History of the World.* New York: Harper and Row, 1981.

Gathercole, Susan E. "Models of Verbal Short-Term Memory." In *Cognitive Models of Memory.* Ed. Martin A. Conway. Cambridge, MA: MIT P, 1997, 13–45.

Gerow, Edwin. "Bhāsa's Urubhanga and Indian Poetics." *Journal of the American Oriental Society* 105.3 (1985): 405–412.

Giffen, Lois Anita. *Theory of Profane Love among the Arabs: The Development of the Genre.* New York: New York UP and London: U of London P, 1971.

Gilbert, Daniel T., and Timothy D. Wilson. "Miswanting: Some Problems in the Forecasting of Future Affective States." In *Feeling and Thinking: The Role of Affect in Social Cognition.* Ed. Joseph P. Forgas. Cambridge: Cambridge UP and Paris: Editions de la Maison des Sciences de l'Homme, 2000, 178–197.

Gokulsing, K. Moti, and Wimal Dissanayake. *Indian Popular Cinema—A Narrative of Cultural Change.* Stoke on Trent, Staffordshire: Trentham Books, 1998.

Gopinath, Gayatri. *Impossible Desires: Queer Diasporas and South Asian Public Cultures.* Durham, NC: Duke UP, 2005.

Gould, Stephen Jay. *The Structure of Evolutionary Theory.* Cambridge, MA: Belknap P, 2002.

Grodal, Torben. "Film Lighting and Mood." In *Moving Image Theory: Ecological Considerations.* Ed. Joseph D. Anderson and Barbara Fisher Anderson. Carbondale: Southern Illinois UP, 2005.

———. *Moving Pictures: A New Theory of Film Genres, Feelings, and Cognition.* Oxford: Clarendon P, 1997.

Hart, George L. *The Poems of Ancient Tamil: Their Milieu and Their Sanskrit Counterparts.* Berkeley: U of California P, 1975.

Hatfield, Elaine, John T. Cacioppo, and Richard L. Rapson. *Emotional Contagion.* Cambridge: Cambridge UP, 1994.

Hawley, John Stratton, in association with Shrivatsa Goswami. *At Play with Krishna: Pilgrimage Dramas from Brindavan.* Princeton, NJ: Princeton UP, 1981.

Hjort, Mette, and Sue Laver. "Introduction." In *Emotion and the Arts.* Ed. Hjort and Laver. New York: Oxford UP, 1997.

Hoffman, Donald D. *Visual Intelligence: How We Create What We See.* New York: W. W. Norton, 1998.

Hogan, Patrick Colm. *Cognitive Science, Literature, and the Arts: A Guide for Humanists.* New York: Routledge, 2003.

———. *Colonialism and Cultural Identity: Crises of Tradition in the Anglophone Literatures of India, Africa, and the Caribbean.* Albany, NY: State U of New York P, 2000.

———. *Empire and Poetic Voice: Cognitive and Cultural Studies of Literary Tradition and Colonialism.* Albany, NY: State U of New York P, 2004.

———. "Imagining What You Can Do: The Brain, Free Will, and Art." *PsyArt: An Online Journal for the Psychological Study of the Arts,* article 050718, http://www.clas.ufl.edu/ipsa/journal/2005_hogan01.shtml, 18 July 2005.

———. "Laughing Brains: On the Cognitive Mechanisms and Reproductive Functions of Mirth." *Semiotica* 165 (2007): 391–408.

———. *The Mind and Its Stories: Narrative Universals and Human Emotion.* Cambridge: Cambridge UP and Paris: Editions de la Maison des Sciences de l'Homme, 2003.

———. "Narrative Universals, Nationalism, and Sacrificial Terror: From *Nosferatu* to Nazism." *Film Studies,* forthcoming.

———. "Narrative Universals, National Sacrifice, and *Dou E Yuan.*" *Ex/Change* (Hong Kong) 12 (2005): 18–25.

———. "Rasa Theory and Dharma Theory: From *The Home and the World* to *Bandit Queen.*" *Quarterly Review of Film and Video* 20.1 (January–March 2003): 37–52.

———. "Shakespeare, Eastern Theatre, and Literary Universals: Drama in the Context of Cognitive Science." In *Shakespeare East and West.* Ed. Minoru Fujita and Leonard Pronko. Richmond, Surrey: Japan Library, 1996.

Hogan, Patrick Colm, and Lalita Pandit. "Ancient Theories of Narrative (Non-Western)." In *The Routledge Encyclopedia of Narrative Theory.* Ed. David Herman, Manfred Jahn, and Marie-Laure Ryan. London: Routledge, 2005, 14–19.

Holland, John, Keith Holyoak, Richard Nisbett, and Paul Thagard. *Induction: Processes of Inference, Learning, and Discovery.* Cambridge, MA: MIT P, 1987.

Hutchins, Edwin. *Cognition in the Wild.* Cambridge, MA: MIT P, 1995.

Ilangô Adigal, Prince. *Shilappadikaram (The Ankle Bracelet).* Trans. Alain Daniélou. New York: New Directions, 1965.

Ingalls, Daniel H. H., ed. *The Dhvanyaloka of Anandavardhana with the Locana of Abhinavagupta.* Trans. Ingalls, Jeffrey Masson, and M. V. Patwardhan. Cambridge, MA: Harvard UP, 1990.

Ireland, Doug. "Iran's Anti-Gay Pogrom." *In These Times* 30.01 (January 2006): 8–9.

Jauss, Hans Robert. "Literary History as a Challenge to Literary Theory." *Toward an Aesthetic of Reception.* Trans. Timothy Bahti. Minneapolis, MN: U of Minnesota P, 1982, 3–45.

Johar, Karan, dir. *Kabhi Khushi Kabhie Gham . . .* Screenplay by Sheena Parikh and Karan Johar. Edited by Sanja Sankla. Photography by Kiran Deohans. Production design/art by Sharmishta Roy. Produced by Yash Johar. Dharma Productions, 2001.

Johnson-Laird, Philip N., and Keith Oatley. "The Language of Emotions: An Analysis of a Semantic Field." *Cognition and Emotion* 3.2 (1989): 81–123.

Joshi, Sam. "In the Eyes of the Beholder: 'Seeing More' into the Erotic Vision of *Romeo & Julian.*" *South Asian Popular Culture* 1.2 (2003): 161–173.

Jourdain, Robert. *Music, the Brain, and Ecstasy: How Music Captures Our Imagination.* New York: Quill, 2002.

Kabir, Nasreen Munni. *Bollywood: The Indian Cinema Story.* London: Channel 4 Books, 2001.

———. *Guru Dutt: A Life in Cinema.* New Delhi, India: Oxford UP, 1997.

———, dir. *In Search of Guru Dutt.* Edited by Martin Roche. Produced by Nasreen Munni Kabir, 1989.

Kahneman, Daniel, and Dale T. Miller. "Norm Theory: Comparing Reality to Its Alternatives." *Psychological Review* 93.2 (1986): 136–153.

Kanda, K. C. *Urdu Ghazals: An Anthology (from 16th to 20th Century).* New Delhi, India: Sterling Publishers, 1994.

Kane, Julie. "Poetry as Right-Hemispheric Language." *Journal of Consciousness Studies* 11.5/11.6 (2004): 21–59.

Kapoor, Raj, dir. *Shree 420.* Story and dialogues by K. A. Abbas. Screenplay by K. A. Abbas and V. P. Sathe. Edited by G. G. Mayekar. Photography by Radhu Karmakar. Lyrics by Shailendra and Hasrat

Jaipuri. Music by Shankar Jaikishan. Produced by Raj Kapoor. R K Studios, 1955.

Kapur, Shekhar, dir. *Bandit Queen.* Screenplay by Mala Sen. Edited by Renu Saluja. Photography by Ashok Mehta. Music by Nusrat Fateh Ali Khan. Produced by Sundeep S. Bedi. Film Four International and Kaleidoscope, 1994.

Kautilya. *The Arthashastra.* Ed. and Trans. L. N. Rangarajan. New Delhi, India: Penguin, 1992.

Kay, Hugh. *Salazar and Modern Portugal.* New York: Hawthorn Books, 1970.

Kazmi, Fareed. *The Politics of India's Conventional Cinema: Imaging a Universe, Subverting a Multiverse.* New Delhi: Sage, 1999.

Kennedy, Miranda, and Matthew Power. "The Buddha's Teardrop." *In These Times* 27.15 (23 June 2003): 20–23.

Khan, Mehboob, dir. *Mother India.* Dialogues by Vajahat Mirza and S. Ali Raza. Edited by Shamsudin Kadri. Photography by Faredoon Irani. Songs by Shakeel Badayuni. Music by Naushad. Mehboob Productions, 1957.

Khizer, Mirza M. "Sufism and Social Integration." In *Sufism and Communal Harmony.* Ed. Asghar Ali Engineer. Jaipur: Printwell, 1991, 102–127.

Kinsley, David. *Hindu Goddesses: Visions of the Divine Feminine in the Hindu Religious Tradition.* Berkeley, CA: U of California P, 1986.

Kiparsky, Paul. "On Theory and Interpretation." In *The Linguistics of Writing: Arguments between Language and Literature.* Ed. Nigel Fabb, Derek Attridge, Alan Durant, and Colin MacCabe. New York: Methuen, 1987, 185–198.

Knappert, Jan. *Indian Mythology: An Encyclopedia of Myth and Legend.* New York: Aquarian P, 1991.

Kosslyn, Stephen. *Image and Brain: The Resolution of the Imagery Debate.* Cambridge, MA: MIT P, 1994.

Kuan Han-ch'ing. *The Injustice Done to Tou Ngo.* In *Six Yüan Plays.* Ed. and trans. Liu Jung-en. New York: Penguin, 1972, 115–158.

LeDoux, Joseph. *The Emotional Brain: The Mysterious Underpinnings of Emotional Life.* New York: Touchstone, 1996.

———. *Synaptic Self: How Our Brains Become Who We Are.* New York: Viking, 2002.

Levy, Reuben. *An Introduction to Persian Literature.* New York: Columbia UP, 1969.

Lichtenstadter, Ilse. *Introduction to Classical Arabic Literature.* New York: Schocken, 1976.

Liu Jung-en. "Introduction." In *Six Yüan Plays.* Ed. and trans. Liu. New York: Penguin, 1972, 7–35.

Lorca, Federico García. *The Selected Poems of Federico García Lorca.* Ed. Francisco García Lorca and Donald M. Allen. New York: New Directions, 1955.

Mahar, J. Michael. "Editor's Preface." In *The Untouchables in Contemporary India.* Ed. Mahar. Tucson, AZ: U of Arizona P, 1972, xxix–xxxii.

Maltby, Richard. "'A Brief Romantic Interlude': Dick and Jane Go to 3½ Seconds of the Classical Hollywood Cinema." In *Post-Theory: Reconstructing Film Studies.* Ed. David Bordwell and Noël Carroll. Madison, WI: U of Wisconsin P, 1996, 434–459.

Marques, A. H. De Oliveira. *History of Portugal.* 2 vols. New York: Columbia UP, 1972.

Martin, Leonard L. "Moods Do Not Convey Information: Moods in Context Do." In *Feeling and Thinking: The Role of Affect in Social Cognition.* Ed. Joseph P. Forgas. Cambridge: Cambridge UP and Paris: Editions de la Maison des Sciences de l'Homme, 2000, 153–177.

Marx, Karl. *Capital: A Critique of Political Economy. Volume I: The Process of Capitalist Production.* Ed. Frederick Engels. Trans. Samuel Moore and Edward Aveling. New York: International Publishers, 1967.

Matthews, Gary G. *Neurobiology: Molecules, Cells, and Systems.* 2nd ed. Malden, MA: Blackwell Science, 2001.

McDermott, Rachel Fell, ed. and trans. *Singing to the Goddess: Poems to Kālī and Umā from Bengal.* Oxford: Oxford UP, 2001.

McGaugh, James L. *Memory and Emotion: The Making of Lasting Memories.* New York: Columbia UP, 2003.

Mehta, Deepa, dir. *Fire.* Screenplay by Deepa Mehta. Edited by Barry Farrell. Photography by Giles Nuttgens. Art Direction by Sunil Chabra. Produced by Deepa Mehta. Kaleidoscope Entertainment and Trial by Fire Films, 1996.

Mehta, Tarla. *Sanskrit Play Production in Ancient India.* Delhi: Motilal Banarsidass, 1995.

Mishra, Vijay. *Bollywood Cinema: Temples of Desire.* New York: Routledge, 2002.

Mukherjee, Prabhati. *Beyond the Four Varṇas: The Untouchables of India.* Delhi, India: Motilal Banarsidass, 1988.

Nanda, Serena. *Neither Man Nor Woman: The Hijras of India.* Belmont, CA: Wadsworth, 1990.

Nandy, Ashis. *The Intimate Enemy: Loss and Recovery of Self under Colonialism.* Delhi, India: Oxford UP, 1983.

———, ed. *The Secret Politics of Our Desires: Innocence, Culpability, and Indian Popular Cinema.* New Delhi, India: Oxford UP, 1998.

Nandy, Ashis, Shikha Trivedy, Shail Mayaram, and Achyut Yagnik. *Creating a Nationality: The Ramjanmabhumi Movement and Fear of the Self.* Delhi, India: Oxford UP, 1998.

Narayan, R. K. *The Ramayana: A Shortened Modern Prose Version of the Indian Epic (Suggested by the Tamil Version of Kamban).* New York: Penguin, 1972.

Nārāyaṇa. *Hitopadeṣa.* Ed. and trans. M. R. Kale. 6th ed. Delhi, India: Motilal Banarsidass, 1989.

Oatley, Keith. *Best Laid Schemes: The Psychology of Emotions.* Cambridge: Cambridge UP and Paris: Editions de la Maison des Sciences de l'Homme, 1992.

———. "Emotions and the Story Worlds of Fiction." In *Narrative Impact.* Ed. Melanie Green, Jeffrey Strange, and Timothy Brock. Mahwah, NJ: Lawrence Erlbaum, 2002, 39–69.

———. "Writingandreading: The Future of Cognitive Poetics." In *Cognitive Poetics in Practice.* Ed. Joanna Gavins and Gerard Steen. New York: Routledge, 2003, 161–173.

Oatley, Keith, and Philip N. Johnson-Laird. "Toward a Cognitive Theory of Emotions." *Cognition and Emotion* 1.1 (1987): 29–50.

Ochsner, Kevin N., and Daniel L. Schacter. "A Social Cognitive Neuroscience Approach to Emotion and Memory." In *The Neuropsychology of Emotion.* Ed. Joan C. Borod. New York: Oxford UP, 2000, 163–193.

O'Flaherty, Wendy Doniger. "The Clash between Relative and Absolute Duty: The Dharma of Demons." In *The Concept of Duty in South Asia.* Ed. O'Flaherty and J. Duncan M. Derrett. N.C.: South Asia Books/School of Oriental and African Studies, 1978, 96–106.

———, ed. and trans. *Hindu Myths.* Baltimore, MD: Penguin, 1975.

Ortony, Andrew, Gerald L. Clore, and Allan Collins. *The Cognitive Structure of Emotions.* Cambridge: Cambridge UP, 1988.

Pandit, Lalita. "Inside the Mind of a Suicide Bomber: Santosh Sivan's

*The Terrorist*." In *Understanding Terrorism: Threats in an Uncertain World*. Ed. Akorlie A. Nyatepe-Coo and Dorothy Zeisler-Vralsted. New York: Prentice Hall, 2003, 91–111.

Patanjali. *Yoga, Discipline of Freedom: The Yoga Sutra Attributed to Patanjali*. Ed. and trans. Barbara Stoler Miller. New York: Bantam, 1998.

Persson, Per. *Understanding Cinema: A Psychological Theory of Moving Imagery*. Cambridge: Cambridge UP, 2003.

Pinker, Steven. *How the Mind Works*. New York: Norton, 1997.

Plantinga, Carl. "Gender, Power, and a Cucumber: Satirizing Masculinity in *This Is Spinal Tap*." In *Movie Music, The Film Reader*. Ed. Kay Dickinson. New York: Routledge, 2003.

———. "The Scene of Empathy and the Human Face on Film." In *Passionate Views: Film, Cognition, and Emotion*. Ed. Plantinga and Greg M. Smith. Baltimore, MD: Johns Hopkins UP, 1999, 239–255.

Prabhupāda, A. C. Bhaktivedanta Swami. *Kṛṣṇa: The Supreme Personality of Godhead (A Summary Study of Śrīla Vyāsadeva's Śrīmad-Bhāgavatam, Tenth Canto)*. 3 vols. New York: Bhaktevedanta Book Trust, 1970.

Prasad, M. Madhava. *Ideology of the Hindi Film: A Historical Construction*. Delhi: Oxford UP, 1998.

Provine, Robert. *Laughter: A Scientific Investigation*. New York: Viking, 2000.

Raghavan, V. "Introduction." In *The Wondrous Crest-Jewel in Performance*. Ed. Clifford Reis Jones. Trans. Raghavan. Delhi: Oxford UP, 1984.

Ramachandran, V. S., and Sandra Blakeslee. *Phantoms in the Brain: Probing the Mysteries of the Human Mind*. New York: Quill, 1998.

Rangoonwalla, Firoze. *Guru Dutt 1925–1965*. Poona, India: National Film Archive of India, 1973.

Richman, Paula. "Introduction: The Diversity of the *Rāmāyaṇa* Tradition." In Richman, *Many*, 3–21.

———. *Many Rāmāyaṇas: The Diversity of a Narrative Tradition in South Asia*. Berkeley, CA: U of California P, 1991.

Richmond, Farley P. "Characteristics of Sanskrit Theatre and Drama." In *Indian Theatre: Traditions of Performance*. Ed. Richmond, Darius L. Swann, and Phillip B. Zarrilli. Honolulu, HI: U of Hawaii P, 1990, 33–85.

Robinson, Andrew. *Satyajit Ray: The Inner Eye*. Berkeley, CA: U of California P, 1989.

Rubin, David. *Memory in Oral Traditions: The Cognitive Psychology of Epic, Ballads, and Counting-Out Rhymes.* New York: Oxford UP, 1995.

Russell, Ralph. *The Pursuit of Urdu Literature: A Select History.* London: Zed Books, 1992.

Sardar, Ziauddin. "Dilip Kumar Made Me Do It." In *The Secret Politics of Our Desires: Innocence, Culpability and Indian Popular Cinema.* Ed. Ashis Nandy. New Delhi, India: Oxford UP, 1998, 19–91.

Schacter, Daniel L. *Searching for Memory: The Brain, the Mind, and the Past.* New York: Basic Books, 1996.

Sidney, Philip. "An Apology for Poetry." In *The Critical Tradition: Classic Texts and Contemporary Trends.* 2nd ed. Ed. David H. Richter. Boston, MA: Bedford Books, 1998, 134–159.

Sippy, Ramesh, dir. *Sholay* (*Flames*). Screenplay by Javed Akhtar and Salim Khan. Edited by M. S. Shinde. Photography by Dwarka Divecha. Music by R. D. Burman. Produced by G. P. Sippy. 1975.

*Śiva Purāṇa.* Delhi, India: Motilal Banarsidass, 1988.

Sivan, Santosh, dir. *The Terrorist.* Screenplay by Santosh Sivan, Ravi Deshpande, and Vijay Deveshwar. Edited by Sreekar Prasad. Photography by Santosh Sivan. Music by Sonu Sisupal Rajamani. Phaedra Cinema, 1999.

Smith, Greg M. *Film Structure and the Emotion System.* Cambridge: Cambridge UP, 2003.

Smith, Jeff. "Movie Music as Moving Music: Emotion, Cognition, and the Film Score." In *Passionate Views: Film, Cognition, and Emotion.* Ed. Carl Plantinga and Greg M. Smith. Baltimore, MD: Johns Hopkins UP, 1999, 146–167.

Smith, Murray. *Engaging Characters: Fiction, Emotion, and the Cinema.* Oxford: Oxford UP, 1995.

Spear, Percival. *A History of India (Volume Two): From the Sixteenth Century to the Twentieth Century.* New York: Penguin, 1978.

Swamy, M. R. Narayan. *Inside an Elusive Mind: Prabhakaran.* Delhi, India: Konark Publishers, 2003.

Tagore, Rabindranath. *Chandalika.* In *A Tagore Reader.* Ed. Amiya Chakravarty. Boston, MA: Beacon P, 1961, 169–179.

Tan, Ed S. *Emotion and the Structure of Narrative Film: Film as an Emotion Machine.* Trans. Barbara Fasting. Mahwah, NJ: Lawrence Erlbaum Associates, 1996.

Tan, Ed S. H., and Nico H. Frijda. "Sentiment in Film Viewing." In *Passionate Views: Film, Cognition, and Emotion.* Ed. Carl Plantinga and Greg M. Smith. Baltimore, MD: Johns Hopkins UP, 1999, 48–64.

Taylor, P. J. O., ed. *A Companion to the "Indian Mutiny" of 1857.* Delhi, India: Oxford UP, 1996.

Thoraval, Yves. *The Cinemas of India.* Delhi, India: MacMillan, 2000.

Tucker, Don M., Douglas Derryberry, and Phan Luu. "Anatomy and Physiology of Human Emotion: Vertical Integration of Brain Stem, Limbic, and Cortical Systems." In *The Neuropsychology of Emotion.* Ed. Joan C. Borod. Oxford: Oxford UP, 2000, 56–79.

Tulasidasa. *Shriramacharitamanasa (The Holy Lake of the Acts of Rama).* Trans. R. C. Prasad. Delhi: Motilal Banarasidass, 1990.

Utpaladeva. *IŚvara Pratyabhijñā Kārikā of Utpaladeva: Verses on the Recognition of the Lord.* Translation with commentary by B. N. Pandit. New Delhi: Muktabodha Indological Research Institute and Delhi: Motilal Banarsidass Publishers, 2003.

Valicha, Kishore. *The Moving Image: A Study of Indian Cinema.* London: Sangam Books, 1988.

Vālmīki. *Srimad Vālmīki Ramayanam.* Trans. N. Raghunathan. 3 vols. Madras: Vighneswara Publishing, 1981.

van Leeuwen, Cees. "Perception." In *A Companion to Cognitive Science.* Ed. William Bechtel and George Graham. Oxford: Blackwell, 1998, 265–281.

Vijay, project director. *Alaap: A Discovery of Indian Classical Music.* Mumbai, India: Times Music, n.d.

Waines, David. *An Introduction to Islam.* Cambridge: Cambridge UP, 1995.

Walter, Henrik. *Neurophilosophy of Free Will: From Libertarian Illusions to a Concept of Natural Autonomy.* Trans. Cynthia Klohr. Cambridge, MA: MIT P, 2001.

Wolpert, Stanley. *Gandhi's Passion: The Life and Legacy of Mahatma Gandhi.* Oxford: Oxford UP, 2001.

———. *India.* Berkeley, CA: U of California P, 1991.

———. *A New History of India.* 4th ed. New York: Oxford UP, 1993.

Zajonc, Robert B. "Feeling and Thinking: Closing the Debate over the Independence of Affect." In *Feeling and Thinking: The Role of Affect in Social Cognition.* Ed. Joseph P. Forgas. Cambridge: Cambridge UP and Paris: Editions de la Maison des Sciences de l'Homme, 2000, 31–58.

Zerubavel, Eviatar. *Social Mindscapes: An Invitation to Cognitive Sociology.* Cambridge, MA: Harvard UP, 1997.

Zinkin, Taya. *Caste Today.* London: Oxford UP, 1962.

Zunshine, Lisa. *Why We Read Fiction: Theory of Mind and the Novel.* Columbus, OH: Ohio State UP, 2006.

# Index